You Know My Method

You Know My Method:

The Science of the Detective

J.K. Van Dover

Bowling Green State University Popular Press
Bowling Green, OH 43403

Other books of interest from the Popular Press:

Stephen King's America
Jonathan P. Davis

H.R.F. Keating: Post-Colonial Detection
Meera Tamaya

Martians and Misplaced Clues:
The Life and Work of Fredric Brown
Jack Seabrook

Stewards of the House:
The Detective Fiction of Jonathan Latimer
Bill Brubaker

Alarms and Epithets: The Art of Eric Ambler
Peter Wolfe

Yesterdays Faces: Volume 6
Robert Sampson

The Spirit of Australia: The Crime Fiction of Arthur Upfield
Ray B. Browne

The Boys from Grover Avenue:
Ed McBain's 87th Precinct Novels
George N. Dove

Copyright © 1994 by Bowling Green State University Popular Press

Library of Congress Catalogue Card No. 93-72934

ISBN: 0-87972-639-3 Clothbound
     0-87972-640-7 Paperback

Cover art and design by Gary Dumm.

For Sarala, again

Contents

Acknowledgements

I have always appreciated the convention which allows a scholar to buttonhole the agreeable reader at the beginning of a book and declare some of the more or less relevant sources of his scholarship and his happiness. It allows some insight into the author's humanity, a quality which other conventions encourage him to suppress in his text. Disagreeable readers may avoid the imposition easily enough.

You Know My Method began in 1984 when, in a spasm of interdisciplinary good will, some faculty at Lincoln University conspired with some colleagues at Pennsylvania State University to initiate a program in Science, Technology and Society. As the English Department's volunteer, I developed a module intended to encourage students to think about the scientific method by thinking about the method of Sherlock Holmes. As I pushed the idea a bit further, I wrote a sequence of articles—on Sherlock Holmes, Father Brown, Craig Kennedy and Dr. Thorndyke—which were published in *Clues*; traces of these articles may be found in the appropriate chapters here, though the emphasis, and in places the basic argument, has evolved considerably in the course of writing the book. I must, therefore, thank Pat Browne twice, first for her support as editor of *Clues* and now for her support as editor at the Popular Press.

Lincoln University supported the research with small grants for materials from the Lilly-Lincoln Grant and from Research and Publications funds. Lincoln's crucial contribution, however, consisted in granting me a long-awaited sabbatical in 1992-93; without it, I could not have undertaken the book.

ii You Know My Method

My main library resource has been the Morris Library of the University of Delaware; I have come to expect a lot of its collection, and it has rarely disappointed. In the summer of 1992, I had the good fortune to be able to exploit the vaster (and dustier) reaches of the stacks in Yale's Sterling Memorial Library. I found much there—Craig Kennedy novels and turn-of-the-century popular magazines as well as obscure scholarly monographs—which I might have found with difficulty, if at all, elsewhere. I owe this good fortune to Professor Robin Winks and the National Endowment for the Humanities. Professor Winks offered an NEH Summer Seminar entitled "The Historian as Detective"; it was a stimulating seminar which sparked dozens of ideas about History and Detectives which I would never otherwise have considered. None, I think, have worked their way directly into this book, but they certainly broadened the contexts in which I view the detective. And the access to the nine million volumes in the SML was invaluable.

Had Brian Tracy not given me a copy of *The Detective and the Professional Thieves*, I would probably have omitted Pinkerton from my argument and thus, I think, missed an important link.

A more modest acknowledger would stop here, but undeterred, I press on. I cannot, regrettably, provide a list of scholar-friends who read the manuscript thrice and whose suggestions have improved it immeasureably but who should not, of course, be held responsible for its errors. I can, however, thank a few of the people who have improved my life immeasurably (and, indeed, should not be held responsible for its errors). My parents, as always, deserve more credit than I can express in this (or any other) place. Two of their three children pursued science in some form: Bruce as research physicist working on magnetism, superconductivity and other arcane technologies; Cindy as a research marine biologist and submersible pilot, who has pursued vent worms and other arcane life forms at the ocean's bottom.

I'm the one the Ancient Mariner (and other arcane poets) stopped. This book is as close to science as I am likely to get.

My father, who died last year, has a special relevance to the thesis of this book. He was omnicompetent in the technologies of the middle 50 years of this century. He repaired radios, televisions, and tape recorders, fixed plumbing, remodelled attics, welded leaks in car radiators, laid cinderblock foundations, carved wooden jewelry boxes, designed and built Tiffany lamps, constructed steam engines (cutting necessary parts on a metal lathe) and ran a School Board. These were his avocations; as an electronics technician for the Signal Corps from 1945 to 1982, he worked on printed circuits and other space age devices that remain well beyond my comprehension. The main strand of my argument is that identifying with the detective helps salve the anxieties of readers troubled by the changes—ideological and physical—caused by the triumph of the scientific method in the nineteenth century. These changes are writ large in the matters of Evolution and Entropy and Nuclear Fission; but they are also writ small in intimate, domestic worlds we inhabit. We no longer know how to make the routine machinery of our lives work. We cannot comprehend the mechanical principles of a parking meter, let alone those of a television; we know the levers to press, but have no idea of how the mysterious wheels and tubes within the box get us our 30 minutes of parking or sitcom. The portion of our necessary environment whose operation we can describe, let alone repair (let alone reproduce) is infinitesimal. We need not think about the origins of life or the effects of a multi-megaton explosion to feel anxiously ignorant of the world in which our century has placed us. My father had his epistemological anxieties, no doubt, and he seemed to prefer Rex Stout as his salve, but unlike me, he could fix whatever went wrong in the physical apparatuses of his domestic world. I try, Lord knows, but I cannot. I earned my Ph.D., but I know much less about the workings of my world than he did.

iv You Know My Method

It is difficult to make exciting fiction with a hero who knows how to solve plumbing problems, though the original Tom Swift series came close. Knowing how to solve murder mysteries—if the *knowing how* is emphasized—is a productive substitution. It is, for example, rather more dramatic than plumbing can hope to be. The detective proves his methods through the active investigation of violent crime. But if I am right, the detective is, in a sense, only a sort of sublimated plumber—or a sublimated auto mechanic, or a sublimated tax preparer. He proves himself competent to solve the melodramatic problems of his world, and—though the problems of our world are more likely to involve plumbing, autos and taxes—we identify with him and enjoy vicariously the competence which we fail to achieve in our worlds. We cannot fix a toaster, but he can fix a time out of joint.

Of course, there may be some devoted readers of detective stories whose sleep has never been troubled by spectres of broken toasters. Well, perhaps they are sufficiently disturbed by thoughts of Darwinian evolution or nuclear holocaust or gene splicing. As I suggest in the introduction, the detective speaks most directly to these matters. Or perhaps I've gotten it entirely wrong and the common reader, like W.H. Auden, is driven by a Christian sense of guilt and a need for redemption to identify routinely with the circle of suspects rather than with the detective. Or something else.

Final acknowledgements are to children and wife. Lara and Andrew are seven and five; they will read this page someday I hope. And they should know then that despite their sometimes untimely eruptions into my study, they, and not this book, have been the best part of this sabbatical year.

And then there is Sarala. These are awkward times for men who wish to thank their wives; but awkwardness has always been one of my gifts, as grace has always been one of Sarala's. We have had a bit over 20 years together now; she has made them extraordinarily happy years. In the end, knowing the right person matters more than knowing how to know anything. I've known the right person.

Chapter 1

The Detective as Hero
of Methodical Thinking

Neither modern science nor the detective story existed in 1800; a century later, the one had unquestionably transformed the intellectual and physical environment of western man and the other had established itself as the pre-eminent genre of popular literature in western culture. Railroads, electricity, vaccines, the theory of evolution, the laws of thermodynamics—and Sherlock Holmes: science and the detective story may not be of comparable consequence in the history of civilization, but they are not unrelated either, and an examination of their inter-dependence may cast a revealing sidelight on the significance of the world-historical phenomenon as well as upon that of the trivial. The detective offered himself as a special model of the new scientific thinker; his distinction lay in his decision to apply the new method to concrete human problems rather than to abstract mechanical problems. He was a hero who possessed a method of knowing how to know—he was a scientist; but what he knew how to know was innocence and guilt—he was a moralist. He knew how to know who was who, rather than what was what. He promised to combine the most powerful method of thought with a fundamental commitment to traditional ethics (and, as a further attraction, to exercise his method and his commitment on the sensational matter of violent crime), and the public embraced him.[1]

2 You Know My Method

The twentieth century has only confirmed the respective hegemonies of the scientist and the detective. Science, for better or worse, continues to alter our world and to define what passes for legitimate thought in it; and the detective story, with significant mutations in form, has remained by far the dominant genre of popular fiction. Developments such as Hiroshima and the hard-boiled style may have altered our views of science and of the detective story, and the distance between Robert Oppenheimer and Mike Hammer may appear to be indeed immeasurable. But in a significant way, even the work of the atomic scientist and of the tough P.I. are connected, and that connection is the object of this inquiry.

The scientific method did not, of course, spring into existence at the beginning of the nineteenth century; any reasonable account of its source must start no later than the seventeenth century and might well pursue its subject into the Middle Ages, to classical Greece, or even beyond. And yet the nineteenth century can legitimately be described as the period when "Modern Science," signifying a powerful, coherent entity, was invented by scientists (the term "scientist" itself being invented in 1834) and accepted by the popular imagination. The various fields within this entity struggled to define their separate disciplines, but all claimed a common method in order to justify their inclusion under the rubric, Science. By the end of the century, the power of this method to interpret the world theoretically and to alter the world practically was acknowledged by everyone. Scientific thought—thought which claimed to be scientifically derived and scientifically verifiable—had become the new orthodoxy.

Though they have been fancifully traced to classical Greece and the biblical Palestine, the origins of the detective story can even more definitely be assigned to the nineteenth century. Edgar Allan Poe invented the story whose hero's heroism lies in his ability to detect. His detective, the very methodical Dupin, appeared in the 1840s at the moment when western science was first achieving self-consciousness about its methodical basis; the detective hero was apotheosized by Sir Arthur Conan Doyle in the 1890s at the moment when the method of western science had won the undisputed authority to discriminate sense from nonsense but was in the process of professionalizing itself, excluding the mass of citizens from genuine participation in its progress. The new orthodoxy seemed to reserve its secrets for initiates, for men (and the occasional woman) who devoted years to advanced study. Sherlock Holmes offered laymen an easy and reassuring access to the mystery of the method.

The history of the detective story may be divided into five main movements, the first two dominated by single individuals, the last three being generic developments. The first movement belongs to Poe; in the person of Monsieur Dupin, Poe invented the fictional detective. Dupin is a peculiar case; though thoroughly methodical, he can best be described as incipiently scientific in his method. The next movement, the Sherlock Holmes movement, establishes the detective as a generic hero of unprecedented popularity. Poe invented the figure; Conan Doyle made it a popular type. And the Holmesian type is thoroughly scientific in his technique. After Holmes, the deluge. The third movement, usually known as The Golden Age of Detective Fiction, overlaps the late career of Holmes. This is the tradition of the Great Detective, with its emphasis more upon the detective's eccentric genius than upon his empirical, rational methodology. An allusion to "little grey cells" may suffice to explain the source of his power of knowing, though he will often enough use "science" or "scientific" as a casual word of praise. Science is, for the Great Detective, an admirable tool, but one more honored as a sort of Masonic emblem of his caste than as a practical device. Science is too much a mechanical art for him to pursue it actively.

The fourth movement, the Hard-boiled school of Hammett and Chandler, would seem to mark a decisive break with the scientific character of the detective. It appears even anti-scientific in its proletarian orientation. Not that proletarians are inherently anti-scientific, nor even that the middle- and upper-middle-class writers who produced the hard-boiled novels were necessarily anti-scientific, but the hard-boiled detective almost makes a boast of his intellectual deficiencies, and science, in any recognizable form, plays almost no direct role in the world of his experience. The fifth movement of the detective story is the present heterogeneous one: all things are possible, and the method of the detective may be colored by a wide spectrum of sources— national, ethnic, or religious origins, gender, police or military procedures, etc. Indeed, the only culture conspicuously absent is the scientific. No prominent scientific detective operates in any best-selling fiction today.

And yet every detective betrays his scientific heritage, because every detective has a method of knowing. Defining himself as the modern hero, Sherlock Holmes made repeated reference to his "method," and he made very clear that he meant *the* method of his century, the scientific method. His followers, having inherited his heroism and his audience, have had less need to proclaim their method (and more need to distinguish themselves from their brethren). Still, the detective formula instituted by Holmes required not only that the detective know the villain in the end, but that he convince the reader that he knows. Being right is not enough: the detective's "J'accuse," even if it is followed by a confirmatory confession, does not satisfy the generic demand for demonstrated method. The detective must always show (or at least imply) that his accusation has been based upon incontrovertible (or at least plausible) inferences, and these inferences, willy-nilly, constitute his method. Even the most neolithic of hard-boiled dicks owes his readers an explanation. His practical method may have consisted of kicking in teeth, but in the end, he takes a page or two to point to the irrefutable signs of guilt which were posted along his tooth-littered path to the ultimate evil-doer. The detective story always ends with a retrospective reconstruction of the hidden skeleton of the action; though he is articulate about nothing else, the detective must methodically articulate this skeleton. He may be no Cuvier, but in this sense, at least, he supplies a scientific satisfaction. The reader must know how the detective knew whodunit.

ii

The addiction to the detective formula coincided with the emergence of two consequences of Western scientific and technological progress. On the one hand, the rationalized, empirically-verifiable methods of science were clearly effective; they provided reliable bases for interpreting and manipulating the phenomena of everyday life. They explained the eruption of mountains and the evolution of life. They produced steam engines and telegraphs and vaccines. (Or seemed to: nineteenth century scientists and engineers certainly pretended that technology was applied science. Historians of science now seem persuaded that technological advances were made largely independently of science, at least until the late nineteenth century.[2]

But on the other hand, the methods of science seemed to destabilize radically the known world. The displacements caused by the new technologies of the Industrial Revolution were tangible; the old rhythms of life succumbed to the schedules imposed by the clock, and urbanization altered landscapes and social environments. Once the brutal excesses of early industrialization had been ameliorated, the new technologies provided an increasing portion of the population an undreamed of Age of Comfort. But for the common man, they also ushered in the Age of Incompetence. An untutored eye might comprehend the principles upon which a medieval grist mill operated, but in the nineteenth century, the motions of the new engines were, for most eyes, a blurred spectacle. The operations of the machinery of the industrial world would remain permanently mysterious to the mass of laymen. Their environment became full of things which, having been produced by man, were not natural or divine mysteries, inherently unknowable, yet they were of such a technological complexity as to be practically unknowable. One might envy the initiates who manipulated the chemistry of coal tar derivatives or the electricity of telecommunications. One might resent them. But one knew one couldn't join them; one knew that one was incompetent to recreate or even to repair the ubiquitous products of human industry which underlay Modern Life. (And the complex social technologies of Modern Life—its mysterious bureaucracies— expanded in company with the material.) For the first time in history, everyone knew that everyone couldn't know how ordinary things—the man-made things of everyone's everyday life—worked.

The new machines had to be taken on faith: one pressed the levers and enjoyed the benefits, but one did not presume to inquire into the arcane logic that linked the lever to the benefit. And, ironically, as one schooled one's self to accept this necessary new faith in scientific technology, one discovered that the scientific method was undermining the larger, older Faith which one's ancestors had schooled themselves to accept. The process had begun with the innovations of Copernicus, Galileo and Newton, but nineteenth-century geology, biology, astronomy and physics seemed continually to be declaring the obsolescence of yesterday's verities. Much like today's frustrated dieter, who finds last week's cure for heart disease appearing on today's list of carcinogens, a moderately well-informed citizen of Victorian England or Gilded Age America, having abandoned the centuries-old certainties of the Bible in favor of new scientific doctrines, often found himself obliged, a decade later, to abandon those new doctrines for newer ones.[3]

The Bible's authority, for example, had allowed Bishop Ussher, applying interpretative methods developed over a millennium to date Creation with some accuracy: 8 p.m., Saturday, 22 October, 4004 BC. By 1850, the work of uniformitarian geologists like Hutton and Playfair had convinced most thinkers that the world was immeasurably old, sufficiently old for the processes of Darwinian evolution to have operated. (In *The Origin of Species* Darwin had suggested a need for something on the order of 300 million years.) Even if the layman remained oblivious to the micro-debates which led to the new, science-based consensus, he would have been cognizant of the macro-adjustment of the early 1860s, when, arguing from a different scientific basis (thermodynamics), Lord Kelvin placed the habitable age of the earth as not more than 200 million, and in 1899 reduced the figure to no more than 20 to 40 million years. Darwin professed himself disturbed by Kelvin's calculations. The common reader who followed the conclusions rather than the arguments might well feel even more unsettled. Then, in 1904, Ernest Rutherford applied new ideas about radioactivity to refute Kelvin, restoring the earth's possible age to billions of years, and the calculations have since been several times adjusted, a few billion years this way or that. The scientific method, having indisputably defeated the old authorities, provided no permanent new ones, no new ones that even *seemed* permanent; its victories were in their essence provisional. A major product of technological change was the expectation of further technological change. The solutions of science seemed dissolutions only.

As a result, while the scientific method seemed to offer an undeniably powerful way of knowing, it also redefined and diminished "knowledge." Bacon, the prophet of the new science, had proclaimed that "Knowledge is Power"; the new science surrendered the noun for a participle: "Knowing is Power." The scientist achieved success by methodically investigating a given problem (or, in revolutionary science, a new problem) and proposing a solution sufficient to save the appearances. If his theory survives experiments designed to disprove it, then he has written his chapter in the history of science. He will have written over the chapter of his predecessors, and he can be sure that his successors will write over his. His contribution is "knowledge" until another theory more efficiently saves the appearances or until new appearances require saving. By the end of the nineteenth century, it was accepted that no scientific "law" could claim exemption from supersession. The criteria for excellence in scientific achievement ceased to include irrefutability. Though Rutherford achieved greatness, in part, by refuting Kelvin, he did not thereby diminish Kelvin's greatness. Newton remains Newton, despite Einstein's coup.

But even the scientist who appreciates the radically provisional character of "knowledge" in his science is likely to tolerate less comfortably a comparable uncertainty in moral principles or judgments. Science may disdain infallibility even as an ideal, but morality does not; permanently provisional conclusions are practically unacceptable. All moral conclusions may be subject to review and reversal in a Higher Assize; but in order to act, the moralist must assume certain principles and certain judgments will endure. If yesterday's murderer is today found innocent, the miscarriage of justice is a dreadful event, not a footnote to the progressive history of moral discovery. Similarly, if yesterday's pleasure is today declared a criminal activity—or vice versa—the consequent reappraisals may be devastating.

Further, scientific thinking professes to be neutral as well as provisional. It boasts the impersonality of its approaches and the universality of its conclusions. It makes no allowances for a special providence in the fall of a man, let alone in that of a sparrow. But the common man, like Tolstoy's Ivan Ilych, sooner or later realizes that the syllogism that begins with "All men are mortal" ends with "Socrates [or Ivan] is mortal," and that this makes a difference. Galileo's experiment from the top of the tower would have proven equally conclusive as regards gravity had he dropped two men of equal mass and different size instead of two balls; the difference would have been that in dropping men, Galileo would have proved himself a proficient murderer as well as a proficient scientist. Science and morals, then, operate on radically different epistemological bases: Reason versus Faith, Universal versus Particular, The Two Cultures, and all that.

But the detective is the timely figure who makes the argument in popular literature that the opposition can be reconciled, that scientific method can serve a moral function and that the common man can comprehend the method of scientific thinking. The machinery of science can be mastered and, mastered, can be bent to ethical purposes. The detective proves that the scientific method can yield the sort of absolutely certain, concrete conclusions which moral inquiries demand. He may, like any scientist, err and be compelled to revise his ideas in the course of his investigation; but his final judgment is never provisional, never subject to revision. His Newtonian dicta will never be unsaid by an Einstein.

And his ambitions are decently modest. He applies his method to the detection of innocent and guilty individuals, not Good and Evil. He does not challenge or subvert the traditional pieties which sanction the standards by which villainies and heroisms are measured. There may be a Logic of Scientific Revolutions, but the logic of the detective is never revolutionary; he never challenges the ethical paradigms of his society. His occasional impulse to free a killer only proves the rule: he does so, always, by appealing to a popular ethical sentiment (i.e. that this type of killer who has killed this type of victim for this type of reason ought not be punished). He always submits to the tacit (if not the legal) standards espoused by his readers.

And though he is invariably successful in his scientific investigations, the detective is never guilty of scientific hubris. *He* never retreats to the high Alps to apply his knowledge to the reinvigoration of dead body parts; *he* never isolates himself on an island to breed man-beasts. He is a citizen; he lives in the city amidst his fellow citizens for whom he works, and if he distinguishes himself through his eccentricities, they are always eccentricities of manners, not morals. He may seem Dickensian in his idiosyncrasies; he never seems Byronic in his ambitions.[4] The detective is an old-fashioned man using the newest methods of knowing to verify the oldest moral distinctions. His popularity, then, can be tied to the rise of the scientific and technological—in short, methodological—understanding of the world in the nineteenth century and to the rise of an accompanying anxiety that this understanding might not be entirely progressive or humane. The scientific method made the fictional detective possible and it made him popular.

iii

The very common reader in the post-Darwinian, post-Edisonian world may well derive some subconscious theological or psychological satisfaction from the plot of the detective story as a Christian interpreter like W.H. Auden or a Freudian like Gertrude Pederson-Krag would have it, but even if at some deep level his repeated purchases can be explained by a compulsion to satisfy such a need, at the superficial level he buys detective stories because he has enjoyed and expects to enjoy again observing how the detective negotiates the moral complexities of his world to arrive at a certain moral truth. Whatever subsidiary thrills he may anticipate from his detective story—sex, violence, erudition, gaslights and hansom cabs—the common reader certainly expects a melodramatically complicated moral world, and he expects one character to confront this opaque world and, exercising the method of his school, to discover the transparent moral truth: the primary moral truth—whodunit—and, in passing, any number of secondary moral truths, identifying the uncle who has a gambling problem, the girl who secretly admires the butler's soldier-son, the shopkeeper who sells drugs under the counter.

This individual who can infallibly read the moral reality of his world is the figure the very common reader identifies with. It must be the very rare reader who joins Auden in sympathizing primarily with the innocent community of bystanders, those parishioners who view the body in the vicarage library and labor through the novel under the pall of being thought guilty. The high percentage of detective stories narrated in the first person, either by the clear-eyed detective or by the half-sighted Watson, surely only confirms the obvious point that the reader normally identifies with the investigator, the man who has the ability to understand his world—or, more easily, with the man's companion, one who has, like the reader, the desire to understand and almost the ability. The significant meaning of the detective as popular figure, then, is this: he is essentially an epistemological hero, a hero of knowing. He may have other virtues (and vices), but the detective necessarily knows how to know; he possesses a *method* of knowing that serves him in the moral crises that confront him. That is detecting; that is his essential profession and practice.

The significance of this peculiar and popular heroism can be easily seen by contrasting it with other qualities of heroism which have more ancient pedigrees. Strength and Courage, for example, have long and honorable heroic heritages; Passion, Will, Humble Integrity, Pluck, Leadership, Faith: all have characterized heroic types. The great heroes of methodical knowing are far fewer; the list of men or women whose unqualified heroic stature derives entirely from knowing how to know may begin and end with Socrates, who, with his dialectical method and his ethical intent, might well serve as a proto-detective. In two important respects, however, his epistemological heroism differs from that of the detective: Socrates's method pursues generalizable ethical conclusions, not particular judgments of guilt or innocence; and his tolerance of aporetic (inconclusive) conclusions contrasts with the invariable certainty of the detective's empirical inquiries.[5]

12　You Know My Method

The absence of heroic knowers in western literature is not surprising. A Christian culture might well prize other virtues over the worldly pursuit of knowledge; it might justly shudder at a Faust. Further, there was little in what Lewis Mumford has called the eotechnic period, the "water-and-wood" phase of slow technological change (1000-1750), to inspire popular interest. If the benefits of scientific inquiry were dubious in intellectual life— and men like Giordano Bruno and Galileo served widely known lessons—they were at most marginal in everyday lives. With the arrival of the Industrial Revolution—Mumford's paleotechnic ("coal-and-iron") period—in the late eighteenth century, the effects of science and technology, both beneficial and detrimental, became inescapably visible. Still, in popular literature, the man who devoted himself to scientific investigation was portrayed as a villain, indeed, often as a monstrous villain. Dr. Lydgate, in George Eliot's *Middlemarch*, is a significant exception, but a series of much more popular and very villainous doctors—Dr. Frankenstein, Dr. Rappaccini, Dr. Jekyll and Dr. Moreau—suggested that modern science might be an inherently immoral profession, leading its initiates into unnatural and destructive (usually self-destructive) exercises of intellect. Mastering the methods of knowing seemed necessarily accompanied by abandonment of any regard for the morality of knowing.

And then came the detective, who reversed the association: his adventures argued that the achievement of moral ends necessitated a mastery of methodical knowing. In his first great incarnations—as M. Auguste Dupin and Mr. Sherlock Holmes—the emphasis upon the methodicalness with which he worked to these moral ends is unmistakable. As the types of detective have proliferated, his technique of knowing has assumed many different bases: deduction, induction, and abduction; Catholic theology and Confucian thought; little grey cells and hard-boiled toughness; dreams and intuitions and behavioral echoes of the inhabitants of St. Mary Mead. In the hands of the multitude of second-rate writers, the detective's method dwindles to a nearly invisible quantity, a mere pretense that he somehow arrived intelligently at the conclusions which the narrative has crudely forced upon him. This diversity of methods is a glory of the form; the heroic knower is not tied to any cultural prejudice; the addicted reader must open himself to many ways to truth.

But this flowering of methods is a secondary development in the form. The original detectives embodied versions of the method which was transforming the material and intellectual character of western civilization in the paleotechnic period. Poe called his detective's version "ratiocination." "Ratiocination," it should be admitted immediately, is not Poe's private label for "scientific method," though, in fact, in his first appearance, Poe's great ratiocinator, Dupin, comes close to practicing scientific investigation. In his later appearances, however, Dupin clearly moves away from identifying himself with crude scientific methodology, and defines his ratiocinative practice as a peculiar, though still distinctly methodological art. With the appearance of Sherlock Holmes, in his own time and since, *the* detective, the scientific method becomes explicitly the detective's profession. Holmes first extremely popular American epigone—advertised, in fact, as "The American Sherlock Holmes"—was purely scientific in profession and practice: Arthur B. Reeve's Craig Kennedy. These two figures, with the addition of R. Austin Freeman's Dr. Thorndyke and a half-dozen minor related figures, are the crucial ones in the history of the genre. They made it a genre. Before them, there was the eccentric invention of Poe and the miscellaneous experiments of Gaboriau, Collins, Anna Katharine Green and others; after them came the Golden Age. The unequal achievements of Arthur Conan Doyle, Arthur B. Reeve, and R. Austin Freeman created an audience which has long outlasted their lifetimes.

These achievements were historically conditioned: the authors' imaginations were inevitably stimulated and limited by the late nineteenth century world into which they were born. Three chronological coincidences may serve to suggest some contexts. Conan Doyle was born in 1859, the year in which Charles Darwin published *The Origin of Species* and changed fundamentally the normal vision of man's place in the world. Freeman's birth in 1862 coincided with one of the more celebrated of Victorian murder cases, that of Jessie M'Lachlan, who was convicted of murdering a fellow servant, Jess M'Pherson. And Arthur B. Reeve's lifetime (1880-1936) coincided precisely with that of the notorious herald of the decline of the west, Oswald Spengler. The scientist, the murderer, and the herald have very little in common, and yet they do frame a troubled time. The scientific method demonstrated its power; Darwin's theory was so readily embraced in part because it crystallized existing tendencies, but also because his exposition was so incontrovertibly scientific. Spengler too owed his wide reception to his crystallization of the notion that the Faustian spirit of western civilization was moving organically toward its twilight and extinction. Poor, ignorant Jessie M'Lachlan may seem out of place in this company, but it might be argued that her brief celebrity also marked a crystallization of a pervasive fascination with murder in domestic, middle-class milieus throughout the Victorian period.[6] The thoughts of Darwin and Spengler threatened the complacent pieties of their audience; the actions of Jessie M'Lachlan had only local physical consequences, but they represented a widely felt threat to a fragile normalcy.

The scientific method of the detectives of Conan Doyle, Freeman and Reeve worked to relieve the anxieties without disturbing the pieties. It was not iconoclastic; quite the opposite. The detective was engaged in a process of methodically restoring the idols of certain truth and justice. His method never projected the revaluation of all values. Grandfather had taken comfort in the knowledge that there was right and wrong, innocence and guilt, but suffered the qualification that man could never infallibly know the one from the other; that knowledge grandfather comfortably enough assigned to God. Science tended to detach God's active interest in the world (when it wasn't tending to deny his very existence), but the scientific detective, by demonstrating that innocence and guilt were empirically and infallibly distinguishable by men, reclaimed those old moral categories, and in so doing he made himself into *the* modern hero.

iv

Sherlock Holmes clearly placed a premium upon his exercise of a prescribable technique; he repeated his encouragement to Dr. Watson—"You know my method"—no fewer than five times (*The Sign of Four*, "The Blue Carbuncle," "The Boscombe Valley Affair," "The Stockbroker's Clerk" and *The Hound of the Baskervilles*). But this emphasis upon the detective's deliberate adherence to a rational method was present in the conception of the first as well as of the most famous detective. The first paragraph of the first detective story, "The Murders in the Rue Morgue" ends: "His results, brought about by the very soul and essence of method, have, in truth, the whole air of intuition" (I.397). Poe begins his story with an extended dissertation introducing his detective's method ("analysis"); only then does he introduce the detective. This priority is existential as well as temporal: his method is, indeed, the very soul and essence of the detective. And though many techniques may qualify as methodical, methodical technique is not a uselessly vague concept. It implies the canonization of rationality and, even more, of efficiency as the measures of success.[7] "Method," for Dupin and Holmes and all detectives, means a process for detecting crime that is rational and efficient. ("Rationalizable" can be substituted for rational; that is, even if the detective does not use formal logic to reach his conclusions, he must justify conclusions logically. The villain is logically the guilty party even in hard-boiled fiction.) Investigation proceeds through a sequence of verifiable steps; these discrete steps appear as units of experience as they occur, but in retrospect they function as logical units in an argument about innocence and guilt. The detective's method consists in acquiring these units in a chronological sequence during the narrative of his inquiry (i.e. selecting these persons to interrogate in this order and in this manner; selecting these objects—ashes, shavings, etc.—for notice) and in rearranging the units in a rational order during the narrative of his explanation of the case. Neither sequence can be accidental; though accident will, of course, play a role in the process of acquisition, even here there must be direction and selection, and this direction is method.

In this respect, then, all detectives adopt a technology of investigation. The detective doesn't look like a reasoning machine. Method is the core of his character—his soul and essence—but it is usually masked behind his all-too-human eccentricities. The first detectives, precisely because they had to go so far to establish their methodical soul and essence, went furthest to overlay the method with personal eccentricity. After sketching Dupin's method, the narrator of "Rue Morgue" sketches Dupin as the exotic scion of aristocrats who prefers the darkness of a dilapidated, shuttered mansion. Watson's list of Holmes's competences begins with sciences—chemistry, geology, anatomy—but ends with "plays the violin well": the Bohemian Holmes masks the Methodical. The early detective who least affected a manner of human eccentricity—Professor Augustus S.F.X. Van Dusen, "The Thinking Machine"—enjoyed his vogue in 1905-07 in part because his machine-likeness was so explicit, but the same quality probably militated against his permanent enshrinement as a popular hero. As later detectives have been able to assume (rather than to demonstrate) their methodical souls and essences, it has become important for writers to distinguish their protagonists more from other detectives than from the unmethodical mass of men, and as a result the emphasis upon the personal qualities (physical, moral, religious characteristics) has increased.

Nonetheless, the detective, insofar as he detects, remains a methodical detector. His method may be as rudimentary as that of the Continental Op in Dashiell Hammett's *Red Harvest*, who responds to Dinah Brand's mockery of his technique ("So that's the way you scientific detectives work...you've got the vaguest way of doing things I ever heard of") with a very short, pragmatic discourse on method: "Plans are all right sometimes...And sometimes just stirring things up is all right—if you're tough enough to survive, and keep your eyes open so you'll see what you want when it comes to the top" (Chapter 10). The Op's hard-boiled technique may appear vague and unscientific, but it is deliberate. His success is, in the end, never accidental. "Just stirring things up" is not a ratiocinative technique, but it is a rational, efficient technique in Personville. And in the end, as he explains what has happened, the Op exposes a logical plot of action, committing more than one logical inference in the process.

Dinah Brand's slur on the Op's want of science allows the Op to place himself in the vanguard of the new hard-boiled school of detection. The old school had consisted of the insistently methodical detectives of the founders—Poe, Conan Doyle, Freeman and Reeve—and the more cavalierly methodical detectives of the Golden Age (1920-40). But all schools, even the hard-boiled, assume that the truths of this world are knowable to a man who makes it his profession to know how to know. The detective's existence is predicated upon his convincing his clients—and his readers—that he has a reliable, repeatable, verifiable way of knowing. His way may be more or less systematic, and more or less explicit, but it is always there. He may disdain "science" in the manner of the Continental Op, but the premise of his existence remains rooted in the expectation that a rationally selected method will yield certain conclusions. The multicultural heirs of the original scientific detectives may protest their autonomy, but their methodological consanguinity betrays them.

v

It remains to describe the narrow meaning of "scientific method" which stimulated the invention of the detective and defined his character. Three things, at least, could be meant by "scientific method" in this context: the method practiced by nineteenth-century scientists, the method nineteenth-century scientists professed to practice, or the method which twentieth-century historians and philosophers of science assert that nineteenth-century scientists practiced. Even a quick survey of the literature on the subject reveals significant differences between each of these meanings. Only the second is relevant here. Though Conan Doyle and Austin Freeman were medical doctors, and Conan Doyle actually made some early gestures toward original medical research, neither would have described himself as a scientist. And while the twentieth century debates on scientific method between thinkers such as Popper, Toulmin, Kuhn and Feyerabend may lead to a surer understanding of what really happens in scientific inquiry and what its results really amount to, little of this has, even yet, filtered down to popular culture, and it certainly casts no light upon the character of scientific method as it appeared to the nineteenth-century observer.

But what scientists then said they were doing is of central concern. That they said anything about their method—and they said a great deal—is itself important. Discussions of method ceased in the early nineteenth century, to be relegated to forewords and footnotes. "For almost the first time, entire books rather than prefaces or chapters were devoted exclusively to the subject [of the philosophy of science]" (Laudon 29). And these books included such major statements on the subject as Sir John Herschel's *Preliminary Discourse on the Study of Natural Philosophy* (1830), William Whewell's *Philosophy of the Inductive Sciences* (1840), John Stuart Mill's *A System of Ratiocinative and Inductive Logic* (1843, 1850, 1872). All of these works were addressed to a broad audience of informed non-specialists. This unprecedented pre-occupation with effective methodology persisted throughout the century. "Victorian science was, in most areas, self-consciously concerned with its own methods. In few other eras before or since, were men of science so given to elaborate analyses of their own practice" (Basalla *et al.* 399).

This self-consciousness was not a private matter. The debate over the most efficient method of obtaining certain new knowledge, though it was carried on by "men of science" (what would now be called scientists and historians or philosophers of science), was, from the first, treated as an issue of importance to the broader public. Although the course of the nineteenth century saw science move steadily toward specialization and professionalization, in the first decades of the century, the men of science still saw themselves (and wanted to see themselves) as representative men. By 1900 they preferred the cachet of expertise, of being engaged in advanced investigations incomprehensible to anyone lacking advanced degrees and laboratory experience. In 1800, with the typical man of science still an amateur naturalist, and with even advanced scientific discoveries being announced and debated in non-specialist quarterlies and magazines, the nature of scientific inquiry could still be regarded as a topic for general debate.

Indeed, the debaters could still assume that the correct scientific method was not a craft mystery, applicable only in the laboratory. Rather, once its procedures could be clarified, it would provide an intellectual discipline that might be applied fruitfully in all fields of human experience. Hershel, Whewell and

Mill were attempting to clarify how men of science reached their
conclusions, but all three were also inspired by Francis Bacon's
vision of the extension of the scientific method to the study of
social and political problems (Yeo, "Scientific Method and the
Rhetoric of Science" 268). Moreover, practicing scientists felt
obligated to communicate their methods and their discoveries to
the mass audience. The British Association for the Advancement
of Science was founded in 1831 as a forum for professional
scientists (as opposed to the amateur-dominated Royal Society),
but one of its principal activities lay in the sponsorship of
"workingmen's lectures." T.H. Huxley was only the most
prominent of its members to devote himself to making such
attempts to inform non-scientists about the methods and the
discoveries of science.

American men of science contributed little original to the
theoretical debates, but they were as actively engaged in the
practice of scientific inquiry and in the dissemination of scientific
innovations. Science had had the good fortune in the early
republic to be widely associated with such public and patriotic
figures as Jefferson, Rittenhouse, and, above all, Franklin. In the
second decade of the century, its intrinsic merits began to be
recognized. "Somewhere around 1815, Americans became
interested in the pursuit of science to a greater extent than ever
before. They founded journals, organized societies, appealed to
the federal government for aid—mostly without success—began
sending their students to the scientific institutions of France and
Germany in unprecedented numbers, and began bitterly
resenting the scientific superiority of Europe" (Daniels 3).[8] Thus
Americans were also being trained to admire science.

In England and America, the key figure in the debate over
scientific method was Francis Bacon, under whose auspices most
scientific methodologies declared themselves. Bacon had
announced his *Novum Organum* in the early seventeenth
century, but aside from occasional nods from practicing scientists

like Newton, Bacon's advocacy of his inductive method received little credit in the pre-methodological seventeenth and eighteenth centuries. Locke was the dominant figure in England and America; Bacon's influence was greater in France than in England during the eighteenth century (Bruce 68). But at the beginning of the nineteenth century, partly as the result of his adoption by the rising school of Scottish common sense philosophy and partly as the result of the tangible advances in scientific understanding and technological applications, he was reclaimed and installed, with Newton, as the presiding genius of scientific inquiry.

Exactly what constituted Baconianism, however, remained in dispute. In its least sophisticated form, endorsed by none of the major theorists but widely recognized nonetheless, it argued for mere induction: the inquirer accumulated facts until they, in effect, spontaneously arranged themselves in a pattern which could be labeled a scientific law. This naive interpretation was, in fact, the one to which Darwin appealed when he justified his revolutionary conclusions as the result of basic Baconian practice: "I worked on true Baconian principles, and without any theory collected facts on a wholesale scale" (Darwin, *Life and Letters* 68).[9] The distinctive features of the basic Baconian method, then, were practical activity (accumulation of data), intellectual passivity (avoidance of theory and hypothesis), and consequent certainty (laws of nature).[10] The hero of this method of knowing was Newton, who, in his statements on methodology, had denounced the intrusion of "hypothesis" into scientific inquiry (*hypothese non fingo*[11]). Newton was praised for his patience in collecting facts and for the humility of his submission to them; the un-Baconian villains were speculators such as Kepler and Descartes, who were convicted of the crime of *a priori* hypothesizing.[12]

Improved versions of Baconianism ranged from John Stuart Mill's effort in his *System of Logic* to preserve as much as possible the straightforward empiricism of the original Baconianism, through Sir John Hershel's added emphasis upon the need for hypothesis to actively guide the accumulation of facts and for mathematical thinking in the analysis of data in his *Preliminary Discourse on the Study of Natural Philosophy* (1830), to William Whewell's Kantian argument that the world can only be known through the active operation of the knowing mind and consequently that mental activities—hypotheses, theories—are prerequisites in true scientific thinking. Yet even though Whewell departed from Baconian orthodoxy— abandoning the claim to certain objective knowledge which Mill and Hershel still endorsed and elevating Kepler over Newton—he too appealed to the imprimatur of Baconianism: "Bacon stands far above the herd of loose and visionary speculators who, before and about his time, spoke of the establishment of new philosophies. If we must select some one philosopher as the Hero of the revolution in scientific method, beyond all doubt Francis Bacon must occupy the place of honour" (Whewell 230). Nor did the Atlantic Ocean prove a bar to Bacon's pre-eminence. An appeal to his name was "a mark of scientific orthodoxy" in antebellum America as well (Daniels 64-65).[13]

Two incidental elements of the Baconian orthodoxy have special relevance for the scientific detective. Bacon encouraged his nineteenth-century apostles to expect the inductive method to yield certain, not probable knowledge (see Hull 17). Long after scientists abandoned the expectation as delusory, the detective continues to realize it, although within a severely limited world of singular events. The other common Baconian expectation lay in the projected universality of the method's operation. In the 127th aphorism of *Novum Organum*, Bacon had advised his readers that "my method of interpretation" was applicable to "other sciences, logic, ethics, and politics" (536). The nineteenth-century Baconists embraced with enthusiasm this vision of the potential transferability of the scientific method to social and political problems.[14] The detective enacted the transfer in a crucial sphere of human experience; again, however, only in single, concrete exercises.

The first phase of the popular debate over scientific method in England and America in the nineteenth century may be labelled the Baconian period. It lasted into the 1840s and was characterized by the assumption that the new consciousness about method was rooted in an old orthodoxy and that it therefore threatened no revolution and was really a simple, purely empirical technique accessible to anyone. "The deference to Baconianism in the early decades of the century, related, in part, to the need to advertise the sober, empirical character of scientific inquiry and to distance it from speculation and hypotheses which had controversial political or theological overtones" (Yeo, "Scientific Method and the Rhetoric of Science" 272).

A second phase of the debate over scientific method, extending from the 1840s into the 1870s, saw a manifest expansion of the power of science to alter perceptions and environments and retreat from the naive methodological assumptions of the early decades. Celebrations such as The Great Exposition in London (1851) and the Columbian Exposition in Philadelphia (1876) encapsulated the changes which science was making throughout society. This phase saw science retreat from the Baconian claim to universal access; simple empirical induction was devalued; hypothesis and theorizing were exalted; and the special genius of the great scientist began to be promoted.[15] Scientists like Huxley might still persist in addressing themselves to workingmen, but there was an emerging consensus that the popular audience were incompetent to judge the merits of scientific thinking.[16] Specialization began to isolate scientists from the general public, and even from scientists in other fields. Science was becoming professionalized and institutionalized: associations such as The British Association for the Advancement of Science (1831) and its American cousin, The American Association for the Advancement of Science (1848)—though they retained as one of their objectives the popularization of scientific knowledge—reflected this withdrawal into professionalism; and the proliferation of new university science departments and government commissions provided opportunities for scientists to pursue highly specialized fields of knowledge.[17]

In the third and final phase of the century, beginning in the 1870s, science abstracted itself from popular discourse.[18] Scientists no longer expected understanding from the general public; indeed, they expected incomprehension. "Popularization" was now something of an embarrassment to real scientists. In response, the general public naturally grew suspicious of a method which no longer was willing or able to explain itself, yet which clearly had the power to alter the character of their world— and not necessarily to their advantage.[19] The public, and even many scientists, began to doubt that secular salvation could be achieved through the scientific method.[20] Scientists began to admit that elements of uncertainty were inherent in their conclusions; statistics and probabilities became an accepted basis for scientific thinking,[21] but this acceptance was not transferrable logically or rhetorically to moral or aesthetic discourse. Morality and art deal with concrete realities. Schrödinger did not care whether the particular cat in his box was alive or dead; a moralist or an artist does. C.P. Snow's problem of the two cultures begins here. The detective, who claims to speak the language of the thinking scientist yet who acts morally in the sphere of the common man, offers an imaginative bridge between the diverging worlds of the scientist and the layman.

As science moved toward amoral abstraction and probability, the detective applied it heroically to the concrete exigencies of the modern world and derived from it absolutely certain conclusions. For several decades, he sustained this heroic illusion. But by the end of the First World War, the detective had forced upon him an awareness of the discredit into which his scientific positivism had fallen, and while never entirely renouncing his original soul and essence, he ceased to advertise it as his primary virtue. In his debut, he credited his success first to his disciplined method and then, perhaps, to his peculiar genius; as the Golden Age began, he promoted his genius and wore his method lightly.

Thus the evolution of science and popular attitudes toward science has a bearing on the evolution of a popular genre. The debate over scientific method in the early nineteenth century made thinking about knowing a topic of wide interest to the popular audience. Method was in the intellectual air when Poe invented the methodical detective; it is not surprising that contemporary editors, reviewers and readers singled this thinking hero out for praise and, more specifically, singled out the methodicalness of his thinking. There is more than a trace of Baconianism to Poe's Dupin in his first appearance, though Poe suppressed it in the two later stories, moving his intellectual hero toward a less empirical mode of thinking. It was, perhaps, this movement away from the Baconian consensus that prevented other writers from seeing the full advantages of a detective hero. Dupin's method became too idiosyncratic and esoteric at a time when real science in England and America was proclaiming itself thoroughly exoteric.

The next great detective—the detective who struck such a responsive chord in the popular imagination that he became the most written-about character in the history of literature and whose innumerable progeny continue to perform so successfully in the literary marketplace—was Sherlock Holmes, and he appeared during the third phase, as the divorce between scientific and popular culture was taking place. His method was that of the new science—empirical Baconianism enhanced by the appealing soupçon of individual genius—and his exercise of it was often deliberately mystifying: crawling over carpets with his lens, silently reviewing evidence with his pipe in his mouth, dropping cryptic hints. But Sherlock Holmes always explained the mystery: the mystery of the crime and the mystery of his method. He alluded to his authorship of abstruse treatises on the variability of human ears or the polyphonic motets of Lassus, but he explained his investigations—how he reached his conclusions as well as what he concluded—in terms that Watson and his intellectual peers might readily comprehend. Where the Dupin series dramatized the alienation of the scientific genius at a time when science seemed commonplace, the Holmes series argued for the reconciliation of the scientist and his society at the historical moment when many of the sciences were abandoning the pretense that the lay reader could comprehend the complexities of their concepts.

Of course, Holmes's scientific method was not comparable in its complexity to the methodologies of those real sciences. It may not have been comparable to the legitimate methodology of any science. But it seemed to be, and that was sufficient. What the detective story did was provide readers with two pleasures: one sensational and one logical. They knew they would encounter a sequence of crime, suspicion and clarification. But they would also encounter a *process* of investigation. This process should mystify them with cryptic clues and comments (such as the famous one about the curious incident of the dog in the night), but the obscurity is an intended part of the game, and it is always clarified in the end. The nuclear physicist does not, and can not, end his article in *The Journal of Nuclear Physics* with a translation of his algebraic mysteries into the common sense language of everyman. The hard sciences reached the point in the nineteenth century where Anglo-Saxon nouns and verbs were unequal to the task of conveying the necessary concepts and details (and even where they seemed to be—e.g. the "charm," "color," and "spin" of "quarks"— they were not). The scientific detective always can and does end by demystifying his mystifications; it is part of his contract. Dr. Watson (or Dr. Jervis or Walter Jameson) will be baffled by the detective's detecting as he detects, but in the end he (and the reader) comprehends every step, every deduction.

And there is as much satisfaction in learning how the detective knew as there is in learning what he knew. The reader anticipates not only the pleasure of discovering whodunit, but of discovering how the detective reasoned his way to the discovery. The formulaic end of the detective story requires satisfaction of both expectations. In the puzzle-oriented detective stories of the Golden Age, this led to the familiar convention of the post-discovery dissertation by the detective in which he seizes the final chapter or two to deliver a detailed exposition of the progress of his inquiry. The actions of the actors—criminals, victims, suspects—claim the interest of most of the narrative; the thoughts of the thinker—the detective—claim the ultimate interest. His terminal lecture becomes as essential to the detective story as the dramatic revelation of the murderer. Less patient (or less intellectually rigorous) readers have permitted many modern detective story writers to imply more and explicate less, but even today, very few readers will be completely satisfied with simply knowing who did it; we want the detective to tell us how he (or she) knew, even if, instead of a chain of reasoning, he offers only the overlooked clue of the tell-tale stain on the business card. Even writers who reserve the surprise discovery of the criminal to the final sentence or word precede it, sometimes awkwardly, with an exposition of how the about-to-be-announced discovery was discovered.

The lending library in hell might, as the old line would have it, be stocked with Agatha Christie novels with the last page, identifying the villain, torn out. The sinners would suffer equally, however, were that page retained, but those crucial pages in which Poirot tells us how he identified the villain were missing. We require both satisfactions: we want to know and we want to know how to know. We close every good detective story with two reactions: "Oh, that's who it was!" and "Aha, that's how he knew." The first response is not superior to the second. If we are suitably pious, we may continue the first thought with, "There, but for the grace of God, go I"; the second, less piously, leads us to: "That, if I knew his method, I too might have known."

And this, I think, is why we read detective stories.

Chapter 2

Edgar Allan Poe

M. Auguste Dupin may not have been the first detecting hero, but he was the first detective hero. His predecessors, however ingenious their inferences, were dilettantes. Dupin professed detection; it was his raison d'etre. It was also the source of his special appeal: from the very beginning, contemporary reviewers took note of his distinctive character as a thinking hero.[1] Dupin became the original of all fictional detectives because he was the first hero to invite readers to identify with an intellect that uses methodical analysis to disentangle sensational moral crises. The hero's virtue displays itself entirely in mental activity, not in physical action. The violence is past before the detective engages in his heroic struggle: the victims are dead, the letter stolen before the narrative begins. And Dupin's methodical analysis is completely secular in its origins and applications. Though it is not exactly scientific in nature, it is certainly not religious or transcendental. The detective uses worldly techniques to investigate a world which, as it consistently happens, yields indisputable truths to that worldly technique.

The detection skills of the hero of the political fable (Godwin's *Caleb Williams*) or the oriental romance (Voltaire's *Zadig*) or the Greek tragedy (Sophocles's *Oedipus Rex*) or the Biblical Apocrypha (*The History of Bel*) may be entertaining and even illuminating,[2] but they are not definitive: they do not imply that the world consistently yields truth to such skills; they do not imply that such skills completely define the character of the hero. As Zadig walks in a wood in the third chapter of *Zadig* (1747), he deduces from a pair of tracks in the sand the existence of a lame, long-eared Spaniel bitch and a fast horse with 23-carat gold studs on its bit. The exercise is impressive, and Zadig's method may be, as T.H. Huxley would later assert, a prototype of the true scientific method—what, in his famous lecture to working men, "The Method of Zadig" (1880), Huxley called "retrospective prophecy."[3] And, of course, for this chapter, Voltaire had to design the surfaces of Zadig's world—the sand in which the bitch's dugs had dragged, the touchstone against which the horse's bit had rubbed—in order to make his deductions possible. But this wood is the only place in Zadig's world contrived to permit such deductions. The reader may extrapolate the lesson, of course, and take the wood as the epitome of the world, but the narrative moves on to other places and other actions. In the true detective story, the power of method to know the world is actual, central, and comprehensive. No extrapolation, either logical or imaginative, is required. The detective (and the reader) may scan any scene presented by the author for concealed meanings; indeed, he must, for every scene conceals meanings.

The detection skills of the detective hero do define the detective's world. The narrative of the detective story depends entirely upon his ability to uncover the moral order of his world through a methodical observation and interpretation of its surfaces. His need to detect determines in a very practical way the actions of every character and the features of every scene. Those actions and features must always allow two plausible readings, one erroneous and one true. The first is the easy reading, the one toward which the inertia of our prejudices inclines us (and, usually, the uniformed police); the second is the hard reading, the one derived from the detective's thoughtful analysis and active interrogation of persons and things. Both must be justified by reference to the superficial appearance of events, though only one—the detective's—sufficiently (and therefore conclusively) explains *all* of the appearances.

The detective of the detective story thus inhabits a peculiar world, a world whose ontology is defined by its epistemology. The plot, the scene, the thoughts and behavior of characters—in short, the world of the story—everything is subordinate to the detective's ability to know the truth through methodical analysis. Critics may debate the types and degrees of realism in the subgenres of the detective story, but the essential quality of Reality in all of them is Knowability. The Knower and his Knowable World are the primary determinants of what is real in the detective story; matters such as dropped "g's" and criminal argot, country estates and mean streets are secondary. Readers of detective stories know they can enjoy the sensational violence and deceptions of the narrative because the genre, as part of its fundamental contract with its readers, guarantees that the human intelligence of the detective will penetrate the deceptions and secure just punishments for the agents of violence.

Edgar Allan Poe was the first writer to create a realistic fictional world that exists to provide a stage for the operation of the interpretive intelligence of a hero. In order for his detective, Dupin, to infer meaning from his world, Poe had to infer Dupin's world from Dupin's inferences: the shutters of Madame L'Espanaye's house in "The Murders in the Rue Morgue" are "of the peculiar kind called by Parisian carpenters *ferrades*" (419) because that kind of shutter affords "an excellent hold for the hands" and so, Dupin can eventually deduce, a homicidal orangutang might make his escape. Dupin's analytic mind, then, and not the tools of a Parisian carpenter, is the real creator of Madame L'Espanaye's shutters, and of a host of other details as well. The detective's methodical mind is existentially prior to his world, and this priority is, of course, a practical priority for the writer. Poe had to construct his story backwards, as his friend,

Thomas Dunn English, confirmed in a review in October 1845. This notion of backward-construction was a novelty at the time— Poe himself had been impressed to learn from Dickens that Godwin had practiced it in the composition of *Caleb Williams*— but it became a standard technique in detective story writing.

Dupin's method was more than the ontological basis of the fiction that featured him; it was, as Poe realized, the main source of Dupin's appeal.[4] In a letter to Poe of 4 August 1846, Philip Pendleton Cooke praised "The Murders in the Rue Morgue" and wrote of Dupin, "I think your French friend, for the most part, fine in his deductions from over-laid & unnoticed small facts, but sometimes too minute & hair-splitting" (*Log* 661). On 9 August, Poe replied:

> You are right about the hair-splitting of my French friend:—that is all done for effect. These tales of ratiocination owe most of their popularity to being something in a new key. I do not mean to say they are not ingenious—but people think them more ingenious than they are—on account of their method and *air* of method. In the "Murders in the Rue Morgue," for instance, where is the ingenuity of unravelling a web which you (the author) have woven for the express purpose of unravelling? The reader is made to confound the ingenuity of the supposititious Dupin with that of the writer of the story. (*Complete Works* 265)

Poe compliments himself on the sleight of hand by which he transforms his own ingenuity at constructing a decipherable world into the detective's ingenuity at deciphering that world. The author begins with "the express purpose of unravelling"; keeping this purpose in mind, he weaves his web—the detective's world; and finally he depicts the detective methodically unraveling it. The reader, moving forward through the story, senses only the epistemological power which the detective's method seems to grant him over his world; he does not see that the power derives simply from having the method define that world in the process of constructing the story. "Method" and "*air* of method": these, according to Poe, are the essential qualities of the detective story.[5]

Poe always asserted a high estimation of the power of method to control the world. There are many instances of Poe flogging method as the surest proof of intellectual excellence and the surest means of imaginative creativity. Early in his career, he published his exposure of "Maezel's Chess-Player" (April 1836), announcing that his conclusions resulted from "a mathematical demonstration, *a priori*" and offering a numbered, 17-point argument. He made much of his success in inferring the course of Dickens's *Barnaby Rudge* after reading the first installments of the novel in May 1841. Having produced his signature poem, "The Raven," Poe wrote "The Philosophy of Composition" to argue that he had composed it in logical sequence of steps, beginning with his choice of meter and of the vowel sounds for the refrain. Poe's well-advertised mastery of cryptography, demonstrated in open challenges to readers and culminating in the essay, "A Few Words on Secret Writing" (July 1841), and the detective story, "The Gold-Bug" (June 1843), also exemplify his infatuation with methodical thought.

The true hero of methodical thought is, of course, the detective.[6] Poe portrayed this hero best in his three Dupin stories, "The Murders in the Rue Morgue" (April 1841), "The Mystery of Marie Rogêt" (November 1842-February 1843), and "The Purloined Letter" (September 1845). ("The Gold Bug," June 1843, and "Thou Art the Man," November 1844, are also usually counted as detective stories, and could also be used to illustrate the point.) In each of the Dupin tales, and under remarkable conditions in "The Mystery of Marie Rogêt," Poe contrived to create a world of surfaces that could yield an abundance of significant meanings to the methodical intelligence of the Monsieur C. Auguste Dupin.

ii

That method is the principal attribute of Dupin's intelligence. The first Dupin story opens neither with a portrait of the detective nor with an account of the crime, but with a substantial Discourse on Method. The narrator, Dupin's nameless companion, offers a three-page prologue to the "The Murders in the Rue Morgue." In it, he discourses on "the faculty of resolution," making the argument that the games of draughts and whist require far more subtle powers of analysis than does the vulgarly more esteemed game of chess. This little treatise—and despite the protest ("I am not now writing a treatise, but simply prefacing a somewhat peculiar narrative by observations very much at random"), it is a treatise—begins with the proposition, "The mental features discoursed of as the analytical are, in themselves, but little susceptible of analysis. We appreciate them only in their effects" (I.397).[7] "Analysis" becomes the label of the method which the narrator announces and Dupin practices.[8] The two other key terms, frequently repeated, are "method," implying the objectivity and the rigor of the thinker's progress, and "acumen," suggesting an especially keen or incisive practice of the analytical method, and perhaps as well the flamboyance with which Dupin displays the results of his analyses: the method should look sharp as well as be sharp.[9]

Having developed his Discourse with illustrations—the games of draughts, whist, and chess—the narrator concludes with a distinction: "The analytical power should not be confounded with simple ingenuity; for while the analyst is necessarily ingenious, the ingenious man is often remarkably incapable of analysis" (I.399). A parallel distinction, he adverts, is that Romantic staple, the distinction between "fancy" and "imagination": "It will be found, in fact, that the ingenious are always fanciful, and the truly imaginative never otherwise than analytic" (I.400).[10] The narrator is riding one of Poe's hobbyhorses—the consanguinity of analysis and imagination (cf.

"The Philosophy of Composition")—and the relationship will be developed further in later discourses.

The opening pages of the initial detective story thus surely make the primacy of method in the genre undebatable. The reader meets the mind—more exactly, the method of the mind— of the detective first, before the detective, before the crime. The story which dramatizes the practice of that method is, explicitly, an appendage to the Discourse on Method: "The narrative which follows will appear to the reader somewhat in light of a commentary upon the propositions just advanced" (400). And the narrative-commentary, when it arrives, transpires in two parts: the first a short thought experiment, and the second a detective story. In the experiment Poe finally gives his method a name and a local habitation: Monsieur C. Auguste Dupin, the scion of an illustrious family now living in reduced circumstances at au troisème, no. 33, rue Dunôt, Faubourg St. Germain, Paris. Poe contrives for Dupin a purely mental exercise: the famous episode of his successful reconstruction of the course of his companion's 15-minute-long silent meditation. Only after having proved the effectiveness of his method in elucidating a sequence of mental events, does Poe allow Dupin to apply it to the problem of elucidating a bizarre sequence of physical events: the murders of Madame and Mademoiselle L'Esplanye. Dupin and his companion read newspaper accounts of the bizarre murder of two women; they visit the scene; and, applying his analytic method, Dupin correctly infers the circumstances of the crime and the identity of the criminal.

The mental experiment is a virtuoso performance; the chain of associations which Dupin traces is fantastic enough to be unforgettable. It cannot be taken at face value; even the naive reader understands that Poe is having his sport in at least some of the connections.[11] Still, for all the playfulness, the exercise does imply that God's omniscience is not the only means for penetrating even the secrets of the mind. Dupin's analytic method works equally well, deriving intangible truth (a history of thoughts and feelings) from tangible signs (glances, murmurs, smiles). The detective story is equally unforgettable in its sensationalism: two women brutally murdered, one stuffed upside-down in a chimney, and the actual villain proving to be an all too brutal orangutang. And yet, as Poe himself saw, the tale's unusual appeal lay not in these unforgettable elements, but in the logic of that preliminary Discourse. Most readers who return to the story probably skip past it, yet it is the source of the narrative and of the genre. As Poe said, "the method and *air* of method" are the essence of his detective story, and even those who skim the Discourse on first reading cannot be unaffected by its placement. "The Murders in the Rue Morgue" is unmistakably about method.

The Discourse calls the method "analysis": "that moral activity which *disentangles*" (I.397). This means a "retrograde" mode of thinking which moves from the visible jumble of consequences backward to the invisible (because past) but necessary causes. The narrator identifies "analysis" as "the highest branch" of mathematical study, contrasting it with the lower branch called "calculation." "Calculation" is, it seems, mere logical elaboration of possible outcomes within a confined field of speculation (the rules of the particular game), and so is the method best adapted to playing chess. Chess merely requires the calculation of the practical consequences of a finite (though huge) number of possible moves. A game like draughts, however, requires more. The possible moves are far fewer in draughts, and so the calculations are correspondingly easier. But the competitor must anticipate the motives which cause his opponent to choose one or another of these fewer options. The chess player must read the board; the draughts player must read a mind. "Deprived of ordinary resources, the analyst throws himself into the spirit of his opponent" (I.398). Through close observation of the opponent's visible movements, he infers his mental habits and anticipates his moves. This, the Discourse asserts, requires calculation to be supplemented by imagination: the result is successful analysis.

The calculator operates expertly within a set of rules, often very complex rules, to be sure. But the analyst goes beyond the rules. Developing the whist illustration, the narrator writes: "Our player confines himself not at all; nor, because the game is the object, does he reject deductions from things external to the game. He examines the countenance of his partner...considers the mode of sorting the cards in each hand...notes every variation of face" (I.399). The analyst differs from the calculator, then, "not so much in the validity of his inference as in the quality of observation. The necessary knowledge is that of *what* to observe." The analyst—the detective—knows *how* to know because he knows *what* to know. In Poe's vocabulary, he adds "imagination" to "inference" (or "calculation"): the union of these two qualities produces the methodical genius which may discover the truth.

The heroic dimensions of Dupin's practice of intellectual method in "Murders in the Rue Morgue" emerges in the contrast to the story's antihero. The murderer is an orangutang, a beast, as the quotation from Cuvier declares, of "gigantic stature...prodigious strength and activity...wild ferocity, and...imitative propensities" (I.424); whatever else he is, the villain is unmethodical. The imitative propensity leads him to mime shaving Madame L'Espanaye; the ferocity leads him to decapitate her; the strength and activity enable him to escape down the lightening rod. The homicidal orangutang is the antithesis of the deliberate Dupin. In his preliminary thought experiment, Dupin proved that his method could disclose the abstruse cogitations of his intellectual companion; in the detective narrative, Dupin proves that the method works equally well when applied to the spontaneous actions of a brute.

Unfortunately, even within the small universe of the three Dupin tales, the method of the detective cannot be easily reduced to a single rule. The term "Analysis" (and "method" and "acumen"), which the Discourse so carefully expounds, does not survive the first story.[12] Replacing it in the later stories are two new ones: "ratiocination" and "mathematics." Though it is the label most often associated with the method of Dupin, the term, "ratiocination," actually appears only three times, and then in the least read Dupin tale, "Marie Rogêt." (Its only other appearance in Poe's fiction is in "Mesmeric Revelation"). Poe himself, however, sanctioned the term by referring to "my tales of ratiocination" (e.g. to James Russell Lowell, 2 July 1844), and it can be used to distinguish Dupin's later method from his earlier (i.e. analysis).

The two methods are, of course, versions of a single approach; only the emphasis has shifted, but the shift is a significant one. The elevation of mathematics is part of the shift. "Mathematical," with its aura of a priori exactness and verifiability, had been applied by reviewers to the reasoning of the ratiocinative tales and by Poe in "The Philosophy of Composition" to his demonstration of the technique employed in the Composition of "The Raven." "Mathematical" is used only once in "Murders in the Rue Morgue," in the passage which precipitates "analysis" from the broader category of "mathematical study." In the two later stories, Poe allowed his detective to make his appeal directly to mathematics, abandoning "analysis" as an intermediary subset.[13] Poe acquires two results from this shift. The first is a clearer association of the detective's technique with a discipline that has a long and prestigious heritage, from Pythagoras and Plato to Descartes. It affiliates Dupin with the line of rationalists who pursued the purest, least empirical of the sciences.[14] The second result is the obliteration of the Discourse's carefully drawn contrast between two types of mathematics: Dupin's method now implicitly includes the "calculation" which the narrator had disparaged in the opening Discourse. This does not, however, mean an abandonment of the imaginative element which there distinguished "analysis" from mere "calculation." On the contrary, rather than subordinate imagination as a differentia between two species of mathematics, Poe elevates it as a coordinate value in his detective's method.

Coleridge—a thinker frequently cited by Poe—had made imagination a central concept in Romantic aesthetics and epistemology, and Poe was surely conscious of the complexities of his allusion. He was also conscious of the paradox of linking imagination to methodical analysis. Even in a Romantic vocabulary which associates Imagination and Reason, method would seem to belong to Understanding, a mode of knowing which is opposed to Reason as Fancy is opposed to Imagination. In any event, to the common reader—a reader who shares the surprise of Inspector G—— and the narrator at Dupin's linkage of mathematics and poetry—imagination is likely to be viewed precisely as the irrational, anti-methodical component of genius.[15]

Poe's elevation of mathematics as a model of precise thinking has implications for the method of his detective. Mathematics is most often invoked in the last Dupin adventure, "The Purloined Letter." There, echoing the narrator's earlier remarks about "analysis," Dupin argues that mathematics, in itself, is mere sterile reasoning. Mathematicians tend to confuse their logic observations with reality, and are thus baffled by a world "where $x^2 + px$ is not altogether equal to q" (I.692-92). Inspector G—— is such a baffled investigator. In a world where the rules stipulate that "hide" equals "conceal," the Inspector would be a genius, able to discover any purloined letter, even one tightly rolled and squeezed into a hollow chair leg. But when the logic of the mathematician is combined with the imagination of the poet, the result will be a more powerful method, the method of a great villain like Minister D—— ("As poet and mathematician, he would reason well; as mere mathematician, he could not have reasoned at all," I.691) or of a great detective like Dupin.

"Ratiocination," as expounded and practiced in "Marie Rogêt" and "Purloined Letter," then, is a method composed of equal parts of poetical imagination and mathematical logic. The "Analysis" of "Murders in the Rue Morgue," on the other hand, is a form of mathematical logic which relies essentially upon the power of imagination. The distinction may seem slight, very slight, but it seems to reflect Poe's hesitation between pushing his epistemological hero toward what could be understood as a scientific discipline and pushing him away. Analysis might be scientific; Ratiocination is not. In his original conception, Dupin betrayed his roots in the new promise of scientific method; in his later adventures, Poe reintroduced an element, however small, of the transcendental thrust that characterized most of his fiction.

iii

"Scientific method" was, in Poe's life-time, an indefinite concept which was just acquiring definition and prestige. Poe came to maturity at the moment when American intellectual culture was just beginning to appreciate the potential power of science. "Throughout the antebellum decades, the prestige once associated with Locke and natural rights was gravitating massively toward Bacon and the inductive philosophy." (Bozeman 26). The Baconian method had, wrote Edward Everett in 1823, "become synonymous with the *true* philosophy."[16] The American notion of what constituted the Baconian scientific method was, however, rather vague. It "evoked a cluster of related ideas: a strenuously empiricist approach to all forms of knowledge, a declared greed for the objective fact, and a corresponding distrust of 'hypotheses,' of 'imagination,' and, indeed, of reason itself" (Bozeman 3). This is a distinctly un-Poe-like cluster, but Poe was nonetheless fascinated by the new Baconian science, and he was sophisticated enough to read Mill's *System of Logic* and to insert a serious criticism of it in *Eureka*. A final element of the popular conception of the Baconian method lay in a bias toward taxonomy as the paradigm of true empirical science, a development related to the prestige of the French anatomist, Georges Cuvier (1769-1832) (Daniels 65).[17] Poe's first book—his redaction of *The Conchologist's First Book , In Which the Animals, According to Cuvier, Are Given...*(1839)—was a work of taxonomic science.[18] Jacques Barzun, setting the context for the emergence of the detective story as a distinctive genre, observes: "The literary imagination of the first half of the nineteenth century was caught by what it understood of method in the new sciences (especially fossil reconstruction in geology) and by its sympathy for the new criminology, which called for the accurate use of physical evidence" (Barzun 13). Poe's genius was to perceive the new use to which Cuvierian science might be put.

Poe was well-informed on contemporary science and scientific method. In his early poem, "Sonnet——To Science" (1829), he makes a familiar Romantic accusation that science commits crimes against the organic vision of imagination (dragging Diana from her car, driving the Hamadryad from the wood, tearing the Naiad from her flood, and, in the last line, tearing "the summer dream beneath the Tamarind tree" from the poet). And Poe's predilection for gothic horrors and anti-modernist satire might imply an instinctive aversion to the consequences of Bacon's *Novum Organum*. In a story like "The Thousand-and-Second Tale of Scheherazade" (1845) he does align himself with those who despise the mere material progress which Baconian science seemed to promise. But he did not therefore prefer ignorance to torn Naiads; he did not place Science on his personal index. Throughout his career, he displayed—even flaunted—his awareness of the achievements of contemporary scientists.

It is easy enough to sneer at signs of the superficiality of his knowledge. Much of his information evidently came from digests; what is impressive is how much information he digested. Poe wrote intelligently of scientific matters in his journalism, but even more noteworthy is his pioneering work in science fiction. Harold Beaver has identified 16 stories that justify inclusion in *The Science Fiction of Edgar Allan Poe.*[19] These demonstrate a wide range of scientific reference: astronomy, chemistry, physics, electricity, botany, engineering, and, to be sure, mesmerism and phrenology. Nor are all the references superficial. In *Eureka* alone, Poe comments upon the ideas of von Humboldt, Laplace, Aristotle, Bacon, Kant, John Stuart Mill, Jean Francois Campollion, Kepler, Pascal, Baron de Bielfeld, Maskelyne-Cavendish-Bailly, Jacob Bryant, John Pringle Nichol, Wilhelm Olbers, Plato, Newton, F.W. Bessel, John Baptiste Fourier, Johann Heinrich von Mädler, Sir John Hershel, Friedrich Wilhelm August Argelander and Johann Franz Encke. Some references are certainly glib, but most show a quite respectable grasp of often complex data and concepts.[20]

Still, *Eureka* offers itself as an alternative to the vision of the scientists it surveys. It uses science against itself to argue for Poe's singular vision of a universe that throbs between unity and multiplicity. In this respect, it only reiterates at the end of Poe's career the message of the early "Sonnet—To Science," But it is a "prose-poem," not a poem, and the key difference between the two lies in *Eureka's* confidence that the anti-scientific vision can be scientifically elaborated in a treatise. Eureka is a methodical exposition, and it declares its method in its first pages. Poe opens *Eureka* as he opened his first detective story, with a Discourse on Method. Furthering the parallel, the Discourse on Method in both the detective story and the cosmology is delivered by a secondary voice. Dupin is primary in "Murders in the Rue Morgue"; the Discourse is assigned to the narrator. A neutral persona—Poe, presumably—is primary in *Eureka*; the Discourse is assigned to a letter-writer from the *Mare Tenebrarum*. And, lest these connections between his methodological tales of ratiocination and his methodological essay on cosmology be overlooked, Poe inserts an explicit sign. In the course of a discussion of the nature of the universe as radiation from a unified origin, Poe stops to make a methodological point: "Now, I have elsewhere observed that it is by just such difficulties as the one now in question—such peculiarities—such roughnesses—such protuberances above the plane of the ordinary—that Reason feels her way, if at all, in her truth" (I.1293). Elsewhere, as Poe's footnote informs us, is in "Murders in the Rue Morgue," where Dupin somewhat more succinctly makes the same point.[21] The logic that works in criminal investigation works as well in cosmological speculation.

In *Eureka*, Poe directly challenges the scientific methods of Aristotle ("Aries Tottle") and Bacon ("one Hog"). He first dismisses Aristotle's "*deductive or à priori* philosophy" (I.1263) then turns to Hog's "*à posteriori or inductive*" system. This latter plan, the Discourse reports, "referred altogether to sensation. He [Hog] proceeded by observing, analyzing, and classifying facts...and arranging them into general laws." Poe's summary reflects quite accurately the tenets of contemporary Baconism, even to the taxonomic inclination to "classify" after the model of Cuvier. The dominance of these two systems of knowing, and "especially" that of Hog, has put a virtual stop to all creative thinking (I.1264).

The disparagement of the Baconian method as "the crawling system" has particular relevance to the evolution of Dupin's method. *Eureka* asserts that "The vital taint...in Baconianism—its most lamentable fount of error—lay in its tendency to throw power and consideration into the hands of merely perceptive men—...the diggers and pedlers of minute facts, for the most part in physical science" (I.1265). Poe proposes as his alternative a method that proceeds by speculation and theory (I.1269; he also advocates that bogey of the Baconians, "hypothesis," see e.g. I.1301). He offers Kepler and Laplace as appropriate models for imitation. Poe was in advance of his time in this regard. Mistrust of hypothesis and imagination was still scientific orthodoxy. Advanced scientific thought was just arriving at the same criticism of naive Baconianism. If science meant militantly pedestrian collection of data, then Poe's hero of knowing would prefer heresy.

In his discussion of the solar system in *Eureka*, Poe pauses to contrast "the three immortal laws guessed by the imaginative Kepler" with subsequent demonstrations of "the patient and mathematical Newton." It is, Poe asserts, "far too fashionable to sneer at all speculation under the comprehensive *sobriquet*, 'guess-work'." It all depends, he points out, on *who* guesses. "In guessing with Plato, we spend our time to better purpose, now and then, than in hearkening to a deep demonstration by Alcmæon" (I.1332). Poe's pantheon of geniuses (the "guessers" in this self-deprecating passage; otherwise,the ratiocinators) then, includes Kepler, Plato—and Dupin. The crawlers, the "diggers and peddlers," include Aristotle, Bacon, Newton and Inspector G——. Plato, as the supreme poet-mathematician in western civilization, is, indeed, the ideal prototype of Dupin, and it is Plato's speculative, ratiocinative method that Dupin ultimately embodies.

The Baconian scientist par excellence in the Dupin saga is, of course, the ineffectual Inspector G——. In "The Purloined Letter," it is *his* method that relies upon crawling inch by inch over Minister D——'s rooms and even over the bricks in his courtyard. He is the one who depends upon the instruments of physical science, patiently seeking the truth by carefully measuring the Minister's cabinets, using "fine long needles" to probe seat cushions and book covers, examining furniture joints "by the aide of a most powerful microscope." Dupin's ratiocination, on the other hand, has no use for quantification. That sort of demonstration belongs to the "patient and mathematical Newton," not to the "imaginative Kepler." Only by adding Keplerian imagination to Newtonian mathematics does he achieve the ratiocinative method. It is precisely the Newtonian (Baconian) "patience," which implies a slavish pursuit of matters of fact, that must be subtracted in order to liberate the ratiocinator to practice his method.

Dupin collects none of the insignia of the scientist. Even in the 1840s, the scientist could be recognized by his instruments, especially his chemical apparatus. When in 1818 Mary Shelley wanted to give Victor Frankenstein a veneer of scientific authority, she had him attend chemistry lectures and boast "at the end of two years, I made some discoveries in the improvement of some chemical instruments which procured me great esteem and admiration at the university" (Shelley, *Frankenstein* 53). Poe makes no effort to endow Dupin with the accoutrements of any hard science. On the contrary, he inhabits "a time-eaten and grotesque mansion" and makes fetish of blocking sunlight from his experience. He succeeds in "The Purloined Letter" because, through speculative reasoning—identifying with mind of his antagonist—he enters Minister D——'s apartment looking for the letter in an obvious place. He succeeds in "Marie Rogêt" by analyzing newspaper accounts, never leaving his apartment. The experiments that verify his speculations are left to the Baconian Inspector. And, even more telling, Poe felt it unnecessary to provide the results of the verification: at the conclusion of the story, he merely inserted an editorial parenthesis informing the reader, "we have taken the liberty of here omitting, from the MSS. placed in our hands, such portion as details the *following up* of the apparently slight clew obtained by Dupin" (I.553).

Though pre-eminently methodical in a Platonic, Keplerian, ratiocinative way, it would seem, then, that nothing could be less correct than to insist that Dupin "is all scientist....Dupin is scientist, scientific process, and scientific object" (Woods 21). The error is to confuse science with method. And yet Dupin might have been a scientist. As the "analyst" of the first story, he was poised to become a scientific, even Baconian inquirer. In the manner of the true scientific detective, he interrogates things. He does examine the scene of the crime. He surveys the house and the neighborhood "with a minuteness of attention" that bewilders his companion and suggests a Newtonian patience. Inside, he scrutinizes everything. He detects the broken nail in the window-frame and the tuft of orangutang hair in the widow's fist; he even executes "a fac-simile drawing" of the pattern of bruises on the widow's throat, and is so exact in his sketch that his companion is able to identify the pattern as corresponding to the description of the digits of an orangutang in Cuvier (I.424). This certainly seems to be objective, quantified scientific inquiry, and the extended allusion to the work of the famous anatomist (and paradigm for early nineteenth-century Baconianism), Georges Cuvier, seems an overt claim to scientific auspices. To be sure, as he later reveals, Dupin's prior reading of the newspaper accounts had led him to certain hypotheses which he intended to test, and this indicates a deviance toward the Keplerian model, but Dupin himself describes his thinking as "à posteriori" (I.418).

In the end, however, these signs of scientific method were discarded, and Poe turned his hero toward a more speculative method, constructing for him worlds in which patient Baconian accumulation of facts leads only to accumulations of facts. The Inspector knows, to "the fiftieth part of a line," the dimensions of the Minister's cabinet, but he will never know where the purloined letter is. He has a method—one method—and he works it inflexibly. Dupin knows that method, and applied it successfully in the Rue Morgue; but Dupin knows that the best craftsman selects his tools according to the task. Dupin is, in a sense, a meta-methodician; he selects from a palette of methods, and in "The Purloined Letter" he prefers imaginative ratiocination to Baconian analysis of detail.

Poe was free in the 1840s to permit his methodical hero this license. The scientific method had not yet proven its claim to exclusive authority. Its power was apparent and growing, but not absolute, and its nature—what is the true scientific method?—was still debatable. That Dupin began as a near-scientist is a tribute to the emerging orthodoxy. A hero of methodical thinking was first conceivable at the dawn of methodical science: Poe was doubtless influenced by the scientific precedent as were the reviewers and readers who were struck by Dupin's new type of intellectual heroism. But Poe was still at liberty to have his detective try other, more metaphysical methods. As the century progressed and the hegemony of the scientific method became more apparent and more accepted, this liberty was lost. By the time Sherlock Holmes appeared in 1886, the only possible method for detecting truth was the scientific.

Chapter 3

Gaboriau, Pinkerton, Green

The interval between the publication of Dupin's last case in 1845 and of Sherlock Holmes's first case in 1887 was not entirely a wasteland for the detective. Histories of the genre have filled it with a host of transitional figures, several of them quite imposing. Charles Dickens, with Inspector Buckett of *Bleak House* (1853) and Wilkie Collins with Sergeant Cuff of *The Moonstone* (1868) made the most prominent contributions to developing the popular figure of the detective, unless Dostoevesky's Porfiry Petrovich (*Crime and Punishment* [1866]) is counted in the category. The detectives of Dickens and Collins cannot be casually dismissed, but they are not masters of method. They inquire, and they advance plots, and they are interesting as characters, but the narratives in which they appear have not been constructed to display their intellectual power to methodically infer the hidden plot of a moral action. As H. Douglas Thomson has observed, Sergeant Cuff is the first detective "with a sensibility greater than his sense" (Thomson 63); it is his sensibility that matters. Inspector Buckett and Sergeant Cuff show that the problem of knowing how to know in moral crises remained a concern of writers and readers; but the primary interest of the novels of Dickens and Collins lies in the ramifications of the crisis upon the minds and actions of the principal characters, not upon the method by which knowledge is achieved.

49

Considerably less prominent but somewhat more relevant is the work of Andrew Forrester, Jr. Forrester himself seems to be a bit of a mystery. He published a number of stories in periodicals, and these were collected in three volumes—*The Revelations of a Private Detective* (1863), *Secret Service* (1864), and *The Female Detective* (1864)—but it is not even clear whether "Andrew Forrester, Jr." is a name or a pseudonym.[1] His best work appears in the stories collected in *The Female Detective,* and his protagonist here, Mrs. G———— of the Metropolitan Police, functions as a didactically methodical investigator. In "The Unknown Weapon," for instance, she pauses at several junctures to detail the "inferences" ("if I may use so pompous a word") which she has made and which will guide the next stage of her inquiry. At one point, she enumerates twelve distinct inferences which lead her to the conclusion ("the condensed inference of all these inferences") that she must find a mysterious box (Forrester 47). Toward the end of the story, she makes an explicit (and explicitly methodological) allusion to "Edgar Poe," referring to Dupin's discourse on concealing objects in open places in "The Purloined Letter." The rigor of Mrs. G————'s thinking is impressive; Forrester entertains no brief for feminine intuition. But the slightness of Mrs. G————'s personality, implied in the omission of lower case letters in her name, prevented her from becoming a popular embodiment of methodical thinking. Forrester's stories were appealing enough to justify reissues, but they failed to capture the public imagination.

Three quite popular writers during the interval between Poe and Conan Doyle did succeed in writing about detectives who were in different ways methodical. Emile Gaboriau created Monsieur Lecoq, unquestionably the most important detective between Dupin and Holmes; Allan Pinkerton composed semi-factual narratives which best exemplify the contemporary image (self-image) of the real detective; and Anna Katharine Green invented Ebenezer Gryce, who comes somewhere between the

Dickensian-Collinsian detective-in-a-story and the Conan-Doylish detective-in-a-detective-story.

i

Etienne Emile Gaboriau was born 1832, the year that Cuvier, Dupin's scientist, died. It was also the year in which the French physicist, Nicholas Carnot died, having completed pioneering work in thermodynamics and in which a demonstration of the power of the new technology was supplied when the first passenger-carrying railroad in France began operation. Gaboriau was, however, evidently not impressed by these coincidences; his detective, Lecoq, does not claim to be a scientist, though he never disdains science either. Gaboriau was, however, much impressed by Monsieur Dupin, especially the more empirical Dupin of "The Murders in the Rue Morgue"; though neither a poet nor a mathematician, Lecoq performs creditable feats of analysis based on careful observation of behavioral and physical evidence. Poe's tales of ratiocination had been among those translated into French in his own lifetime.[2] Gaboriau's admiration of these tales was evidently strong enough to inspire him to attempt to imitate them early in his own career as a writer (Gaboriau vii).[3] Gaboriau made his living working in whatever literary genres paid. He published some 20 books between 1861 and 1881 (the last four being issued after his death in 1873). Of these, nine, beginning with *L'Affair Lerouge* (1866), can be classified crime or detective novels; and Gaboriau's principal detective, Lecoq, appears in five of these.

Lecoq plays a minor role in *L'Affaire Lerouge*. He appears as a reformed criminal in the service of the police. This background was surely intended to echo that of the famous Vidocq. François Eugène Vidocq (1775-1857) is usually honored as history's first professional detective. After an early career as a thief, he enlisted as an informer under Napoleon, becoming chief of the Paris

Sûreté in 1811. His conversion to the side of the angels was apparently incomplete; charges of corruption pursued him. He was not, in any event, a hero of method. Disguise was his most notable device; his most effective seems to have been solving robberies perpetrated by his own agents. Forced to resign in 1827, he spent his last 30 years as a writer (the four volumes of his *Mémoires*, 1828-29, were immediately translated into English), a private detective, and occasional policeman. Despite his fame, he died in poverty.

The great popularity of *L'Affaire Lerouge* led to four encores for Lecoq, but Gaboriau chose not to pursue the criminal/policeman ambivalence of the Vidocqian model (Balzac, in the figure of Vautrin, showed what might be done with it). In the next three Lecoq novels (*Le Crime d'Orcival*, 1867; *Le Dossier no. 113*, 1867; and *Les Esclaves de Paris*, 1868) the detective plays a larger role and plays it straight, exercising a genius for methodical, Dupinian investigation which places him in the main line of development of the detective story. But he also retains a Vidocqian reliance upon disguise, and this requires a comment. Disguise is probably the clearest alternative to methodical inquiry. It is a physical rather than a mental technology; its discoveries are actual rather than inferred (the disguised detective tricks an admission from a witness or overhears a confession from a suspect); it is sensational—visible, dramatic, active—rather than cerebral; and it certainly works. Lecoq uses disguise, and explicitly values it. He declares to a magistrate in *Monsieur Lecoq*, "A detective who can't equal the most skilful actor in the matter of make-up is no better than an ordinary policeman" (197). In the police stories of Gaboriau's English contemporary, "Waters," disguise serves the detective as his principal device, and as a result, *Recollections of a Policeman* (1852) remains a Neanderthal curiosity in the prehistory of the detective story.[4] Lecoq exploits the dramatic possibilities of investigation-by-disguise in the manner of Vidocq and Waters, but he also declares allegiance to the Dupinian creed of investigation-by-intellectual method, and it is the latter addition which earns him his high place in the history of the development of the detective story.

By most accounts, Lecoq's finest performance in both modes comes in his last appearance, *Monsieur Lecoq*. Here Lecoq enters the narrative as a novice, the youngest member of a party of detectives which happens upon a murder. In a sign of Gaboriau's evolving concept of his detective, there is now no reference to Lecoq's criminal past. Rather, he is the son of "a respectable, well-to-do Norman family." The premature deaths of his parents threw him upon his own resources; eventually he obtained a place "solving bewildering and intricate problems" for a "well-known astronomer." He has, however, too vivid an imagination and too great an ambition, and he spends his solitude devising fantastic (and nefarious) schemes to make himself rich. The astronomer decides his fate by advising him that with his special skills, he must become either a famous thief or a great detective (14-15). He chooses detection, and the astronomer writes him a recommendation.

The role of the astronomer is brief and incidental, but instructive. Lecoq neither professes nor practices scientific inquiry, but through this allusion to the astronomer, Gaboriau endows him with a sort of scientific sponsorship. His genius at solving the astronomer's problems is presumably related to his skill at solving the moral mysteries of crime. Further, the nature of that problem-solving genius is, presumably, mathematical, and when to this is added "the work of his imagination" which makes him such an uneasy scientist's apprentice, he even becomes a version of the poet-mathematician which Dupin advocated in "Purloined Letter." This episode of scientific patronage occupies no more than a page of the second chapter of *Monsieur Lecoq*; and even there, Gaboriau makes no effort to concretize the science. The astronomer might as easily have been a lawyer or a merchant. But he was an astronomer, and this suggests that Gaboriau did intend to exploit at least some association with science.

A second very minor incident in *Monsieur Lecoq* reinforces the sense that Gaboriau realized the usefulness of tinting his detective with scientific methodology. Much later in the narrative, Lecoq adopts the strategy of eavesdropping on his imprisoned suspect through a funnel-shaped hole bored through the cell's ceiling. His nominal superior, Gevrol, contemptuous of all the methods Lecoq employs, visits him in his concealed location and comments: "You will look just like one of those silly naturalists who put all sorts of little insects under a magnifying glass, and spend their lives watching them." Lecoq turns the simile to his own advantage: "You couldn't have found a better comparison, General...I owe my idea to those very naturalists you speak about so slightingly. By dint of studying those little creatures—as you say—under a microscope, these patient, gifted men discover the habits and instincts of the insect world. Very well, then. What they can do with an insect, I will do with a man!" (181). The exchange has no further consequence, but its insertion here is revealing. Gevrol exhibits the vulgar contempt for the mysteries of any investigative technique; Lecoq proclaims the prestige of those techniques. And he does so at a revealing moment. Ratiocinative analysis of the evidence of the footprints in the snow had required no apology, but espionage does. Lecoq is, after all, about to crouch and apply eye and ear to eavesdrop on a prisoner, a method that seems unoriginal and even dishonorable. By identifying himself with successful, objective scientific investigators, Lecoq cloaks himself with the dignity of science. And the science he embraces is the safe taxonomic science—the science of Cuvier. Like Dupin, Lecoq prefers a scientific paradigm that takes classification as its task: the detective discovers the habits and instincts of the human world in order to pin men to the proper moral and social categories.

These occasional gestures toward scientific credibility are all that Lecoq makes. He does not lecture on his methodology, though he might easily have. He has ready audiences in either the dim-witted, loyal Father Absinthe or the sharp-witted Magistrate Segmuller. His silence may be partly excused by his age; pontification may be disagreeable in a youth of 26; but even his aged advisor, Tabaret (Tirauclair), the real consulting detective who, at the end of the novel, points out the truth that Lecoq, for all his clever deductions, missed—even Tabaret neglects the opportunity to discourse on method in the manner of Dupin, or to allude to dissertations on method in the manner of Sherlock Holmes.[5] Gaboriau's interest as a novelist lay elsewhere. He preferred the label "le roman judiciare" for his fiction; his purpose was to use criminal cases to cast a light on contemporary society. Ultimately, Balzac, more than Poe, was Gaboriau's model. Even in *Monsieur Lecoq*, the detective, after dominating the first half of the novel with his techniques of investigation, abdicates the second half to the narration of the dynastic history that has led to the crime.

For Gaboriau, then, methodological issues are secondary. He would exploit the example of Dupin to provide local effects, but ratiocination was not, as it was for Poe, the soul and essence of the detective and his story.[6] Lecoq's deductions—as when he reads the history of the footprints in the snow at the beginning of *Monsieur Lecoq*—are spectacular, and, after he has explained them, commendably rational and naturalistic. But it is their spectacularness, not their deductiveness, that matters most. Lecoq's successful use of disguise and his project to eavesdrop on his prisoner work to the same effect: whatever method Lecoq uses, he uses inventively and effectively, but the variety of methods yields an impression of ingenious improvisation rather than one of deliberate methodology. Meditations on method are alien to his nature, and this distinctly separates him from Dupin before him and Holmes after him.

Lecoq's catholic embrace of diverse methods offers some justification to the sneer Conan Doyle placed in the mouth of Sherlock Holmes. In Holmes' first adventure, *A Study in Scarlet*, Conan Doyle had his detective identify his most important predecessors by having him repudiate them. Holmes dismisses Dupin as "a very inferior fellow" (in allowing Dupin "some *analytical* genius" [emphasis added], Holmes at least shows he attended to the Discourse on Method in "Rue Morgue"). He calls Lecoq "a miserable bungler" who "had only one thing to recommend him, and that was his energy." He specifically censures the long investigation into the identity of the captured murderer that comprises the *Monsieur Lecoq* : "I could have done it in twenty-four hours. Lecoq took six months or so" (I.162). (Holmes overlooks the even more telling point that Lecoq, with all his months, fails. It is Tabaret who, from his armchair, identifies the villain after hearing Lecoq's recital of the details of his investigations.) Energy is indeed Lecoq's salient virtue. He throws himself into each of the methods he employs, and Holmes is correct to observe that the effect, at least to readers raised on post-Holmesian scientific detectives, is one of dissipation of talents.

None of this diminishes Gaboriau's stature as a novelist. But it does show that the principal fictional detective between Dupin and Holmes failed to take method as his soul and essence. Lecoq was a popular invention: Gaboriau's detective stories were frequently reprinted in France, and he became wealthy from his writing. After his death, Lecoqian pastiches continued to be published. Anglo-American appreciation came more slowly. A plagiarized version of *Le Dossier 113* was published in New York in 1868, and beginning in 1873, a series of cheaply printed translations of Gaboriau's works was issued in Boston. The first editions of Gaboriau did not appear in England until the 1880s, just in time for Conan Doyle to read them and include Lecoq as the miserable bungler with whom Sherlock Holmes disdains comparison.

ii

Allan Pinkerton (1819-84) was a detective, not a novelist, and, in the Anglo-American world, at least, he has surpassed Vidocq as the most famous non-fictional detective in history. (That dozens of fictional detectives are more famous than either of these non-fictional ones speaks to the power of the genre.) Pinkerton was also the purported author of what purported to be non-fictional narratives of his detective agency's investigations. Sixteen of these thick narratives were published between 1874 and 1884, usually with titles in the form of "x and the Detectives": *The Molly Maguires and the Detectives, The Spiritualists and the Detectives*, etc. In fact, Pinkerton's role was limited to dictating notes to a stenographer and editing the final version produced by one of up to four professional writers he kept on his staff. The writers fleshed out the narratives with invented circumstantial detail and dialogue. And even the authenticity of Pinkerton's dictated skeleton might be doubtful. Many of the cases he selected for publication occurred before the Chicago fire of 1871 which destroyed the agency's archives and as a result, his memory was the only warrant for their historicity.[7]

There are, then, significant elements of fiction in the Pinkerton narratives. The plots are neatly completed; the motives and thoughts as well as the actions of the characters are often depicted with impossible clarity; the style is amused and superior. And Pinkerton was certainly aware of the new type of fictional detective which was appearing in dime novels at precisely the moment he began issuing his own stories. Kenward Philip's *The Bowery Detective* (1870) seems to have been the first of these; the most famous, Harlan Page Halsey's Old Sleuth, began his long career with *Old Sleuth, the Detective* in 1872. Old Sleuth's principal detective technique, like that of Vidocq and Lecoq, was disguise; Pinkerton's detectives carried on the tradition. But for Pinkerton, the tradition posed a problem in methodology: disguise worked, but was it moral?

Pinkerton did not offer his stories as fiction. He explicitly rejected a dime novel format (Morn 82). His volumes would be imposingly massive—250 to 600 pages in length, hard-cover, with his organization's open-eye emblem and "We Never Sleep" motto embossed in gold on the cover. They were designed as advertisements for his agency in particular, but also for the profession of detective in general. The profession required defense in the post-Civil War era. It was often equated with espionage, an activity whose honor was dubious even in wartime. Pinkerton had first made his name as a spy during the Civil War, and the taint persisted as he made his name as a detective. When an undercover Pinkerton operative testified at a trial in 1867, the judge cautioned the jury to be especially doubtful of his testimony: "the character of the detective—and it is simply another word for spy—has always been, and always will be, an unpopular one. There is an element in human nature—and it is an element that humanity may be proud of and not ashamed—which looks with suspicion necessarily upon that calling in life and that kind of business, because there is necessarily connected with it more or less deception and deceit" (Morn 70).

Pinkerton's books were, in effect, appeals to public opinion against this prejudice. Though the detective did use disguise and did insinuate himself under false pretenses into the confidence of witnesses and criminals, his practices were, Pinkerton argued, the exercise of a deliberately chosen and demonstrably effective method. Beneath the disguise, Pinkerton always emphasized, was a decent young man (or, occasionally, young woman) dedicated to the apprehension of malefactors. As Frank Morn observes, most of Pinkerton's narratives were not mysteries. "Generally, the criminal was already known, and the story concentrated on the methodical tracking down of the suspect or the accumulation of evidence for a conviction" (84). As a result, the focus is upon how the detective knows rather than upon who done it; Pinkerton's basic apology for the profession of the detective is that its apparent deviations from the code of gentlemanly behavior are the consequence of an intelligent, justifiable method.

His strategy can be illustrated through an examination of "The Edgewood Mystery and the Detective," included in *Professional Thieves and the Detective* (1881, ed. G.W. Carleton, New York). Its 17 chapters occupy just over 100 pages, and it provides a complete account of the 1869 murder of an immigrant artist in Edgewood, NJ. A body is discovered beside a path on the village common. Local authorities are unable even to identify the body. Town elders resort to the Pinkertons, and the case is supervised by George H. Bangs, Pinkerton's well-known General Superintendent, and Robert A. Pinkerton, Pinkerton's son. Bangs and young Pinkerton interrogate the town elders who commission them. Pinkerton observes that it is his invariable rule to require "full and explicit accounts": "I have frequently found that some apparently unimportant incident, some half-remembered fragment of conversation, or some trifling, ill-considered remark have been the means of affording a perfect clue" (300). Pedantic asides of this sort become Pinkerton's substitute for Dupin's Discourses on Method; they are periodical reminders that Pinkerton investigators govern their inquiries by adherence to a defined set of methodological rules.

Bangs and Robert Pinkerton visit the scene of the crime; they trace footprints; and they discover initials sewn into the victim's shirt. Their first action is to deploy an agent disguised as a journeyman painter to make further inquiries in the neighborhood. By Chapter Four, newspaper notices have elicited the names of the dead man and of a principal suspect; the remaining 13 chapters are devoted to locating the suspect and proving the case. (Two of the chapters transport the reader to the Alsatian homeland of the victim and suspect, giving an account of their origins that recalls the fables of industrious and idle apprentices.) Another operative in disguise ("the garb of a mechanic") serves as the primary agent in the pursuit. The final chapter offers two vignettes: the victim's parents grieving in Strasbourg, and the murderer raving insanely in his cell. "Reader, our story is done. The detective has performed his mission; the weight of punishment has fallen upon the guilty transgressor, and now we draw the curtain…" (394).

"The Edgewood Mystery and the Detective" is padded with sentimental interludes and with an overlong pursuit of the killer. But it is also padded with statements of method. Pinkerton is almost Poe-like in his insistence upon the primacy of methodological considerations. The initial inquiry of Bangs and Robert Pinkerton provides a neat illustration. It opens with a reminder of the Pinkerton "rule" about attending to "apparently unimportant incidents"; the narrative that follows climaxes with the apparently trivial discovery of the initialled shirt. Before reporting the meaning of the initials in the next chapter, Pinkerton returns to his methodological point with a short lecture: "It is a remarkable subject of consideration what small and apparently insignificant causes will oftentimes produce wonderful and revolutionizing effects; and yet the world's history contains many marked evidences of the great forces which have sometimes grown from and been produced by comparatively trifling inceptions and circumstances" (306). He then adduces four illustrations of this principle: Galileo noticing the movement of a pendulum, Newton noticing the fall of an apple, and someone— he doesn't give a name, though he presumably refers to James Watt—noticing the hissing of a steam kettle, and Benjamin West drawing in a farm-house kitchen. Three of the four examples are derived from science and technology (how Art, in the person of West, entered the equation, is unclear, though the victim of the Edgefield murder was a would-be artist). Pinkerton is transparently claiming the essential identity of the work of his detective and that of the great scientists. All his detectives did was notice a stitched "A.B.," advertise for information regarding a missing man with the initials "A.B.," and greet the landlord who replied to the notice; but the scientific context makes this routine sequence into a model of ingenious method.

The importance of method is evident in the larger structure of narrative too. Like the first paragraphs of "Murders in the Rue Morgue," the entire first chapter of "The Edgewood Mystery and the Detective" functions to make the narrative a pendant to a discourse. Pinkerton's discourse is more diffuse than that of the narrator of "Rue Morgue." It includes his thoughts on the prevalence of "the grim, hideous monster" of murder in contemporary society and upon that society's misguided sympathy for the murderer. But it concludes with several paragraphs specifically on Method in the detection of crime, and particularly on the undervaluation of circumstantial evidence. This, he announces, is the whole point of the succeeding narrative: "In the following pages I shall attempt to depict a crime, the detection and punishment of which clearly illustrates the important nature of circumstantial evidence, in the development of a theory of criminal action, in which no positive proof could be addressed upon which to base an examination or to construct a theory of operation" (292). Lacking the detective story writer's complete liberty to construct a world in which circumstances may indeed point infallibly toward a single culprit, Pinkerton does not quite justify his boast. His operatives do construct a good case of circumstantial evidence, but the narrative carefully confirms the case by having the killer cry out a virtual confession in his sleep and, in the end, a complete confession in his prison cell.

"The Edgewood Mystery and the Detective" casts two other relevant sidelights on the development of the detective story, both further linking Pinkerton to Poe as opposed to Gaboriau. Lecoq was a member of the official police force (and one of Gaboriau's strengths lay in his intimate knowledge of the operations of the official justice system). Pinkerton's agents, like Dupin and Holmes, were private investigators, and Pinkerton could commend their performance by contrasting it with that of a bumbling officialdom. The Inspector G—— of "The Edgewood Mystery" is Mr. James Byerly, county sheriff. Byerly makes only a brief appearance, but it is situated immediately following the lecture on "apparently unimportant incidents," and so Byerly's methodological incompetence is directly contrasted with the scientific competence of the Pinkerton detectives. The treatment of Byerly is rough—"it must be confessed that his intellectual acquirements (he could not write his own name) eminently fitted him for the duties he so magnanimously took upon himself" (309)—but his methodlessness merits it. He arrests an innkeeper and his wife because the victim reportedly visited their hotel prior to his murder; when his case is dismissed, he apprehends a boy who had worked for the innkeeper; when that case too proves unsustainable, he arrests a householder at whose house the boy had slept prior to the murder. (Pinkerton adds: "I verily believe that, had the boy slept in a cow-shed, the pertinacious criminal-hunter would have procured a warrant for the arrest of the inoffensive bovines upon the morrow," 310.) The sheriff's random follies obviously highlight by contrast the informed procedures of true, methodical Pinkertonian detective.

Pinkerton also pauses, late in the narrative, to explicitly distance himself from the European (Vidocqian) model of detective. Like Vidocq, his operatives rely heavily upon disguise, but underneath the mask, they are honest men and dedicated professionals. "It is true," he admits, "that in many cities of the Old World the leading tenet of detective belief seems to be that 'to set a thief to catch a thief' is the true secret of success" (359). Pinkerton refutes this tenet; he has never employed a thief, and he has yet to fail of success ("when success was possible"). Earlier, just before narrating the misadventures of Sheriff Byerly, Pinkerton had emphasized a related point: "I never work for rewards" (309). Pinkerton and his operatives are professionals, not opportunists. "My operations are based entirely upon a distinct understanding and agreement of a business character."

Pinkerton's detective narratives are a refutation of that judge's depreciation of a detective's testimony. The detective—Pinkerton's detective—is a methodical, sober businessman.

A Pinkerton detective, then, has more integrity than an Old World detective and more intelligence than a New World sheriff. He "is required to be of a well-developed mind, to possess a clear and comprehensive under-standing, and to be able at all times to assume any position that may be requisite for the accomplishment of the object he has in view" (359). ("Assume any position" presumably refers to disguises, and its placement behind "well-developed mind" and "comprehensive under-standing" may be a bit ingenuous, but it shows the priorities of the Pinkertonian method as it was preached, if not practiced.) Although like Lecoq, he appears to the post-Holmesian reader to be possessed of more energy than intellect, it is his intellect upon which he prides himself and by which he defines himself. Amid the contingencies of the real world (and to the extent that the contingencies of Pinkerton's ghostwritten narrative *are* those of the real world), simple routines, accidental discoveries, and especially clever disguises may work more productively than ratiocination. But Pinkerton clearly saw that an appeal to method was the best guarantee of the integrity and professionalism of his occupation.[8]

iii

The great popularity of the writings of Anna Katharine Green (1846-1935) in England and especially in America has proven as ephemeral as that of Gaboriau and Pinkerton. Her contemporary reputation exceeded theirs, and as if in compensation and despite some recent tremors of rehabilitation, so has her succeeding obscurity. None of the three seems much read today,[9] but Gaboriau survives in all histories of the detective genre as the principal mediator between Poe and Conan Doyle, and Pinkerton's eponymous organization has kept his name alive.

Anna Katharine Green, when she is noticed at all, is usually reduced to the epithet, "The Mother of Detective Fiction," and perhaps a paragraph explaining that her sentimental romances had once enjoyed a now inexplicable vogue.

Her first novel, *The Leavenworth Case* (1878), was an enormous success. It was the first important detective novel (in clear contrast to the Dickens' and Collins' novels with detectives in them), and it was the first best-selling detective novel, passing through many editions and selling, by one account, a million copies. In a long career as a popular writer, Miss Green published some 33 novels and six volumes of short stories, all involving matters of crime. In addition to her main series of novels featuring the New York City police detective, Ebenezer Gryce, she also developed recurring unofficial detectives such as the spinster Amelia Butterworth and the debutante Violet Strange.

But the end of her active career as a writer coincided with the inauguration of the post-Holmesian "Golden Age" (her last Gryce novel appeared in 1917, her last novel in 1923), and while the new style embraced some elements of her craft—careful plotting and informed use of forensic and legal details—it repudiated a major element—the melodramatic rhetoric and sentimental characterization which occupied a central place in Miss Green's narratives. S.S. Van Dine rated the injunction "There must be no love interest" third in his list of 20 rules for writing detective stories. And in his 1927 introduction to *The World's Great Detective Stories*, Van Dine specified the case against Miss Green (or, as he preferred, Mrs. Rohlf): "many of us to-day, who have become accustomed to the complex, economical and highly rarified technic of detective fiction" find her novels "over-documented and...too intimately concerned with strictly romantic material and humanistic considerations" (15). Although, as the chief exponent of "to-day's technic," Van Dine might have blushed at the self-praise implied in "complex, economical and highly rarified," he evidently did speak for writers and readers of the late twenties, and Anna Katharine Green's reputation began its precipitous decline.[10]

But though he was contemptuous of the technique of the writer, Van Dine praised the technique of her detective. He followed his criticism of Miss Green's distracting addiction to "romantic material and humanistic considerations" with a commendation of the "convincing logic" and "sense of reality" with which her books narrated the investigations of her detective.[11] Both aspects are important. Miss Green's elevation of "logic" as the detective's technique—to the virtual exclusion of disguise and other such energetic techniques—marked an advance over Gaboriau, and her "sense of reality" established verisimilitude as a core value in the detective story aesthetic.

Poe made method the soul and essence of the detective, but, being Poe, was less dogmatic about stipulating the character of the tangible world which the soul inhabited. He required a functional verisimilitude—buildings had to have plausible (i.e. orangutang-accessible) windows and shutters; apartments had to have plausible furnishings—but non-functional matters such as geography and politics did not matter. Dupin's Paris was not France's Paris. Mary Rogers or Marie Rogêt, the Hudson or the Seine—these details did not affect the method of Dupin's inquiry and might be treated cavalierly. Poe could even mock superfluous verisimilitude: in the mind-reading episode in "Rue Morgue" he seems to have gone out of his way to devise an implausible chain of associations for Dupin methodically to recreate. Gaboriau's great contribution lay in his thrust toward verisimilitude; his detectives operate in the real physical and social world that Gaboriau himself knew intimately. Knowability remains the first priority: the snow falls in the courtyard and along walls so that Lecoq can deduce a man is tall, of middle age, wearing a soft hat and shaggy brown overcoat, and married; but the trail of footprints leads the detective out into the real streets of Paris.

Miss Green did not know the streets of her world, but she did know the interiors of middle- and upper-class New York and, through her lawyer-father, she knew the routines of judicial procedure. By fitting the action of her novels to a world defined by this knowledge, she rooted her detective in his historical moment.[12] If the transcendental virtue of knowing how to know is the detective's soul and essence, the cognate, entirely immanent virtue of knowledge of the contingencies of the world of here and now has, since Gaboriau and Green, been the distinction of the best detective stories. Sherlock Holmes is inseparable from Victorian gaslights, and the Continental Op belongs to the Prohibition 1920s.[13]

It is a truism that great literature achieves its universality by locating itself concretely in a particular time and place. What Gaboriau and Miss Green did was show that the popular genre of detective story acquired a special strength by exploiting the truism. They realized that its aesthetic made a virtue of precise observation of concrete locations. By abandoning the arabesque atmosphere preferred by Poe, Anna Katharine Green proved to her late nineteenth-century audience that the detective story might hold a vivid mirror to the social (/economic/psychic/sexual/etc.) realities of the time. And the dimensions of her success gave her realistic bias an inertia which has yet to dissipate. (There are, of course, exceptions: Chesterton is perhaps the most challenging; writers such as Borges, Hiber Conteris, and Paul Auster suggest other escapes from the normal realism of the detective story.)

Both Gaboriau and Miss Green paid for their realisms by taxing Poe's emphasis on method. Miss Green paid the higher assessment. Ebenezer Gryce analyzes; he observes and deduces and acts with praiseworthy forethought; but he is not a ratiocinator; analysis is not his soul and essence. In *The Leavenworth Case*, for example, medical evidence on the gunshot wound, ballistics evidence regarding the weapon employed, evidence regarding the stationery upon which a confession was written all contribute to his solution to the mystery of the murder of Horatio Leavenworth. Ebenezer Gryce must prove himself an acute analyst of this empirical evidence in order to detect the villain. Or, rather, because he doesn't really detect the villain, to detect the innocent. His analyses serve to vindicate in sequence the two sisters who are the prime suspects; but it is only by staging a drama of false accusation that he provokes the actual murderer to self-incrimination. And even then Gryce declares the result "unexpected"; he had, he later explains, anticipated a confession from a different suspect. The detective's energy thus succeeds where his intellect fails.

And so Gryce's method seems significantly limited in its power to know. To be sure, a method that relieves the innocent merits applause. But although his analyses of ballistics and stationery are impressive, the crucial deduction—the deduction which Gryce says determined for him the necessary innocence of the sisters—is, as Julian Symons has observed, rather dubious: " 'Well,' said he, 'there has always been one thing that plagued me, even in the very moment of my strongest suspicion against this woman, and that was, the pistol-cleaning business. I could not reconcile it with what I knew of womankind. Did you ever know a woman who cleaned a pistol?' " (309). Miss Green quite fairly described the cleaned pistol in her report of the inquest toward the beginning of the novel; any reasoner as acute as Ebenezer Gryce might have shared his certainty. But, even allowing for a different century's different reality in the matter of female delicacy, the syllogism may appear unsatisfying.

Ebenezer Gryce dominates the narrative of *The Leavenworth Case*. It is this dominance of the detecting detective which makes Miss Green belong the history of the detective story in a way which Dickens and Collins do not,[14] but though Ebenezer Gryce is the analyst to whom the narrator and reader must ultimately defer, he exercises his mastery through his personal character as much as through his analysis. He never proclaims adherence to a coherent, efficient method in the manner of Dupin, nor do his local exercises in analysis ever take on the magnitude of Lecoq's pursuit of the footprints in the snow at the beginning of *Monsieur Lecoq*. Lecoq may practice several methods, but he practices each with impressive diligence. Gryce is good, but that is all. He is introduced as "a portly, comfortable personage with an eye that never pierced, that did not even rest on *you*" (5). His averted gaze becomes a trademark, and he sees much by seeing indirectly, but he loses something in analytic presence by possessing an eye that never pierces.

As an official detective, Gryce can call upon "innumerable" agents (110); and he may direct his agents to employ the Vidocq-Lecoq-Pinkerton device of disguise (220, 226); unlike the Pinkerton detectives, he permits himself an interest in the disposition of reward money (158, 296); he will read private correspondence which the gentlemanly narrator will not (159); he is, however, at a disadvantage when treating with his social superiors (106). All of these details have methodological implications, and, combined with his moments of straightforward analytic insight, contribute to his weight as a dominating intelligence. Still, there is some justification to Miss Green's own preference for the label "criminal romance" over "detective story."[15] When S.S. Van Dine praised the "convincing logic" of her novels, he referred to the carefulness with which she, as the author, plotted the developments, rather than to the detective's overpowering display of logical deductions within the narrative.

As a result, although Ebenezer Gryce was featured in 12 novels, he never acquired the personal reputation accorded Dupin and Lecoq, to say nothing of the immortality achieved by the Baker Street detective who followed him eight years later. In order to avoid the fantastic atmosphere that colored Poe's conception of the detective story, Anna Katharine Green made two important gestures: she played up the realism of the physical and social environment and she played down the genius of the detective. Arthur Conan Doyle's genius lay in recognizing that the first gesture was sufficient: place a methodological genius in a realistic world and he might be the hero for the age.

Chapter 4

Conan Doyle: Sherlock Holmes

"His reasonings & deductions (which are the whole of his character) would become an intolerable bore on the stage" (qtd. in R.L. Green 9). Though only half-right, Conan Doyle's parenthesis makes a revealing statement. Had his reasonings and deductions been the whole of Mr. Sherlock Holmes, Mr. Sherlock Holmes would not have become the universal hero of reasoning and deduction—of methodical thinking—that he has become. That Conan Doyle's extra-parenthetical judgment has proven entirely mistaken—Sherlock Holmes has in fact triumphed repeatedly on the stage and on the screen—underlines this misperception of his own creation. It is precisely because Holmes is wholly an individual as well as wholly a methodical investigator that he enjoyed his unparalleled triumph as an imaginative figure. Holmes is at once a complete man and a complete detective.

Conan Doyle was correct in thinking the stage required the man, not the method. The theatrical Holmes does emphasize the pipe, the deer-stalker, the lens, the violin, sometimes the cocaine: in short, the 221B-Baker-Street-ness of Sherlock Holmes. What is interesting and relevant is that when Conan Doyle thought of his character, he instinctively thought of the method—the reasonings and deductions—to the exclusion of the man. The quotation comes from a letter to Mrs. Charles Charrington in June 1893, replying to her inquiry about the possibility of Conan Doyle composing a Holmes play. By that time, the character of Sherlock

Holmes had been firmly established: two novels and the first
volume of collected stories had appeared; the seventh story of the
second series would appear that month. And in the mind of
Arthur Conan Doyle, method was the whole of Sherlock
Holmes.[1]

Poe's phrase, "soul and essence," might have expressed the
idea more accurately (and "whole character" might have better
fitted Dupin). Sherlock Holmes was not, as Auguste Dupin was,
an appendage to a Discourse on Method; the contrary is true: the
first two chapters of the inaugural Sherlock Holmes adventure, A
Study in Scarlet, neatly reverse the priorities of "The Murders in
the Rue Morgue." The first chapter is entitled "Mr. Sherlock
Holmes," the second, "The Science of Deduction." And even
"The Science of Deduction" prefers conversation between men to
a methodological monologue. But the first two chapters of A
Study in Scarlet are nonetheless unequivocal about the central
importance of method; Conan Doyle allows his hero's
preoccupation with methodological inquiry to emerge gradually
yet steadily in the course of Dr. Watson's (and the reader's) initial
encounters with his new roommate. And not until it is fully
established does he, in Chapter Three, "The Lauriston Gardens
Mystery," allow his detective to engage actively in the application
of the methods he has been discussing.

The first indication of Holmes's addiction to method
precedes his actual appearance in the narrative. Young Stamford
prepares Watson for his meeting with his prospective roommate
by warning that Holmes is "an enthusiast in some branches of
science." Chemistry and anatomy seem to be his best subjects,
but his studies are "very desultory and eccentric." "He appears to
have a passion for definite and exact knowledge," and this
includes, warns Stamford, definite and exact knowledge about
post-mortem bleeding, a knowledge verified by his own
experiments in beating corpses with a stick. Holmes spends a
great deal of time in the laboratory of St. Bartholomew's hospital,

and that is where, surrounded by "retorts, test-tubes, and little Bunsen lamps, with their blue flickering flames" the meeting between Watson and Holmes takes place (I.148-50).

Background and setting thus point to scientific inquiry; action confirms it. Our first view of Sherlock Holmes finds him actively engaged in experimentally verifying his discovery of a new test for blood. Holding a test-tube, he utters his first recorded words: "I have found a reagent which is precipitated by haemoglobin, and nothing else." Generations of science-oriented Baker Street Irregulars have amused themselves speculating about what Holmes's reagent might have been; it doesn't really matter. One of the very first reviews of A *Study of Scarlet* took the main point: Conan Doyle's "detective is a marvellous creation, and the study of him which is given at the beginning is one of the most carefully elaborated portions of the book.... He is a profound chemist, though ignorant of the Solar System; and he has, furthermore, discovered a re-agent that is only precipitated by haemoglobin (whatever that may be), which he regards as a sovereign detector of blood stains" (qtd. in Green 60). "Whatever that may be": Poe would have been disappointed had an unintelligent reader admitted unrepentant ignorance of a term in one of his Discourses on Method; Poe presented his methods as real (or realistic; even if they are hoaxes, everything depends upon their being apparently verifiable). Conan Doyle was probably undisturbed—or even flattered—by the reviewer's "whatever that may be." Without understanding what Holmes has done or whether it is, in fact, scientifically feasible, the reviewer (and every reader) understands the sort of thing Holmes has done: he has applied an esoteric scientific technique to an exoteric, unambiguous moral problem. Lest the reader shrug at the spectacle of a mountain of science ("retorts, test-tubes, and little Bunsen lamps") struggling to produce a mouse, Conan Doyle has Holmes explain to the shrugging ("interesting chemically, no doubt,...but practically—") Dr. Watson: "Why, man, it is the most practical medico-legal discovery for years. Don't you see that it gives us an infallible test for blood stains?" (I.150). Holmes describes the methods which his supercedes ("the old guaiacum test" and microscopic examination) and the concrete consequences which might follow from it (Von Bischoff of Frankfurt, Mason of Bradford, Lefevre of Montpellier, Samson of New Orleans: all might have hung had the test been applied).

All of this comes in the chapter, "Mr. Sherlock Holmes." Stamford's introductory phrase, "an enthusiast in some branches of science," has been fully realized in the initial impression Holmes makes on Watson and the reader. Less attention has been given to developing Stamford's follow-up line, that "As far as I know he is a decent fellow enough." Holmes's decency and humanity can be allowed to emerge more slowly, but the last lines of the chapter do make a gesture toward extending his character beyond the limits of the wholly scientific. Holmes confesses to periodic bouts of depression and to a weakness for the violin. These quite unscientific habits are the first intimations of the all-too-human half of his character.

Chapter Two, "The Science of Deduction," reverses the order of the first chapter, but retains the proportions. As Watson observes his roommate, he first notes Holmes's routines and oddities. Holmes normally devotes himself to studies at the chemical laboratory or dissecting rooms, but he also falls into fits of lethargy (which, Watson notes, might have suggested narcotic addiction in a less temperate person). Then Watson makes his famous catalog of Holmes's fields of expertise. Holmes scores "Nil" on Literature, Philosophy and Astronomy, and "Feeble" on Politics, but earns considerably higher marks in Botany ("Variable. Well up in belladonna, opium, and poisons generally"), Geology ("Practical, but limited"), and Anatomy ("Accurate, but unsystematic"). His rating in Chemistry is highest of all—"Profound"—and is equalled only by his knowledge of Sensational Literature ("Immense").

Holmes's excellence in chemistry is particularly significant. It was in the chemical laboratory that Holmes first appeared; his first action was the completion of a chemical experiment; and his first words announced the success of that experiment. Chemistry was the hard science which had made the most dramatic progress through the early and mid-nineteenth century (as the progress of physics would in a similar way dominate the later century). By assigning Holmes proficiency in chemistry, Conan Doyle clearly meant to cloak his detective method with the aura of authority that chemistry had won. It was an aura that he worked to sustain in the early Holmes tales. Repeated references to the laboratory bench which Holmes maintains at 221B Baker Street serve this end. In "A Case of Identity," for example, Watson returns to find Holmes asleep. "A formidable array of bottles and test-tubes, with the pungent cleanly smell of hydrochloric acid, told me that he had spent the day in the chemical work which was so dear to him" (I.413). Such references occur regularly in the first two novels and in the first three collections of stories. In the later works, Holmes's reputation as a scientist was apparently secure enough for Conan Doyle to forego this testimony to Holmes's scientific orientation.[2] It might be noted, however, that when he decided to resurrect his hero after his apparent death at Reichenbach Falls, Conan Doyle inserted an explicit reminder of Holmes's skill as a chemist. In the first adventure of *The Return of Sherlock Holmes*, Holmes explains to Watson that prior to his return to London "I spent some months in a research into the coal-tar derivatives, which I conducted in a laboratory at Montpelier, in the south of France" (II.337).[3]

As outstanding as Holmes's mastery of chemistry, however, is his ignorance of astronomy. It was Watson's astonishment at Holmes's ignorance of the Copernican Theory that initially pricked him into compiling his catalog. "That any civilized human being in this nineteenth century should not be aware that the earth travelled around the sun appeared to me such an extraordinary fact that I could hardly realize it" (I.154). And not only is Holmes unaware, he will perversely persist in his ignorance: "Now that I know it I shall do my best to forget it." The geocentric or heliocentric reality of the solar system, he explains, makes no difference to him or his work. (Finding out what does make a difference to Holmes and his work is the purpose of Watson's catalog.) Holmes is right: heliocentrism has never figured decisively in any murder investigation, but there is surely another significance to his spectacular ignorance. Just as Conan Doyle sought to cloak his detective with the authority of chemistry, he sought to shield him from the controversy of astronomy. The Copernican Theory, especially in its role in the famous conflicts between Bruno and Galileo and the Catholic Church, still stands in the popular imagination as the first great scientific challenge to the traditional orthodoxy of the Christian worldview. It has become the symbol of the revolutionary impact of the scientific method. Because the Bible says little about chemistry (or about matters remotely subject to chemical analysis), chemistry's revolutions have never had such metaphysical or theological repercussions; they have upset chemical dogmas only. Chemistry is one of the theologically safest as well as scientifically hardest of the sciences.

Geology, biology, and physics all posed their challenges to received opinion in the nineteenth century, and Holmes treads more lightly here. His geology, for example, is specifically "practical," completely dissociable from the debates on the Effects of The Flood and the Age of the Planet. Holmes's biology is subdivided into the untheoretical fields of botany and anatomy. Taxonomy—with Cuvier as its patron saint—is an inherently innocent technique. Research in those fields underlay Darwin's conclusions, but they were also the primary sciences of the religious scientists like Louis Agassiz or Philip Gosse who opposed Darwin. Watson's catalog, then, portrays a man with a very strong, practical, non-controversial mastery of his century's scientific methods.[4] He is also, as the final items on Watson's list indicate, well-informed on the extremes of human moral behavior ("appears to know every detail of every horror perpetrated in the century") and with the institutions that judge that behavior ("a good practical knowledge of British law"—"*practical*" again). What he does not know and will not know is the speculative sciences which might challenge the basis for traditional values.

And yet, having made the case that Sherlock Holmes's methods were both fundamentally scientific and fundamentally unsubversive, Conan Doyle could not resist inserting a clue that if either quality was dispensable, it was the latter. At the end of the fourth chapter of *A Study in Scarlet*, Holmes withdraws briefly from science and murder to attend a concert by the violinist Norman Neruda. At the beginning of Chapter Five, before re-immersing himself in his case, he comments to Watson, "Do you remember what Darwin says about music? He claims that the power of producing and appreciating it existed among the human race long before the power of speech was arrived at" (I.178). Not only is the reference to that most subversive of contemporary scientists, Charles Darwin, but it is to a passage in *The Descent of Man*, the 1871 work in which Darwin girded his loins and affirmed that natural selection applied to man too.[5] The substance of the allusion is innocent—Darwin's views on music outraged no prelates—but it adds a dissonant note to the burden of conservative, pragmatic scientism which Conan Doyle played upon with the first two chapters. (And, if we identify "the power of speech" with rational analysis, it allows Holmes to reverse the two poles of his character: his devotion to music is, on an evolutionary scale, prior to his devotion to reasonings and deductions.)

The cataloging of Holmes's character in the second chapter of *A Study in Scarlet* certifies his competence in recognized scientific disciplines. It remains for the detective to declare the peculiar discipline of his own science, and this Holmes does in his periodical essay, *The Book of Life*. Watson, less forthcoming than the narrator of the Dupin tales, offers the reader only a precis and a paragraph before dismissing it all as "ineffable twaddle," but this suffices to make Holmes's method clear. The anonymous author (soon to be revealed as Sherlock Holmes) attempts to show, says Watson, "how much an observant man might learn by an accurate and systematic examination of all that came his way." Momentary expressions, twitches, glances: such signs might infallibly reveal a man's inmost thoughts. The observer's empirical conclusions might have the certainty of Euclidian propositions.

And they might have unlimited power. Watson quotes: "From a drop of water...a logician could infer the possibility of an Atlantic or a Niagara without having seen or heard of one or the other. So all life is a great chain, the nature of which is known whenever we are shown a single link of it" (I.159). Ineffable twaddle, indeed! And yet this rhapsody, as much as any chemical test for blood-stains, marks Holmes as a nineteenth-century scientist. John Tyndall (1820-1893) was a well-known research physicist and popularizer of science.[6] T.H. Huxley wrote of him in 1861, "a favorite problem of his is—Given the molecular forces in a mutton chop, deduce Hamlet or Faust therefrom. He is confident that the Physics of the Future will solve this easily" (qtd. in Basalla 19). Huxley is joking and Holmes, evidently, is not, but then the distance from a drop of water to the Atlantic is considerably less than that from a mutton chop to Hamlet. Holmes, Huxley, and Tyndall all shared the confidence that the power of scientific logic was, in principle if not in practice, illimitable.

The final portion of Watson's excerpt from Holmes's *The Book of Life* takes a significantly didactic tone. "The Science of Deduction and Analysis is one which can only be acquired by long and patient study, nor is life long enough to allow any mortal to attain the highest possible perfection in it." Perfect knowing how to know, yielding perfect knowledge, is attainable only by the immortal—i.e. by God; the detective is inherently a limited imitator. "Before turning to those moral and mental aspects of the matter which present the greatest difficulties, let the inquirer begin by mastering more elementary problems" (I.159). Examples include such Holmesian techniques as inferring a man's calling by the state of his fingernails, his coat-sleeve, his boot, etc.

Both the warning against expecting too much from the method and the lesson on learning the method distinguish the Conan Doyle approach from the Poe approach. Dupin's method was apparently illimitable in its applications and, though it might be explained, it could not be taught; one either possessed the genius of the poet-mathematician, or one did not; one could identify with one's antagonist, or one could not. Holmes begins with the assumption that his method cannot, practically, know everything, and that everyone, theoretically, can know the method. In this, Holmes is echoing exactly the Baconian assumptions broadcast about the scientific method by nineteenth-century polemicists like Huxley.

Holmes admits to being the author of the "ineffable twaddle," and declares that the Science of Deduction and Analysis pays his rent: he is a "consulting detective." Other detectives bring him problems. "I listen to their story, they listen to my comments, and then I pocket my fee" (I.160). Now and then a more complex case compels him to "bustle about." The first is the science of Dupin, the second the science of Lecoq. The science of Holmes unites both. His "special knowledge" and "those rules of deduction laid down in that article" are, he declares, the key elements of his success. The chapter ends with two examples of his method in practice. Holmes explains how he deduced Watson had served in Afghanistan; then he deduces the former rank and service of a messenger who brings the letter that draws Holmes into the murder case that constitutes *A Study in Scarlet*.

Of the pure, Dupin-like ratiocination which Holmes claims as his normal pattern little more is heard. Although he does retire into occasional three-pipe meditations on the evidence in a case, Holmes almost always engages in active, empirical investigations. Despite his disparagement of Lecoq as an energetic bungler, Holmes makes frequent use of the principal non-intellectual detective technique—disguise—as well. In nearly a fifth of his cases, he makes himself up as a country parson or a sailor or an American named Altamount. As Inspector Jones tells Holmes, "You would have made an actor, and a rare one." But disguise is always, for Holmes, a secondary tactic, not a primary strategy. He uses it to obtain data upon which to base inferences; it never leads, by itself, to conclusive demonstrations of guilt. Nor does his penchant for impersonation function as a metaphor for a practical intellectual empathy with others, a detective technique endorsed by other detectives such as Father Brown. Rather, it seems basically an expression of Holmes's delight in the dramatic gesture (and of Conan Doyle's judgment that dramatic gestures have their place in well-told stories).

Ratiocination solely from newspaper accounts, in the manner of "Marie Rogêt," is unthinkable for Sherlock Holmes. His deductions regarding Watson and the retired sergeant of the Royal Marine Light Infantry are, however, quite typical. They are clever exercises in the sort of inference for which Conan Doyle's teacher, Dr. Joseph Bell, was noted. Holmes is frequently given the opportunity to perform similar analyses on a person or a walking-stick or an abandoned hat at the beginning of a case. These deductions are often more clever than credible, though they never slip into the mocking extravagance Poe permitted himself in constructing Dupin's mind-reading episode at the beginning of "Rue Morgue." Conan Doyle's homage to Dupin in Holmes's own mind-reading episode at the beginning of "The Cardboard Box" (and sometimes at the beginning of "The Resident Patient") is distinctly more pedestrian in its associations.

And it must be admitted that these clever inaugural deductions are never material to the case at hand.

Rather, like the allusions to chemical experimentation, they contribute to an atmosphere of science and method. For Poe, atmosphere was not enough. It was not aesthetic obtuseness that encouraged him to include those labored Discourses on Method in each of the Dupin tales; they were the source and substance of the tales, and Poe excused no reader from the obligation to comprehend them. Conan Doyle was less demanding (and, perhaps, more of a story-teller); the impression of science and of methodological thinking was for him usually sufficient, and—once the heavy work had been achieved in the first chapters of *A Study in Scarlet* and briefly reinforced in some other early stories—it was all he offered. This was his deliberate policy. In his autobiography, *Memories and Adventures*, Conan Doyle makes clear that the brief episodes of inference like that performed on the retired sergeant were designed as surrogates for more elaborate, more pertinent analyses of evidence: Sherlock Holmes, he wrote, "shows his powers by what the South Americans now call 'Sherlockholmitos,' which means clever little deductions, which often have nothing to with the matter at hand, but impress the reader with a general sense of power" (107).

The first implication of Sherlockholmitos seems to be that Holmes's methodical science is mere smoke and mirrors, a factitious veneer.[7] Even an admirer of Holmesian forensic science, the forensic scientist Sir Sydney Smith, professed puzzlement at the absence of actual, relevant science in the Holmes series: "in not one of the detailed stories does he use his laboratory skill; in not one of these cases does he make a chemical test" (*Mostly Murder* 31).[8] It should be acknowledged immediately that Smith opens his account of his own career as a pathologist with a laudatory chapter entitled "Dr. Bell and Sherlock Holmes" in which he credits Holmes with "the anticipation of modern scientific methods of investigation." Still, just as Poe used an artistic sleight of hand to transpose his cleverness as a writer into Dupin's cleverness as a detective, so Conan Doyle seems to have magically transferred the scientific air of Holmes's chemical corner and his exercises of Sherlockholmitos to the criminal investigations. Holmes seems to be scientifically methodical and he seems to be a successful investigator, and so he seems to be a successful, scientifically methodical investigator.

Even when Holmes's deductions are material to the case he is working on, they often do not contribute directly to the solution. In "The Boscombe Valley Mystery," Holmes applies his lens to the scene of the crime and deduces that the murderer "is a tall man, left-handed, limps with the right leg, wears thick-soled shooting-boots and a grey cloak, smokes Indian cigars, uses a cigar-holder, and carries a blunt penknife in his pocket" (II.146). Although Boscombe Valley is not, as Holmes notes, a populous neighborhood, Inspector Lestrade dismisses this description as mere theory, and declines to pursue it, and the murderer is never caught. Holmes does identify the culprit, but the physical description only ices the cake of other, more practical, less empirical clues which turn Holmes's suspicion toward the only other Australian in Valley. Holmes's deductions from the footprints and cigar ashes are wonderful and right, but in the end, they are virtually superfluous. Still, the exercise works: the reader watches Holmes's observations of the murder site through Dr. Watson's eyes in a long paragraph of description. Both the reader and Watson are astonished when Holmes rises and reports to Lestrade the pith of his conclusions, and both must wait a page or two before, in the presence of the murderer, Holmes explains how his observations led to his conclusions. The resulting impression is unmistakable: the scientific analysis of the scene was the effective cause of the discovery of the criminal.

And this is the real significance of Sherlockholmitos: despite the sometimes dubious quality of their science (as when Holmes infers from a large hat a large intellect) and their sometimes questionable relevance to the investigation at hand, these episodes are absolutely essential, however fraudulent, to sustaining the air of method—of "reasonings & deductions"—which Conan Doyle saw as "the whole of [Holmes's] character." Poe spoke of his detective's "method and *air* of method"; Conan Doyle was satisfied with only the second, but with nothing less. The science may be dubious, but the air of science is genuine. As Christopher Clausen has observed, despite the flaws in Holmes's science, "The important point...is that he is conceived—and conceives of himself—as a man who applies scientific methods to the detection of crime, and that his success as a detective is due to those methods" (Clausen 109). The Sherlockholmitos exercises exemplify a methodical mind drawing accurate knowledge about persons from the interrogation of inert things, and this is the fundamental premise of the Holmes series.

Conan Doyle employs another trick to give a credible scientific coloring to the method which Holmes adopts: he assigns to the detective authorship of scientific monographs. These citations consist of nothing more than a title, but they suggest a systematic foundation to Holmes's isolated observations. "The Boscombe Valley Mystery" provides a good example of this device as well. Holmes had recognized the ash at the murder scene as that of an Indian cigar. In his explication at the story's end, he reminds Watson that this recognition was not serendipitous: "I have, as you know, devoted some attention to this, and written a little monograph on the ashes of 140 different varieties of pipe, cigar and cigarette tobacco" (II.148). Monograph-writing stands for an essential practice of the scientist: he must formulate and publish his results. It is, moreover, a practice particularly important to the basic scientist (as opposed to the applied scientist or technologist). By publishing his discoveries, the scientist stakes his claim to them, and invites additional experiments that may confirm or refute his theories or modify his data. Holmes the monograph-writing scientist further validates Holmes the detective. Other scientific-sounding monographs alluded to in the Holmes stories include those on dating documents, tattoo marks, tracing footsteps, the influence of trade upon hands, and the variability of human ears.

Monographs, clever little deductions, and chemical experiments all testify to Holmes's methodological soul and essence. Though he never lets his detective lecture in the manner of Dupin, Conan Doyle is far more explicit (and far more frequently explicit) about his detective's dedication to scientific methods of investigation than was Gaboriau (or Pinkerton or Green). Watching Holmes work in *Study in Scarlet*, Watson declares, "You have brought detection as near an exact science as it ever will be brought in this world" (I.174), and this is compliment Holmes values most. At the beginning of the second novel, *The Sign of Four*, Holmes makes an ungrateful but revealing return: "Detection is, or ought to be, an exact science, and should be treated in the same cold and unemotional manner. You have attempted to tinge it with romanticism, which produces much the same effect as if you worked a love-story or an elopement into the fifth proposition of Euclid" (I.611).[9] Holmes's "exact science," as he explains it in *The Sign of Four* shortly after reproaching Watson's romanticism, requires three disciplines: observation, deduction, and a wide range of exact knowledge.

That the first and third requirements are proper to the scientific method is certain. There can be some debate over the term correctness of "deduction" as the rubric for the Logic of Scientific Discovery. Holmes uses it invariably; critics have often argued that he ought to have said "induction."[10] That scientific thinking requires some form of logic, however, is undisputed, and Holmes logic as practiced, if not as named, surely qualifies as scientific. Recently, an impressive group of semioticians and historians discovered that their studies of scientific thinking had converged on the realization that the method of the fictional detective Sherlock Holmes corresponded nicely to the method ("abduction") expounded by Holmes's non-fictional contemporary, the important American philosopher of science, Charles S. Peirce (1839-1914). The collection of articles by Umberto Eco, Carlo Ginzburg, Thomas Sebeok that emerged as *The Sign of Three* may have its mock-scholarly quality, but their discussions of abduction as a scientific logic are entirely serious in their implications.[11] That Holmes can inspire and sustain such sophisticated analyses, even playfully, testifies to Conan Doyle's success in imagining an epistemological hero.

Holmes's fullest discussions of his method naturally occur in the two inaugural novels of series. In the succeeding two novels and 56 stories, Conan Doyle was content to insert occasional Holmesian Exhortations on Method, as opposed to Dupinian Dissertations. Less demanding on the reader, these exhortations are nonetheless effective in sustaining the impression that Holmes is a conscious, methodical inquirer. They are distributed throughout the series (though, again, with noticeably diminished frequency in the final two collections of stories). They include the famous, repeated aphorism, "When you have eliminated the impossible, whatever remains, however improbable, must be the truth," and such other injunctions as the very Baconian "It is a capital mistake to theorize before you have all the evidence," or the similar warning, "It is an error to argue in front of your data. You find yourself insensibly twisting them round to fit your theories."[12] Accept "the only hypothesis that covers the facts"; when confronted with several possible explanations, try "test after test until one or the other of them has a convincing amount of support"; "one forms provisional theories and waits for time or fuller knowledge to explode them."[13] These general rules, combined with the concrete illustrations of Holmes's patient explication of his every deduction sustain the impression that his method is a genuine, scientific technique for knowing how to know.[14]

ii

In "The Adventure of the Blanched Soldier," a late story first published in November 1926, Holmes admits that by "cunning questions and ejaculations" Dr. Watson had elevated the detective's "simple art" into a "prodigy." In his fit of modesty, Holmes describes his "simple art" as nothing "but systematized common sense." The phrase has a distinguished ancestry. It would seem to be a reference to the best known definition of the scientific method offered by the best known advocate of science in the nineteenth century, T.H. Huxley. In an early lecture, "On the Educational Value of the Natural History Sciences" (1854), Huxley wrote: "Science is, I believe, nothing but *trained and organised common sense*" (*Science and Education* 45).[15] The phrase encapsulated Huxley's view of the real method of science, but it served at least two secondary purposes. One was parochial. Engaged in the defense of the scientific nature of *his* science (i.e. biology), Huxley had to contend with the argument that "Mathematics...have one special method; Physics another, Biology a third, and so forth," and with the accompanying implication that the least quantifiable was the least scientific. If, as he proposed, all scientific method could be reduced to the formula, "trained and organized common sense," then all sciences might be equally scientific.

But further, if his formula is true, all valid thinking is scientific, differing only in degree from what is usually regarded as mysteriously "scientific." "So, the vast results obtained by Science are won by no mystical faculties, by no mental processes, other than those which are practised by every one of us, in the humblest and meanest affairs of life" (III.45). Huxley was so committed to reassuring his audience that Science was an unexceptional pursuit that his objection to Bacon was not that Bacon demanded too little—too little hypothesis, too little quantification—of the inductive scientist, but too much. Huxley's defense of science was that it was common. The example with which he immediately illustrates a humble, mean affair which employs the scientific method is revealing: "A detective policeman discovers a burglar from the marks made by his shoe, by a mental process identical with that by which Cuvier restored the extinct animals of Montmartre from fragments of their bones" (III.45-46). Writing five years before Darwin's *Origin*, Huxley cites the anatomist Cuvier as the model of scientific inquirer; even more interesting, however, is his perception of the natural analogy between scientific and detective investigation. The method applied to explaining a crime—a methodological pursuit which every citizen must applaud—serves to justify the amoral reconstruction of an extinct animal.

Nine years later, Huxley expanded his suggestive analogy. Three years after the crisis of the publication of *The Origin of Species*, Huxley was giving the most famous of his series of lectures to workingmen. He had begun these lectures in 1855 in the conviction that they ought to comprehend the changes wrought by contemporary scientific advances ("I want the working classes to understand that Science and her ways are great facts for them" [27 Feb. 1855 letter qtd. in L. Huxley I.149]). In 1862 he delivered a course of six workingmen's lectures on the Darwinian theory at the School of Mines in London. Transcribed in shorthand and published in the form of six little blue pamphlets at 4d each, "On Our Knowledge of the Causes of Organic Nature" was extremely popular. It represents Huxley the popularizer at his best. In the third of the six lectures, "The Method by which the Causes of the Present and Past Conditions of Organic Nature are to be Discovered," Huxley pauses to offer a defense of the scientific method which had led Darwin to the conclusions which the other lectures expounded. Again, Huxley's essential argument is that science is "trained and organized common sense": "The method of scientific investigation is nothing but the expression of the necessary mode of working of the human mind. It is simply the mode at which all

phenomena are reasoned about, rendered precise and exact"
(*Darwinia* II.363). And again he offers homely examples of the
commonplace use of the method. A person who samples two
hard, green apples at a fruiterer's shop and finds them sour will
likely decline the shopkeeper's offer to taste a third hard, green
apple. This, Huxley informs his audience, is the operation of
induction, the very method by which Darwin unsettled so many
minds with his explanation of the origin of species.

Huxley then proceeds to offer a more elaborate justification
of the scientific method of reasoning backward from effects to
causes:

> I want to put the case clearly before you, and I will therefore show
> you what I mean by another familiar example. I will suppose that one of
> you, on coming down in the morning to the parlour of your house,
> finds that a tea-pot and some spoons which had been left in the room
> on the previous evening are gone,—the window is open, and you
> observe the mark of a dirty hand on the window-frame, and perhaps in
> addition to that, you notice the impress of a hob-nailed shoe on the
> gravel outside. All these phenomena have struck your attention
> instantly, and before two seconds have passed you say, "Oh, somebody
> has broken open the window, entered the room, and run off with the
> spoons and the tea-pot!" That speech is out of your mouth in a
> moment. And you will probably add, "I know there has; I am quite sure
> of it!" You mean to say exactly what you know; but in reality you are
> giving expression to what is, in all particulars, an hypothesis. You do not
> *know* it at all; it is nothing but an hypothesis rapidly framed in your own
> mind. And it is an hypothesis founded on a long train of inductions and
> deductions. (II.368-69)

His analysis of this example continues for several pages, but
the point is clear. The "knowledge" of the scientist is equivalent to
that of the disturbed householder; it is only more conscious of the
way it achieved its knowledge (and, as a result, that its

"knowledge" is provisional). And once again, now in a more elaborate fashion, Huxley offers his working man audience the reciprocal reassurances 1) that science knows the origin of species the way we know we've been robbed, and 2) that to the degree that science renders that common method more "precise and exact," it may enable us to better identify the criminal who has violated our domicile.

Huxley uses brief dramatic anecdotes to illustrate his argument in favor of scientific method; Sherlock Holmes uses brief exhortations on method in the course of his narrative dramas. Both serve the same cause. Conan Doyle admits, in *Memories and Adventures*, to falling under the influence of "Huxley, Tyndall, Darwin, Herbert Spencer and John Stuart Mill"—"our chief philosophers" (31). In this, he fell in with what Beatrice Webb identified as "the then-called 'religion of science' ": "an implicit faith that, by the methods of physical science, and by these methods alone, could be solved all the problems arising out of the relation of man to man and of man towards the universe."[16] As a young man, Conan Doyle had reacted strongly against the solid Roman Catholicism of his family. During his terms at the Jesuit school of Stonyhurst, he saw the Prefect of Lower Studies, Reverend George Renerden Kingdon, SJ, as the epitome of the failure of religion. Kingdon had had a scientific training, having won the Wix Prize for medicine at St. Bartholomew's for his essay, "On the connexion between Revealed Religion and Natural Science," but by the time that Conan Doyle encountered him at Stonyhurst, Kingdon had retreated into an adamant opposition to modern science, an opposition which impressed Conan Doyle unfavorably then and afterward (Edwards 96-101). (It was then, with a significant irony, that the author placed the introduction of his scientific detective in the laboratory of St Bartholomew's.)

Conan Doyle's study of medicine at Edinburgh confirmed his agnosticism, and the example there of the acute diagnostician, Dr. Joseph Bell, provided him with the inspiration for a new kind of hero.[17] Conan Doyle declared in a 1927 interview: "It often annoyed me how in the old fashioned detective stories, the detective always seemed to get at his results by some sort of lucky chance or fluke or else it was unexplained how he got there.... I began to think about this and...of turning scientific methods...onto the work of detection.... I used as a student [to] have an old professor whose name was Bell who was extraordinarily quick at deductive work" (qtd. in Rodin and Key 199). In *Memories and Adventures*, Conan repeats his story, though here he identifies Gaboriau and Poe as his prototypes, rather than the anonymous "old fashioned" writers (presumably the authors of pulp adventure stories). Seeking an original touch, Conan Doyle thought "of my old teacher Joe Bell, of his eagle face, of his curious ways, of his eerie trick of spotting details. If he were a detective he would surely reduce this fascinating but unorganized business to something nearer to an exact science" (75). In both accounts, science—the organized business of spotting details—was the inspiration of Sherlock Holmes's character. His entire career is dedicated to the proposition that the "methods of physical science" could indeed, in the words of Beatrice Webb, solve "all the problems arising out of the relation of man to man." With deliberate caution, however, he declined to take up her further faith that it might as well solve those arising out the relation of man to the universe. He suggests that scientific reasoning ought to be applied in religion—"There is nothing in which deduction is so necessary as religion.... It can be built up as an exact science by the reasoner" (II.178)—but he himself declines to make the application or to do the reasoning.

Holmes is, in fact, militantly conventional in his moral judgments. This does not mean that he is utterly incapable of personal views; just as he can quote Darwin or praise Winwoode Reade, he can occasionally break into a brief revelation of an individual perspective, as when, in "The Naval Treaty" he praises Board Schools as "Beacons of the future!" or takes a moss rose as the text for a short homily: "Our highest assurance of the goodness of Providence seems to be to rest in the flowers" (II.179, 178). Like his author (who also could entertain original views), however, Holmes is basically a good Victorian. Holmes's application of scientific to criminal investigation is something new, but his ethics are not in the least innovative; he is neither a utilitarian nor a pragmatist; he subscribes to none of the would-be scientific ideologies of his time—Comtean positivism, Marxian historical materialism, Freudian psychoanalysis.

Yet Holmes is not a martinet; he is not a slave to legalism. He accepts the general values of his society, but he is willing to break specific laws to achieve what he assumes will generally be regarded as a good result. Thus he takes it upon himself to exonerate a repentant thief: "I suppose I am commuting a felony, but it is just possible that I am saving a soul. This fellow will not go wrong again. He is too terribly frightened. Send him to gaol now, and you make him a gaolbird for life" (I.467).[18] Such gestures, and more serious ones, such as committing burglaries himself, do not represent a threatening revaluation of values, but simply reflect a pragmatic attitude toward achieving the ends of justice.

And it might be noted that in one of the earliest examples of Holmes's arrogation of judicial authority, "The Boscombe Valley Mystery," Holmes concludes his release of a sympathetic murderer with a significant disclaimer: "You yourself are aware that you will soon have to answer for your deed at a higher court than the Assizes. I will keep your confession, and, if McCarthy is condemned, I shall be forced to use it. If not, it shall never be seen by mortal eye" (II.151). Holmes's allusion to the immortal eye of the Last Judgment hardly amounts to a sober affirmation of Christian eschatology, but even as a conventional piety, it serves to argue that Holmes does not intend to usurp an unlicensed power to evaluate his fellow citizens: he employs his science to discover, not to judge; what judgments he does make are based upon his adherence to traditional values.

iii

I fear that [Dr. Watson] has given an exaggerated view of my scientific methods. ("Sussex" II.468)

That Holmes's method is scientific and that it is powerful, are two important themes of his stories. The third is that it is benevolent. By the last quarter of the nineteenth century, science was, by the very nature of its increasingly sophisticated quantifications, passing beyond the comprehension of workingmen, even those tutored by Professor Huxley. The mechanization of warfare and the degradation of the environment were tangible signs that its power was not universally beneficial. And the Darwinian theory had, as everyone but the Dayton, Tennessee Board of Education seemed to know, upset any complacently fundamentalist view of Christianity.[19] In 1886, the year that Conan Doyle was composing *A Study in Scarlet*, Robert Louis Stevenson published his tale of a scientist whose chemical researches resulted in the liberation of Mr. Hyde. But we need go no further than Holmes's own great antagonist, Professor Moriarty, to find a demonized image of the scientist.[20]

Moriarty, a model of the anti-heroic scientist (Watson epitomizes him as "the famous scientific criminal"), plays an interesting role in the argument of the Holmes saga. He was obviously designed *ad hoc* to provide a suitable antagonist to culminate the career of his scientific detective. Conan Doyle had decided to eliminate the distraction of Sherlock Holmes. He imagined Moriarty as the "Napoleon of crime" and thus a suitable antagonist for his detective's "Final Problem." Moriarty represents an inversion of the values embodied in Holmes. He is also a scientist, but his specialty is esoteric and dangerously Copernican: mathematical astronomy, not chemistry or anatomy.[21] He has authored a treatise upon the Binomial Theorem ("which has had a European vogue") and *The Dynamics of the Asteroid* ("which ascends to such rarefied heights of pure mathematics that it is said that there was no man in the scientific press capable of criticizing it," I.472). Moriarty has deliberately applied his mathematical genius and his scientific method to organizing crime; he is purposefully immoral and anti-social. The methods of physical science, when perversely applied to "the problems arising out of the relation of man to man," might also prove to be the source of great evil. In the drama of the detective story, however, good science *always* defeats bad science; the detecting detective *always* exposes and defeats the villain, and, with rare exceptions such as Holmes's temporarily fatal fall at Reichenbach, the good scientist survives to pursue other villains.

But what makes Holmes a good man who knows how to know and Moriarty a bad man who knows how to know? It cannot simply be the latter's mathematical and astronomical studies. The answer is that although Conan Doyle does portray Holmes as a man whose "whole" character consists of "his reasonings & deductions," by the magic of fiction, he is also wholly unscientific in his habits. There is a dramatic balance in the union of these opposites. The quoter of Goethe and student of the polyphonic motets of Lassus saves the reasoning machine which categorically disdains emotions. Holmes is not a secretive researcher like Frankenstein or Jekyll, nor is he even a withdrawn, nocturnal creature like Poe's Dupin. Though hardly gregarious, Holmes is most literally a man of the streets, afoot or in a hansom cab. And within the walls of his famous suite at 221B Baker Street, he balances his laboratory bench with Bohemian furnishings, his precise methodology with negligent habits. The cigars in the coal scuttle, the tobacco in the Persian slipper, the correspondence transfixed with a knife to the mantle of the fireplace, the "patriotic V.R. done in bullet-pocks" on the wall—all contribute to this effect.[22]

Professor Moriarty, by contrast, pursued a single-mindedly intellectual career: compelled by "dark rumors" to give up his "Mathematical Chair at one of our smaller universities," he set up as an "Army coach." Holmes describes him as a pallid "reptilian" creature with no enthusiasms: "He is clean-shaven, pale, and ascetic-looking, retaining something of the Professor in his features" (II.304). Moriarty did indulge himself in a painting by Greuze, but this seems to have humanized him no more than Holmes's discourse on "the causes of the change in the obliquity of ecliptic" dehumanized him.

Holmes's two most unscientific habits are his addiction to cocaine and his affection for the violin. His seven percent solution has doubtless been the more notorious of the two, but in fact, though Conan Doyle did introduce the cocaine habit in the second Holmes tale as a dramatic way of separating his hero from the commonalty, the violin was used first and reappears most often as a sign of Holmes's special character. Before he agrees to room with Watson, Holmes warns him that violin playing is one of his vices, and immediately after cataloguing Holmes's knowledge in the various fields of science, Watson shifts to a description of Holmes's practice at the violin: "When left to himself, however, he would seldom produce any music or attempt any recognized air. Leaning back in his arm-chair of an evening, he would close his eyes and scrape carelessly at the fiddle which was thrown across his knee. Sometimes the chords were sonorous and melancholy. Occasionally they were fantastic and cheerful" (I.158). Watson finds these idiosyncratic solos "exasperating," but they obviously served as a type of artistic excess designed to balance the scientific excess of the preceding catalogue.

Indeed, throughout the series, the violin serves as the emblem of an artistic impulse that coexists with Holmes's scientific character. The lens, symbol of that character, is referred to in 19 of the 60 tales of the saga; the violin appears in 13. The point is not that Holmes synthesizes the two tendencies; he does not play the violin scientifically, nor does he take his cocaine scientifically. Holmes's Bohemian habits concretize him as an individual—he is not simply a type of the scientist—and they argue that even an extreme advocate of the empirical scientific method—"All emotions, and that one [love] particularly, were abhorrent to his cold, precise, but admirably balanced mind" (I.346)—need not be consumed by the pursuit of his profession. Holmes *is* as cold and precise as a magnifying lens in his investigations, but unlike an obsessive Frankenstein or Moriarty, he can be sonorous and melancholic, or fantastic and cheerful when he operates in a different mode. Cocaine, Holmes explains to Watson, saves his sanity when he is oppressed by the tedious intervals between investigations; oddly enough, it also helps to save him as a scientific hero by emphasizing an unscientific— even anti-scientific—dimension of his character. Holmes is not a Bohemian scientist, but by being a Bohemian as well as a scientist—and by applying his science to matters of immediate moral interest—he has emerged as the heroic type of anti-heroic type of the scientist in nineteenth-century literature.

Chapter 5

Conan Doyle:
Dr. Challenger

Professor George Edward Challenger belongs to the history of science fiction, not that of the detective story, but he provides an occasion to raise some relevant questions about epistemological heroism. An examination of his character can help to clarify the distinction between the detective hero as in his essence the exercise of the scientific method, and the science fiction hero as in his essence the exercise of scientific concepts and/or technological advances. The one takes possession of the method which science had proved powerful; the other is possessed by the consequences of that powerful method. The detective seizes a logic and applies it to the analysis of moral actions. The science fiction hero plays out how humans might act, morally or immorally, under conditions extrapolated from current scientific understanding or technological conditions. The detective defines his world; it must be the common world of the reader's experience, but its particular furnishings and characters have been created expressly for him to decipher through his methodical intellect. The science fiction hero is defined by his world; it is a world of the near or distant future and he has been created expressly to dramatize its novel dimensions.

Dr. Challenger's peculiar career also provides an opportunity to glance at a way of knowing which, in the decades of the detective's rise to generic eminence, offered the greatest contrast to the scientific method. In his third appearance, in *The Land of Mist*, Conan Doyle has Dr. Challenger convert to a faith in the Spiritualist path to knowledge. Spiritualism, as S.S. Van Dine's rules for detectives had decreed, is anathema to the detective. He stands for empirical rationalism, and the least admission of the supernatural in his solutions is sufficient to disbar him. The exposure of fake psychics was, in fact, a preoccupation of early detectives. The actual Pinkerton and the fictional Craig Kennedy both engaged in such exposures.[1] Conan Doyle felt at liberty to bend his popular scientist to submission to the new faith, but he could not turn his popular detective. Only two years before Challenger's conversion, and long after Conan Doyle had made his own commitment to Spiritualism, Sherlock Holmes made a point of dismissing supernatural phenomena: "This Agency stands flat-footed on the ground, and there it must remain. The world is big enough for us. No ghosts need apply" ("Sussex Vampire" II.463). The fictional detective pursues physical effects only to their physical causes; he categorically declines to speculate further.

i

Dr. Challenger was featured in two novels and five short stories: *The Lost World* (1912), "The Poison Belt" (1913), *The Land of Mist* (1926), "When the World Screamed" (1928) and "The Disintegration Machine" (1929). The two novels have most to offer, though the final two stories (which ignore the Spiritualist conversion) might be used to illustrate the hubris of the scientist: Challenger's almost maniac insistence that the earth acknowledge him in "When the World Screamed" and Theodor Nemor's demonic mania in "The Disintegration Machine." These are precisely the excesses which the flat-footed scientific detective avoids by confining his method to murders.

The Lost World establishes Challenger as a scientist, but it does so through assertions and associations, rather than through exhortations to or exercises of scientific thinking. The entire narrative turns on the necessity of personal witness; no amount of circumstantial evidence or inference is sufficient to persuade anyone of the existence of a lost world of dinosaurs in the Amazonian wilderness. Notebooks, drawings, testimonies, photographs: all are insufficient. The scientific community must see in order to accept and understand. At the beginning of the novel, the scientist, Professor Summerlee, dismisses Challenger's proofs and insists that he must personally witness a pterodactyl before he will acknowledge its reality. When he attains that view he makes a handsome apology, but, at the end of the novel, Professor Illingsworth makes exactly the same demand. Truth in science fiction is proved by experience, not analysis. (This is, of course, the point of the genre: the science fiction writer proposes the imagined experience of his narrative as the proof of the reality of his extrapolated new [or lost] world. The world itself is a speculation; speculations by characters within that world are valueless.)

None of the scientists in *The Lost World* performs experiments; none is even associated with experimental tools such as lenses or retorts. There is Observation, of course, as the adventurers view running, flying, and swimming dinosaurs; and there is Knowledge as they recall names and information from paleontological research; but there is little of the third element of Holmes's definition of his science: Deduction. The drama of a protagonist methodically exploring the implications of a physical scene (or of a conversation) is absent. The scene in *The Lost World* simply overwhelms the observers (and readers) and convinces by this experiential overwhelming. The science fiction novel is about witnessing the marvellous, not inferring it.

Professor Challenger's relationship with his Watson, the young journalist Edward Malone, illustrates the same point. There is no interplay between the two. Challenger possesses knowledge which he imperiously imparts to Malone and to everyone else. He is a lecturer, not a talker. Challenger's overbearing manner is a comic humor, but it is, for the want of any other characteristic, his essence as well. As a result, the scientist appears here as a dogmatizing source of information. Holmes condescends to Watson—this is part of his comic humor—but he also enjoins Watson to practice his methods, and he frequently questions Watson with expectation of receiving intelligent replies. There is no intellectual parity between Holmes and Watson; Watson's obtuseness is designed precisely to cast Holmes's acuteness into relief. But there is a dialogue between the unequal intellects, and it is this dialogue that makes the method of thinking a central topic in the series. The absence of a comparable dialogue in the Challenger books produces the opposite effect. Neither Malone nor the reader is invited to think; only to experience and perhaps to learn.

If Challenger's role is merely to lead the narrator to novel experiences, how can it acquire a scientific coloring? Assertion replaces demonstration. There is no such thing as Challengeritos; there are no "clever little deductions, which often have nothing to do with the matter at hand, but impress the reader with a general sense of power." There are assertions of science: Challenger is introduced as "the famous zoologist," assigned memberships in dozens of scientific societies, and credited with authorship of " 'Some Observations Upon a Series of Kalmuck Skulls'; 'Outlines of Vertebrate Evolution'; and numerous papers, including 'The Underlying Fallacy of Weismannism' " (*Lost World* 10). Challenger's quarrel with Weismann suggests another strategy for validating Challenger as a scientist. August Weismann (1834-1914) was the German biologist whose work on germ plasms and genetics in the 1880s anticipated later discoveries about chromosomal mechanics. Weismann was still living when *Lost World* was published; by engaging Challenger in discourse with actual con-temporary scientists, Conan Doyle could endow him with an aura of scientific authenticity. Darwin (1809-82) and

Henry Walter Bates (naturalist and entomologist, 1825-92) were both dead, but comparisons to their scientific excursions in Patagonia and the Amazon basin lend credibility to Challenger's own Amazonian expedition. A reference to the Malayan travels of the still-living Alfred Edward Wallace serves the same function.

Most interesting is Challenger's reference to "an excellent monograph by my gifted friend, Ray Lankester" (21). Edwin Ray Lankester (1847-1929), a prominent zoologist and, at the end of his career, a well-known popularizer of science, was, in fact, Conan Doyle's gifted friend; the excellent monograph may have been Lankester's "book on extinct animals" (*Extinct Animals*, 1905) which, according to John Dickson Carr, inspired Conan Doyle in 1911 to begin writing *The Lost World*. Lankester seems to have followed the narrative's composition, and even offered advice concerning the depiction of the dinosaurs (Carr 316-18). This intermingling of real and fictional scientists helps the illusion that Challenger is an actual member of the scientific fraternity.

Because Malone, the narrator, shares the common man's bewilderment at the esoteric jargon of this increasingly exclusive fraternity, this association of names is sufficient. Early in the novel, Malone attempts to follow Challenger's contribution to the "Weismann versus Darwin" debate. "My scientific education having been somewhat neglected, I was unable to follow the whole argument," he reports, concluding, "Most of the matter might have been written in Chinese for any definite meaning that it conveyed to my brain" (12). Having established his (and our) incapacity to understand scientific discourse, he can from then on content himself with accounts of its gestures rather than its substance as he portrays Challenger and Summerlee engaged in unrecordable scientific disputes. "The voices of the contending men of science rose in a prolonged duet," for example, but we hear nothing of their subject matter, only that Summerlee plays a "high, strident note" against "the sonorous bass" of Challenger

(99). Where the Holmes stories argued that everyman might participate intelligently and morally in the scientific method, the Challenger series dramatizes everyman's exclusion. He might get a laugh from scientific pomposity, and he might go along on a scientific expedition for the spectacle; but he cannot expect to follow the scientist's debates. The terms of those debates have become inaccessible. Challenger cannot, like Holmes, explain his methods simply and clearly at the end. Born a crucial 25 years after Sherlock Holmes, Professor Challenger embodies a different conception of the scientific endeavor. He is, after all, *Professor* Challenger, not some desultory dilettante who experiments on corpses in a medical laboratory. Science, by the beginning of the twentieth century, had fully institutionalized itself.

What scientific substance Malone does include in his narrative usually concerns taxonomy, a natural concern of discoverers of a lost world. Challenger and Summerlee attempt to classify the creatures they encounter. This is genuine scientific thinking, but as presented in the novel, its primary effect is to reinforce the mystery of advanced science. The creatures actually work as plausible monsters to terrify the explorers; assigning them their scientific names afterward—Iguanadon, Pterodactyl, and Stegosaur; Toxodon, Ichthyosaurus, Allosaurus, Megalosaurus— is merely another easy gesture toward sustaining the illusion of science. At one point, Lord John Roxton refers to a "loonie" debate between the scientists over the "scientific classification" of the ape men. "One said it was the *Dryopithicus* of Java, the other said it was *Pithecanthropus*" (131). The substance of this controversy might have been significant, especially in the context of the widely debated search for "the missing link," but once again, an allusion to scientific thinking, rather than an exercise of it, suffices.

Of course, most readers are grateful for the superfluity of the scientific veneer, at least every reader who is either, in the words of Conan Doyle's epigraph for the novel, "the boy who's half a man, or the man who's half a boy." *The Lost World* is a boy's adventure story with enough manly science to allow either of the two amphibious readers to enjoy it. But the action of the story is not, to any serious degree, a fable about thinking scientifically (except for that false implication that in science, only personal eye-witness evidence is admissible). It plays with scientific facts and names, but not with scientific method.

Most significantly, considering the topic of the novel, no effort is made to draw a Lesson on Evolution. This silence is not as curious as the incident of the dog in the night; an adventure novel is under no obligation to provide lessons on any topic. Still, the discovery of the non-extinction of species ought, in a post-Darwinian era, have drawn some comment from the scientific protagonists. The Lost World discovered in the Amazon might have been interpreted as a confirmation of Darwin or even, with its proof of the persistence of species, as a refutation. But though Darwin's name is mentioned, the subject is not pursued. The adventure of discovery is left as an end in itself.

ii

Ironically, the most scientific of the Professor Challenger stories—methodologically-speaking—may be the novel which Conan Doyle constructed as a polemic on behalf of what might seem an anti-science: Spiritualism. In *The Land of Mist*, Professor Challenger and Malone, as principal investigators, are compelled to explore a new meta-physical rather than a new physical territory. Instead of mapping topographies and taxonomies, they must search for ways to accommodate new realities. Challenger, Malone and others engage in a dramatic process of learning how to know about the supernatural. The narrative presents a variety of supernatural events ranging from the fake to the true, from the physical (ectoplasms) to the mental (clairvoyance, messages from the dead), from the benevolent to the horrific, from the spontaneous to the rigorously experimental. The inquirers are faced with the problem of evaluating the legitimacy of this miscellany of phenomena.

To Conan Doyle's credit, he does not seek to make his case merely by overwhelming Challenger and the reader with this profusion of examples, though there is a profusion indeed: honest Tom Linden's trances, the bestial spirit Lord John Roxton encounters in the haunted house, the medical spirit who doctors successfully to Challenger's incurably ill protege, the ectoplasmic hand captured in paraffin by Dr. Mapuis at the Institute Métaphysique. This abundance is impressive (and lest it be dismissed as only fictional, Conan Doyle footnotes several of the episodes to a series of appendices which give their historical prototypes[2]), but Conan Doyle thought that Spiritualism's greatest quality as a faith lay in its character as a scientifically demonstrable faith. Though in the end, each inquirer, including finally the Professor himself, must be convinced by personally experiencing a moving personal communication, much of the thrust of the novel is toward the argument that such communications should really be superfluous, and that any fair, rational examination of the evidence for Spiritualism should suffice to convince an open-minded skeptic. Spiritualism's revelations are the culmination of scientific thought, not its contradiction.

It exasperated Conan Doyle to see scientists refuse to weigh the evidence in only this field of research, and so, in his novel, he presents Challenger as a militant atheist, the epitome of closed-minded scientific materialism. In the course of the novel, Malone, the journalist, proves himself open-minded and moves reluctantly but steadily toward Spiritualism, overcoming his prejudices through a series of experiences. Challenger blindly refuses to read or witness any evidence, ignoring even what proves to have been an early direct communication from his dead wife. In a parody of the Huxley-Wilberforce debate, Challenger speaks for dogmatic scientific naturalism against James Smith, the spokesman for open-minded Spiritualist supernaturalism. The Scientist bellows uninformed denunciations; the Spiritualist responds dispassionately with evidence and argument; and Challenger can end the exchange only with sputtered defiance. Then, in the penultimate chapter, Challenger's willful opposition collapses in the face of a single communication from the spirits.

The Land of Mist is as much a treatise upon Varieties of Response to Psychical Experience as upon Varieties of Psychical Experience. To be sure, Conan Doyle is interested in the metaphysics that must underlie the phenomena—he has some spirits discourse on their levels of happiness and the extent and limits of their power to know and act. But he declines to be dogmatic, and qualifies even the lessons delivered by spirits: they too are fallible, he notes. Conan Doyle concentrates upon the way different individuals approach and understand the novelties of psychic phenomena: how men (and women) grow to accept and understand messages from "the other side" and how this acceptance and understanding affects their lives. Conan Doyle depicts several avenues to acceptance and understanding, but always one consequence: once an individual knows he can trust the signs from the other side, he becomes a happier, more peaceful, more contented, and also more self-confident and independent person. Thus even Dr. Challenger is profoundly relieved by his conversion; he regains his wife, and he learns he was not, as he had feared his entire adult life, an accidental murderer. He grows positively as well: "he was a gentler, humbler, and more spiritual man," though intellectually "ever stronger and more virile" (224).

The Land of Mist, then, dramatizes the efficacy of two ways of knowing. One is the scientific method, which, if applied open-mindedly, serves as a excellent tool for exploring the realities of psychic phenomena (and, as Conan Doyle admitted in his life and in his book) for separating the all-too-frequent frauds from the realities. In this sense, Conan Doyle has not abandoned the

Religion of Science for which he deserted Catholicism as a youth. The appeal of Spiritualism for him is precisely that it subjects itself to the canons of scientific reasoning. Every legitimate medium in *The Land of Mist* welcomes skeptical observers and submits to the indignities of body searches, paraffin molds, and whatever other empirical tests these observers might insist upon. Science, fairly done, serves Professor Challenger as reliably in the metaphysical researches of *The Land of Mist* as it served Holmes in the physical researches of his investigations.

The scientific way of knowing is, however, for the Spiritualist only a preliminary tool. It leads the intelligence to an acceptance of the superior method, and that consists in experience, in listening to the authority of the voices from the other side. Science confirms the legitimacy of the voices; the voices speak for themselves, offering messages of individual or universal significance. The active scientific method with its provisional inferences yields to the passive Spiritualistic method with its infallible communications. The detective acquires knowledge because he applies his method within a limited sphere to reach limited judgments; the Spiritualist receives unqualified knowledge which may be universal in its truth.[3]

Conan Doyle was not, as he well knew, the only man educated in Victorian Scientism to succumb to the attraction of psychic revelations. *The Land of Mist* twice (88, 186) recites a list of contemporary scientist-psychics, a list that includes three eminent English physicists, Sir William Crookes (1832-1919), Sir Oliver Lodge (1851-1940), Sir William Barrett (1844-1925), the Italian criminologist, Cesare Lombroso (1835-1909), the French physiologist/psychologist, Charles Robert Richet (1850-1935), and the co-discoverer of the theory of natural selection, Sir Alfred Edward Wallace. All of these scientific minds came to recognize some validity to psychic phenomena, with Lodge serving as president of the Society for Psychical Research (1901-04; 1932). The list, with its abundance of physicists, is perhaps more imposing than the invocation of naturalists and zoologists like Bates, Weismann, and Lankester in *The Lost World*.

The one name which overlaps the two is that of Wallace, a scientist who participated in the biological scientific revolution of 1859, but beginning in 1865 had grown increasingly fascinated by the possibilities of psychic science. In 1898, Wallace wrote a book celebrating *The Wonderful Century*, making the argument that the nineteenth century had made 24 significant advances in science and technology (e.g. 1. Railways, 2. Steamships... 7. Electric Lighting... 11. Spectrum Analysis... 13. Antiseptic Surgery... 22. Organic Evolution Established...), outdistancing all preceding centuries combined, which, by his count, could claim only 15 (154-55). But among the century's "Failures," he listed first "The Neglect of Phrenology" and "The Opposition to Hypnotism and Psychical Research" (he also listed among the Failures what he took to be an erroneous faith in vaccination). In *The Lost World*, Wallace had served as an example of the type of scientist who devotes himself to the often strenuous empirical investigations which must precede scientific discovery. His travels in the East Indies—or, equally, Darwin's aboard the *Beagle*—stand as heroic versions of the preliminary laboratory work required in all real science; Challenger's expedition to the Lost World is an exact imitation of this sort of dramatically empirical science. In *The Land of Mist*, Wallace embodies the open-mindedness of the true scientist. For the biological scientist, heroism lies in the courage required to explore new territories in pursuit of new ideas; for the psychic scientist, the courage is the same, but the new territories are metaphorical; they represent new geographies of experience rather than of terrain and flora and fauna.

Professor Challenger's conversion may not, therefore, be as radical as it seems. Early and late, he poses as a man who, wherever he goes, goes boldly. The two scenes of action—the Jurassic lost world of 1912 and the Spiritualist land of mist of

1926—may not be so distant from one another. In the early novel, Challenger leads; in the later, he follows. But his boldness is uniform: he acts upon ideas, and while this is not the essence of science, it is surely a sort of intellectual heroism. Although he did not commit himself to Spiritualism, either publicly or privately, until the trauma of World War I forced him, Conan Doyle had been actively interested in psychic phenomena since the early 1880s.[4] The flat-footed, empirical exploration of the Amazon in *The Lost World* and its astonishing results were probably not intended as metaphors for the metaphysical explorations of the ethereal world of the Spirits in *The Land of Mist* and its astonishing results, but the analogy between the two exercises of scientific courage suggests that they may not be incompatible with one another. But it is also clear that the character of neither the empirical nor the metaphysical Professor Challenger is compatible with that of the methodical detective, Mr. Sherlock Holmes.

Chapter 6

Morrison, Futrelle and Leroux

One element contributing to the phenomenal success of Sherlock Holmes was the new type of journal in which his adventures appeared. The literate middle class had expanded sufficiently by the late nineteenth century to justify the publication of a number of magazines whose articles, stories, and illustrations were aimed at gratifying their standards and tastes. The premier journal of this type—the first and the greatest—was *The Strand*. It was founded in January 1891 by George Newnes, whose success with the more plebeian *Tit-bits* encouraged him to aspire to a higher class. He modeled *The Strand* upon American monthlies, especially in his use of illustrations, and the public's embrace of his experiment was immediate. Its initial circulation of 300,000 made it the best-selling periodical in England or America. Its middle-class audience was exactly the audience to whom the methodical detective would appeal. And appeal he did: within six months of his debut in *The Strand's* seventh issue in July 1891, Sherlock Holmes had become the magazine's most popular feature, and Conan Doyle its best-paid contributor.[1] (Huxley's workingmen, more likely to patronize *Tit-bits*, were not, however, entirely excluded from the Holmes fetish; Newnes published reprints of Holmes stories and miscellaneous Holmesian trivia and contests in *Tit-bits*.)

Two series of short stories sufficed to fix Sherlock Holmes's pre-eminence in the public imagination: *The Adventures of*

Sherlock Holmes (stories appearing in *The Strand* July 1891-June 1892) and *The Memoirs of Sherlock Holmes* (appearing December 1892-December 1893). The success of *The Strand* and of its detective insured that the magazine would be imitated, and that the imitators would commission imitative detectives. The two most revealing of the first faux Holmeses were Martin Hewitt and Professor Van Dusen, The Thinking Machine. Hewitt placed himself firmly to Holmes's right: he is much more soundly bourgeois in character and much less scientific in his method; Professor Van Dusen placed himself equally firmly to Holmes left: far more methodical and at least comparably eccentric. These alternatives require some discussion.

But a number of minor figures also flourished in the immediate post-Reichenbach decade (1895-1905), and some of these bear brief examination. In each instance, the detective appeared in a series of stories published in *The Strand* or one of its competitors; and in each instance, the stories proved sufficiently appealing to justify collection in one or more volumes. Finally, in each instance the collections proved insufficiently appealing to justify reprinting, and the detectives declined into antiquarian curiosities. The authors of such stories include L.T. Meade, whose collaboration with Clifford Halifax, *Stories from the Diary of a Doctor*, were collected in 1894 (second series, 1896); M.P. Shiel, whose Prince Zaleski stories were collected in 1895; M. McDonnell Bodkin, whose stories about the detectives Paul Beck, Dora Myrl and their offspring, "Young Beck, A Chip Off the Old Block," were collected in three volumes published between 1898 and 1911; and Baroness Orczy, whose 38 Old Man in the Corner stories filled four volumes (1909-25; the stories began appearing in *The Royal Magazine* in 1901). All occupy recognizable positions in the development of the methodological character of the detective. Dr. Halifax, the hero of the Meade/Halifax collaboration, anticipates in some respects the practice of Dr. Thorndyke, though his detective abilities place him closer to Thorndyke's various medical associates—Drs. Jervis, Berkeley, Strangeways, etc. Prince Zaleski and the Old Man in the Corner in quite different manners revive the Dupinian method; ratiocination remains a minor technique in the 1880-1920 period, but attained its majority in the Golden Age. And Paul Beck proves that if Morrison's experiment with Martin Hewitt was not a spectacular success, it was at least successful enough to obtain a hearing for other pedestrian, "rule-of-thumb" detectives.

Elizabeth Thomasina (Lillie Thomas) Meade (Smith), (1854-1914) is best known as a prolific writer of girl's stories, but in two different collaborations, she also made a contribution to the early detective story. With Robert Eustace (Robert Eustace Barton) she published *A Master of Mysteries* (1898), *The Gold Star Line* (1899), *The Brotherhood of the Seven Kings* (1899), *The Sanctuary Club* (1900). Her more significant collaboration, however, was with Halifax (Edgar Beaumont, 1860-1921). It led to six volumes, of which the most important was *Stories from the Diary of a Doctor* (1894; *Second Series*, 1896).[2] The stories, which began appearing in *The Strand* in 1893, have been praised for their medical/scientific details and for the quality of the writing.[3] Ellery Queen has called *Stories from the Diary of a Doctor* a classic example of a fad in the 1890s for "so-called 'medical mysteries' " ("Queen's Quorum" 241). This trend in itself is an indication of an audience looking for stories that argued for the benevolence of scientific (or, as Queen would have it, "semi-scientific") method. Dr. Halifax draws on a long line of benevolent doctors in Victorian fiction, but his benevolence manifests itself in his mastery of the new technical innovations in medicine. He uses new, scientific medicine to cure physiological and psychological problems.

Stories from the Diary of a Doctor do not, however, emphasize method. Dr. Halifax encounters such peculiar medical conditions as catalepsy, amnesia, vertigo, kleptomania. He is acute in his diagnoses and occasionally bold in his surgical remedies, such as performing delicate trephining operations (once while asleep). The details of these conditions and treatments are convincing; Mrs. Meade's professional collaborators, Drs. Halifax and Eustace, evidently insured verisimilitude in this respect. (It seems that they were also responsible for the plots; Mrs. Meade provided the very competent narration and what Barzun and Taylor praise as the "well-managed English locale" of the stories.) But there is very little detection as such in *Stories from the Diary of a Doctor*. Dr. Halifax analyzes the conditions of his patient, and often sketches the elements of his analysis, but he is not given to active investigations of the external circumstances of the situation. These tend to unfold on their own. Dr. Halifax is no Dr. Thorndyke: he does not press for information; he collects no data and performs no experiments; he certainly delivers no lectures on the principles of medical or scientific inquiry. Mrs. Meade's collaborations with Robert Eustace have the same result. There is usually a scientific context—the villainies may, for example, be perpetrated through rare poisons (and the hero may resort to rare antidotes)—but the detection, such as it is, cannot claim to be scientific or methodical.

M.P. Shiel, 1865-1947, openly claimed the mantle of Poe for his detective, inscribing a copy of *Prince Zaleski*, "But there is no detective but the detective and father of detectives, the 'Dupin' of Poe, of whom this Zaleski is a legitimate son, and the notorious Holmes a bastard son" (qtd. in *Works* III.514). Shiel's claim of descent has some justice; he certainly absorbed some of Poe's affinity for the grotesque and arabesque. Though Shiel adhered to what he called his religion of science, the withdrawn Prince Zaleski seems untouched by the developments in science and technology in the nineteenth century. The Prince Zaleski stories (and Shiel's work generally) have inspired a coterie of devoted admirers, but it is clear that the mass audience for detective fiction in the 1890s (and since) has preferred the methodical bastards to the true heir.

Matthias McDonnell Bodkin (1850-1933) merits brief mention for his attempt to produce a popular detective who proclaims himself basically unscientific. Paul Beck announces his exoteric orientation in the very title of his collected adventures: *Paul Beck, the Rule of Thumb Detective* (1898). Beck is described as "a stout, thick-set man" who pursues his inquiries with pedestrian diligence rather than scientific rigor. Still, even Paul Beck stoops to using a magnifying glass to examine physical evidence in "Murder by Proxy"; the influence of the Holmesian model was irresistible. ("Murder by Proxy," published in *Pearson's* in 1897, anticipates the criminal device made famous by Melville Davisson Post's Uncle Abner in "The Doomdorf Mystery.")

Finally, Baroness Orczy's Old Man in the Corner recalls in some respects the Dupin of "Marie Rogêt": he is an armchair detective. On the advice of her husband, the Baroness began by deliberately avoiding the Holmesian model, attempting to create "a detective in no respect like Sherlock Holmes" (Bleiler, "Introduction" viii). But although she avoids obvious imitations of the Holmesian manner, the Old Man inevitably reflects a measure of the methodical soul and essence which Holmes bequeathed his most successful heirs. The Old Man (his name may be Bill Owen) sits in a corner of the A.B.C. shop tying knots in pieces of string ("scientific knots"[4]) and, drawing upon information derived from reading papers and attending inquests, propounds solutions to recent crimes to "The Lady Journalist," Polly Burton, who narrates the stories. The Old Man summarizes the case, then lays out with irrefutable (or, at least, unrefuted) logic his solution. He does not lecture on method; but in his first appearance, "The Fenchurch Street Mystery," he does speak casually of "following my usual method" ("mind you, I am only an amateur, I try to reason out a case for the love of the thing" [6]). More importantly, he adopts the Holmesian pose of exhorting his auditor to imitate his method: he reproaches the Lady Journalist for never having "studied my methods of reasoning sufficiently" ("The Glasgow Mystery" 67), or he demands, "Confess that I have not yet taught to think logically" ("The Murder of Miss Pebmarsh" 149). "Methods of reasoning" and "thinking logically" may seem uselessly vague as models of investigative technique; and the rhetoric of scientific method is indeed largely absent. But the character of the narration itself—the Old Man's careful laying out of the sequence of action followed by his convincing exercise of logically exposing the hidden connections—emphasizes method in a way that sets The Old Man in the Corner clearly closer to the Holmesian prototype than to the later Golden Age revisions of the place of method.

ii

Nonetheless, the two most important of the first heirs of Sherlock Holmes were Martin Hewitt and Professor Van Dusen. Both Arthur Morrison (1863-1945) and Jacques Futrelle (1875-1912) made their detective stories conform to the basic conventions Conan Doyle had established. They took a detective detecting as the core of the story, arranging setting, plot and character to display the detecting detective to best advantage. Morrison's detective, like Holmes, is a private detective operating in Victorian London. In a bid to distinguish him from the already titanic figure of Holmes, Morrison moved toward eliminating the detective's methodological and bohemian emphases; he would abandon the overt scientism and the balancing eccentricities almost entirely. This shift was not, of course, simply a rebellion against a powerful father; it also reflected Morrison's own sensibility. Morrison was a journalist, not a doctor; he had emerged from the lower classes, and was already publishing naturalistic stories about slum life in London. These much-admired stories, collected in *Tales of Mean Streets* (1894) and *A Child of the Jago* (1896), would be recognized as his major literary accomplishments. Jacques Futrelle was also a journalist and also wrote non-detective fiction, but only produced some little-admired romances. For his detective stories, Futrelle also moved away from Holmes, but in a direction contrary to that of Morrison. He sought to claim the Holmesian succession by retaining some eccentricity and pressing the methodological emphasis to a mechanical extreme.

Morrison's Martin Hewitt enjoyed a special advantage: he appeared initially under the sponsorship of Holmes's own organ, *The Strand.* When Conan Doyle announced Holmes's demise in "The Final Problem" in December 1893, thousands of readers went into mourning. To assuage the grief (and retain the audience), *The Strand* turned to Morrison, who, in March 1894, introduced the adventures of Martin Hewitt, Investigator. The Hewitt stories were well received enough to be later collected in four volumes (1894, 1895, 1896, 1903), and the volumes were popular enough to be reprinted, but *The Strand* gave up the series after the first six (Morrison transferred his detective to *Windsor Magazine*), and Martin Hewitt has since diminished into a literary curiosity.

The Hewitt stories seem in many ways a creditable refuge for the Holmesless. Morrison's stories are well-written; the plots satisfy the formulaic expectations established by Conan Doyle, yet they have original touches. And though Morrison, like Conan Doyle, regarded his detective fiction as a pot-boiling distraction from his more serious work, he brought to them some of the skill and attention to detail which had earned praise for his naturalistic stories of slum life.[5] But in order to make his detective different, Morrison chose to eliminate both Holmes's eccentricities and his method. Hewitt is plump, genial, undramatic; his digs are unpolluted by cocaine or violins. And though he is very clever, he never exhorts anyone to practice his method.

Hewitt's most significant observation on method comes in his debut, "The Lenton Croft Robberies" (March 1894). It seems to echo the Huxley-Holmes definition of scientific method as "trained and organized common sense." In its opening paragraphs, the story's narrator, the journalist Brett, remarks, "Some curiosity has been expressed as to Mr. Martin Hewitt's system, and as he himself always consistently maintains that he has no system beyond a judicious use of ordinary faculties, I intend setting forth in detail a few of the more interesting of his cases" (3). That Brett can so casually allude to a widespread curiosity about his friend's investigative "system" is indeed a tribute to Sherlock Holmes. It was Holmes who created that curiosity by coining systematic, methodical thought (or the appearance of such thought) as a common currency in popular literature. Prior to his ascendency, three years before "The Lenton Croft Robberies," such a beginning—"Some curiosity has been expressed as to Mr. Martin Hewitt's system"—would have been inconceivable and Hewitt's modest repudiation of any "system" laughably incomprehensible.

In another interesting inversion, Brett proposes to narrate detective stories as footnotes to the detective's unsystematic methods. Dupin and Holmes insisted upon the priority of method; the narratives were illustrative and secondary. Again, Holmes's achievement in positing method as the soul and essence of his existence makes it possible for his earliest imitator to take method so much for granted as to slight it. Hewitt justifies Brett's "consistently maintains that he has no system" as he starts the formulaic concluding explication of his investigation: " 'System?' said Hewitt,... 'I can't say I have a system. I call it nothing but common-sense and a pair of sharp eyes' " (14).

A phrase that for Huxley was a weapon in the defense of his science and for Holmes a sign of his intention to affiliate himself with that scientific doctrine, seems here mere honest modesty.[6] Hewitt's abjuration of system reflects Morrison's refusal to apply a veneer of methodicalness to his stories. Hewitt approaches each of his cases with an analytical intelligence, but no profession of analytical principle. He is the heir to the scientific method; he always explains the reasoning which led him to his conclusions, and his reasoning is always based on empirical observations, but he declines to promote himself as an exponent of any science of detection. Morrison's plots are often quite good; he designs complicated problems for Martin Hewitt's intelligence to unravel (an important and plausible accessory to the villainy in "The Lenton Croft Robberies," for example, is, as Hewitt deduces, a trained parrot). But though he may sometimes exercise it less ingeniously, Holmes talks about his method much more, and this talk (with his talk about violins and cocaine) made him heroic in a way Martin Hewitt never was (or, presumably wanted to be).

iii

Professor Augustus F.X. Van Dusen, PhD, LLD, FRS, MD, MDS does present himself as a hero of methodological detection. The first important American rival of Sherlock Holmes did not appear until nearly a decade after Hewitt (and two years after Holmes had enjoyed his resurrection in "The Adventure of the Empty House" in September [US]/October [UK] 1903). Professor Augustus F.X. Van Dusen, "The Thinking Machine," enjoyed a considerable vogue in America and England. His initial adventure, "The Problem of Cell 13" (30 October-5 November 1905) is said to be the most often reprinted of all detective stories. Nonetheless, after a popularity that justified two collections of stories (1906, 1907) and a novel (1906), he too largely faded from view. It would seem that the figure of Holmes was too great and too near. Though neither Martin Hewitt nor Professor Van Dusen could be mistaken for Sherlock Holmes, both were probably overdetermined by their predecessor, an advantage in their immediate appeal to the audience Holmes created, but detrimental to their permanent popularity. Neither quite deserves his present obscurity, but some of the sources of that obscurity are understandable.

Where Morrison sought to distinguish his detective by eliminating the lens and the violin, Jacques Futrelle, inspired by Poe as much as by Conan Doyle, endowed his detective with a surfeit of method and a good measure of eccentricity. Morrison moved the detective story toward naturalism; Futrelle moved it toward comedy. (PhD, LLD, FRS, MD, MDS: Futrelle is presumably playing on the professor's pomposity; there has been some debate regarding the degree of intentional comedy in the Van Dusen series.) Born in Georgia, Futrelle was, like Poe, a Southerner as well as an American, and he seems to have shared Poe's fascination with extreme exercises of rational thinking. Although he usually adopts the Holmsian habit of injunction over the Dupinian preference for lecture, Futrelle's detective is clearly a professor of method. He is, in fact, a Professor; he operates in Boston, and in "The Lost Radium" he seems to be associated with "Yarvard University."

The Professor's method is clearly scientific. Van Dusen is introduced in "The Problem of Cell 13" with his panoply of earned and honorary initials. He is regularly referred to as "the scientist" in all the stories. Though Futrelle does not invoke the authority of chemistry with the frequency of Conan Doyle, he does assign the professor his own "small laboratory" full of "chemical apparatus," and announces that from this laboratory the professor has published "truths that shocked and partially readjusted at least three of the exact sciences" ("The Rosewell Tiara," II.130). Futrelle's comic impulse may be detected in this latter assertion; still, Professor Van Dusen is certainly being portrayed as an effective practitioner of the scientific method. And only of the scientific method: the Professor's superior bearing (and his uncommonly large head and long yellow hair) preclude any indulgence in disguise. Intellectual inquiry is his only method.

And just as Holmes attempted to indoctrinate Watson with his methodological imperatives, so Van Dusen expounds his logic to Hutchinson Hatch. There are, however, two differences, both of which serve to exaggerate the rigor of Van Dusen's method. Dupin assumes that his companion can comprehend his dissertations on method, though comprehension seems to be all he expects: there is no indication that Dupin thinks that the narrator could by understanding him imitate him. Holmes actually hopes to educate Watson; he speaks on the assumption that Watson might conceivably acquire his methods. Van Dusen resembles Professor Challenger rather than either of his detective predecessors. He displays his logic and its results; he does not attempt to teach his logic. The professor attributes his power to scientific thinking, but he is a scientist of the twentieth century. Huxley's rhetoric of mere "trained and organised common sense" seems naive in the face of esoteric disputes in physics, chemistry, genetics, etc. Van Dusen is a scientist of the new, professional type; he assumes that scientific thinking is possible only to initiates, and neither Hutchinson Hatch nor anyone else present in the stories qualifies. He speaks his methodological injunctions with an irritated dogmatism, reproaching everyone (sometimes including himself) for not perceiving the infallible conclusions toward which they lead.

The other difference between Van Dusen's method and Holmes's lies in this apparent infallibility. The Professor really has only two rules, one of which he repeats in almost every story: "Two and two always makes four, Mr. Hatch, not sometimes, but always." (The other rule, less frequently repeated, is equally absolute: "Nothing is impossible.") Van Dusen makes much of his confidence that the solution he arrives at is the only solution. All detectives come to the correct conclusion, of course, but few attribute such a priori certainty to their methods. Holmes often enough allows for error in his calculations. His virtue lies in having a most effective method, one that proves itself consistently in its practice. Even Dupin was more modest. When he drew on mathematics to explicate his method, he cited algebra, with its variables, not arithmetic. Moreover, his algebraic example was cited specifically to illustrate the necessity of imaginative flexibility in thinking: the reason that "mere mathematicians" do not make good detectives is that given an equation such as x^2 + px equals q, the mere mathematician is incapable of coping with the fact that "occasions may occur where x^2 + px is *not* altogether equal to p" ("Purloined" I.693). Professor Van Dusen's "Two and two always makes four, Mr. Hatch, not sometimes, but always" would seem to place him with Poe's mere mathematicians, and with Conan Doyle's assertive Professor Challenger.

Van Dusen's famous nickname, "The Thinking Machine," confirms this placement. Thinking has become the function of a machine. Holmes sometimes seemed flamboyantly to distill his character in a machine—picturing his mind "a racing engine," untouched by emotions—but his bohemian habits always countered the effect. The Thinking Machine has his eccentric qualities—his "enormous head" with his long yellow hair and size eight hat, his magisterial pose—but they do not come close to countering the effect of a genuinely mechanical intelligence.[7] The Thinking Machine is a marvellous device for dissolving complicated plots, but he never emerges as a person. Nor does Hutchinson Hatch. Holmes and Watson set the standard for humanly believable detective teams; imitators have been more or less successful (Nero and Archie, Poirot and Hastings). None (not even Craig Kennedy and Walter Jameson) has been as insubstantial as Van Dusen and Hatch; they are animated neither by being assigned non-functional personalities and backgrounds nor by convincingly human conversations.

Conan Doyle's half-truth, that Holmes's "reasonings & deductions...are the whole of his character," is wholly true of Professor Van Dusen. The Thinking Machine stories propose unadulterated method—"logic" practiced by "the scientist"—as a hero of popular fiction. The twentieth-century public was evidently inclined, for a time, to embrace such an abstract hero. The settings of the stories are concrete, the problems are familiar (murder, theft, kidnapping), and Futrelle was an entertaining writer: even in a detective series, the hero is not all. But he is primary, and the Thinking Machine's popularity would seem to argue for a historical moment when the common reader was prepared to accept scientific method as inaccessible to common thinkers, but powerfully benevolent in practice.

And yet the Thinking Machine is not totally arid in his devotion to scientific logic. Though he never mentions Dupin, he shares Dupin's belief in the importance of imagination, the quality Dupin's "mere mathematicians" lacked. In "Kidnapped Baby Blake, Millionaire," he offers an unusually extended exposition of method. He begins with praise of imagination: "In the higher reasoning which can only come from long study and experiment, imagination is necessary to supply temporary gaps caused by absence of facts. Imagination is the backbone of scientific thinking" (I.194). He develops his theme by citing the role of imagination in technological advances such as Marconi's wireless telegraphy and the steam engine (two of Wallace's wonders of the nineteenth century) as well as such theoretical scientific advances as molecular and atomic theory. Van Dusen thus reflects the view that emerged in the later nineteenth century that science requires more than a Baconian collection of data; a disciplined mind and a visionary genius are also required. By 1905, the professionalization of science was nearly completed; real science (as opposed to popularized science) was the well-guarded province of the trained specialist. Professor Van Dusen, as a working university research scientist, embodies this new type of the scientist.

But in his excursus on method, The Thinking Machine is not only reflecting historical developments in scientific practice and theory, the American detective is also returning to his roots. He seems to be moving toward Dupin's formulation of the detective's method as a synthesis of the mathematician's technique and the poet's. Indeed, in a peculiar, Poe-like extrapolation, Van Dusen pauses to pursue a cosmological speculation that proceeds from atoms to men to cities to worlds, and "then comes the supreme imaginative leap which would make worlds merely atoms, pinpoint parts of a vast solar system itself merely an atom in some greater scheme of creation which the imagination refuses to grasp, which staggers the mind. It is all logic, logic, logic" (I.195). It is the sort of logic Poe might have admired.

The professor then repeats his aphorism, "two and two make four, not sometimes, but all the time" and concludes his lecture with the demonstration of a colorful chemical reaction which, he asserts, also illustrates an analogy between the microscopic and the macroscopic. Normally, the Thinking Machine is satisfied to manifest his methodological credentials with the aphorism, the word "logic," and his title of "the scientist." He does on a few other occasions admit the necessity of imagination. Exactly what possessed Van Dusen (or Futrelle) to interpolate the gratuitous speculations of "Kidnapped Baby Blake, Millionaire" is unclear. Science, logic, imagination and the universe are rolled together in an uncharacteristic rhapsody. Futrelle may have intended a conscious homage to Poe. (Or is it a burlesque? If so, in this respect, too, Futrelle claims a descent from the hoax-minded Poe.) That the villain of "Kidnapped Baby Blake, Millionaire" proves to be an orangutang (and that, like the criminal orangutang of "Murders in the Rue Morgue," the creature is the escaped possession of a sailor) would seem to confirm this intention. Professor F.X. Van Dusen is unquestionably a twentieth century post-Holmesian detective, but Futrelle seems to declare his debt to the American originator as well.

It is his science that distinguishes Professor Van Dusen most clearly from his two great predecessors, and in two respects. The first lies in his professionalism. Dupin and Holmes were, in effect, autodidacts; they invented themselves as experts. Poe gave substance to his detective's expertise by laying out his method in extended, credible discourses on his method; Conan Doyle did so through dramatic fragments: outsider testimonies (young Stamford), the scene of Holmes in the St. Bart's laboratory, the excerpt from "The Book of Life." Dupin was an amateur (in terms of motive, not skill) as a thinker and as a detective; though he sought rewards, he was an aristocrat who would have disdained professionalism. Holmes was indeed a professional private detective, but he was an amateur scientist. Hewitt was a professional private detective, and no scientist at all. (Lecoq and Gryce had been professional police detectives.) Van Dusen is a professional scientist and an amateur detective. As an amateur detective, the Professor escaped the prejudice that detection was a sordid, corrupt occupation; Futrelle did not need to defend his man's ethics (and not having to establish him as an ethical man also meant, to some extent, not having to establish him as man; hence the Thinking Machine).

And as a professional scientist, the Professor acquired the social credentials of the professional as well as the methodological credentials of the scientists. His authority in both matters was institutionalized. Dupin, Lecoq, Pinkerton, Gryce and Holmes had all been outsiders; Pinkerton and Gryce were especially unhappy about their exclusion, while the two most successful— Dupin and Holmes—chose that status. Morrison had attempted to move the detective toward respectability by dressing him in middle-class propriety. The first paragraphs of "The Lenten Croft Mystery," instead of establishing his method, establish his class. Hewitt began work as a clerk for a firm of solicitors; his success there led him to open his "private detective business," which he conducts "in the most private manner." And, Brett reports with satisfaction, his decision to operate independently "has been completely justified by the brilliant *professional* successes he has since achieved" (emphasis added). (Morrison himself seems to have been ambivalent about his own humble origins.) Futrelle moved The Thinking Machine toward respectability by throwing an academic gown of Professorialism over him. (And, though perhaps as an American I should blush to say it, simply by making him smart: in less-stratified American society, intelligence and ingenuity are in themselves warrants for social respectability.)

The second respect in which Professor Van Dusen's science distinguishes him from his detective predecessors relates to its substance. It is a matter raised only occasionally, but significantly. The Thinking Machine's cases sometimes involve quite advanced technologies. Holmes, for all his chemical experiments, remains largely innocent of technological developments. He was, for example, notoriously tardy in his appreciation of fingerprints; to the end, he preferred the telegraph to the telephone. His scientific tools—his lens and tape measure—give the necessary objective, quantitative character to his inquiries, but they are quite rudimentary. Although the last volume of Holmes stories was published in the 1920s, nearly all were firmly set in the Victorian period. Professor Van Dusen is considerably more au courant. Whether dealing with technologies of gas pipes, motorcycles, telephones, air balloons, or even radium, the Thinking Machine possesses the competence to comprehend their mechanisms. There is no Professor Moriarty to embody Villainy in the Thinking Machine stories, but the Thinking Machine does encounter a sort of antithesis: the dangerous unthinking machines of modern life. Crimes in his world are frequently committed through manipulation of these new devices. The devices are not depicted as evils in themselves; there is no hint of the Luddite in Futrelle. But the new machines do open the way for hitherto unthought of tactics in criminal activity. And it takes a Thinking Machine to counter them.

iv

Hewitt and Van Dusen embody the principal directions in which the detective story might evolve; they do not, of course, exhaust them. By looking briefly at an important figure entirely out of the Anglo-American tradition, however, it can be seen that even a detective who is not working directly under the shadow of

Sherlock Holmes cannot escape the scientific, methodological bias which Holmes bequeathed to his heirs. Gaston Leroux's (1868-1927) pair of novels featuring Joseph Rouletabille—*Le Mystère de la Chambre Jaune* (*The Mystery of the Yellow Room,* 1907) and *Le Parfum de la Dame en Noir* (*The Perfume of the Lady in Black,* 1908)—are justly regarded as classic detective stories. They have, to be sure, additional ambitions. As Richard P. Benton has observed, the relations between the young detective, his victimized mother and his villainous father develop mythic dimensions, especially in the second novel where the familial relationships become explicit ("Gaston Leroux" III.1071-77). Because all the major characters repeat their roles in the second novel (and because both plots depend essentially upon locked rooms), Leroux achieves a remarkable effect through repetition with variation. A reader educated by the Anglo-American tradition may find the histrionics in Leroux's novels distracting, and both *The Mystery of the Yellow Room* and *The Perfume of the Lady in Black* can be faulted for over-reliance on coincidence, but they comprise a landmark in the history of the genre.

Leroux's primary theme seems to be a search for identity within a claustrophobic web of disguised relationships; the detective, by 1907, had become a natural candidate for such a searcher. Joseph Rouletabille is an 18-year-old journalist as the first novel opens. When Mademoiselle Stangerson, daughter of the famous physicist Professor Stangerson, suffers a mysterious, near-fatal assault, Rouletabille vows to solve the mystery, and, moreover, to reach the solution in advance of the renowned police detective Frédéric Larsan, who has been called into the case. Rouletabille never discourses on method; his manner inclines more toward enigmatic watchwords and sentimental ejaculations. Still, he prizes method tacitly. When he disparages Larsan, it is on account of his method: "I fancied he was a much abler man. I had, indeed, a great admiration for him, before I got to know his method of working. It's deplorable. He owes his reputation solely to his ability; but he lacks reasoning power—the mathematics of his ideas are very poor" (Leroux, *Mystery of the Yellow Room* 92). Larsan, who possesses a "world-wide" reputation as "the most skillful unraveller of the most mysterious and complicated crimes" (25), seems at times to be a version of Sherlock Holmes, conducting experiments in timing and noticing overturned stones. But he also, like Dupin's Inspector G——, pursues false trails. Like Vidocq, he proves to be a master of disguise and, as well, a former (and not completely reformed) criminal. In the end, Rouletabille's method—reasoning power and mathematics—surpasses that of the police detective, but in doing so, reveals that the police detective (and, presumably his method) is his own father.

The cluster of methodological terms which Rouletabille values in opposition to Larsan—"method," "reason" and "mathematics"—harks back to Poe rather than Sherlock Holmes, and, in fact, Rouletabille seems to evolve backward in his investigative techniques. When he first performs as a detective, he, like Larsan, seems to be a respectable Holmesian. He examines doors and windows and shutters; he "looked at everything, smelled everything. He went down on his knees and rapidly examined every one of the paving tiles" (35). After this "close scrutiny" of the doors, exterior rooms, he enters the laboratory in which Mademoiselle Stangerson was assaulted. The narrator, Sainclair, observes: "My friend, who went about his work methodically, silently studied the room" (36). That the room is filled with scientific instruments—"a large chimney, crucibles, ovens, and such implements as are needed for chemical experiments; tables, loaded with phials, papers, reports, and electrical machine" (Leroux, *Mystery of the Yellow Room* 36)— adds to the impression of scientific inquiry.[8] And Rouletabille emerges from his empirical investigation with a tangible clue, a burnt slip of paper with a partially destroyed and seemingly irrelevant message. He will later notice footprints and carefully cut a paper pattern of the print to measure against others. In all these activities, he seems a son of Holmes.

But midway through the novel he at least half-repudiates the scientific, Holmesian model. He reproaches himself, "Like the least intelligent of detectives I went on blindly over the traces of footprints which told me just no more than they could" (111). Footprints are for Inspector G——'s and Holmes's (and, as well, Lecoq's); Dupin's and Rouletabille's aspire to a higher method. The senses do not, Rouletabille now asserts, furnish proof. "If I am taking cognisance of what is offered me by my senses I do so but to bring the results within the circle of my reason. That circle may be the most circumscribed, but if it is, he has the advantage—it holds nothing but *the truth!*" (112). Something is presumably lost in translation, but it is evident that Rouletabille's "circle of reason" transcends scientific truth. Leroux is defining his own peculiar approach to the detective's method. In *The Perfume of the Lady in Black* Rouletabille is even less bound by naturalistic procedures of investigation; the circle he appeals to now seems one of imagination. The detective's sensitive nose, rather than his observant eye, becomes the emblem of his power to penetrate beneath surfaces. And yet, at the ends of both novels, Rouletabille explains the mysteries rationally, accounting for all the empirical evidence; further, he explains how he rationally moved step by step to reach his explanation. The detective's fundamental obligation to demonstrate the technique of arriving at his conclusions remains inescapable.

Chapter 7

R. Austin Freeman

By 1907, when R. Austin Freeman introduced Dr. Thorndyke in *The Red Thumb Mark*, the proliferation of fictional detectives had begun, and there were clear signs that the main line of the genre's development was being overshadowed by collateral projections. If Dupin were its root, Lecoq and Holmes were the trunk; Freeman placed Thorndyke directly atop this trunk, but all about him exfoliating branches were budding. The detective, by Thorndyke's final adventure in 1942, had put on many masks that diverted attention from his methodological soul and essence. The detective became more an actor than a lecturer; his appeal came to lie in the effortlessness of his performance, and didactic asides about technique began to seem dispensable.

Some of these dramatic masks were already being worn by Thorndyke's earliest contemporaries. A few of these detectives, like Professor Van Dusen, still adhered to the methodological line. But absent the touch of extravagance present in Poe, Futrelle, and even Conan Doyle, severe methodology could become tiresome. (It was Freeman's singular triumph to combine a sober method and a clever but uninebriated narration.) Most of the new detectives, like Martin Hewitt, relied upon a presumption of method. Rather than expound or even enjoin principles of inquiry, they simply inquired. They exploited a presumption of method, a presumption based largely upon the generic expectations which had been established by the preachments of the methodologists (Dupin, Holmes, Van Dusen, Thorndyke). The detective might modestly attribute his success to "common sense" or "rule of thumb" or "little grey cells"; still, the reader knew that the detective, because he was a detective, must have begun his investigation with a deliberate, comprehensive, and effective approach to investigating.

If more than this vague assurance from precedent was needed, the new detectives could depend upon their concluding summary of the case at hand to sustain the illusion that their inquiry had been intelligent from the start. If, in the end, he arrives at a recreation of the crime that is rational, plausible, and unquestionably (because no character does question it, and no reader can) true, then the detective must have begun with methodological deliberation. And if he achieves similarly rational, plausible, and true conclusions in a succession of stories, why then there must be system to his method.

The system need not be overtly scientific, though its necessary rational and empirical aspects clearly affiliate it with the scientific method. Indeed, while on the one hand scientific thinking retained, and still retains, its nearly exclusive claim as the mark of legitimate thinking; the consequences of scientific thinking had grown even more dubious. The retreat into citadels of professionalism at the close of the nineteenth century raised suspicions; twentieth-century theories like relativity and technologies like phosgene gas insured that shadows at least balanced the brighter features of the face of science. Science was no longer a revolutionary novelty, but neither was it a simple and sure tool of progress.

The detective was thus tempted to finesse the question of technique. It was less complicated (and considerably easier) to have him act and then think. To have him think about thinking and talk about thinking, or even to associate him with scientific discipline, was as superfluous as it was tedious. The scientific method had, after all, infiltrated most forms of thought in the modern world; it was the general possession of thinking persons. It was sufficient that the detective's concluding explanation be rational and naturalistic. Few of the Great Detectives who peopled the Golden Age of the 1920s and 1930s indulged in Dupinian lecture or Holmesian injunction. One who did—Van Dine's Philo Vance—was eventually reprimanded for (among other faults) precisely this habit of overtalking his methodology. Even Dr. Thorndyke's nearer contemporaries—detectives introduced between 1905 and 1920—betrayed this inclination to underplay technique as the outstanding virtue of the detective and to prefer action over lecture as the proof of the detective's power to know. Examples of this trend include J.S. Fletcher (*Archer Dawe, Sleuth-Hound*, 1909), G.K. Chesterton (*The Innocence of Father Brown*, 1911), Canon Whitechurch (*Thrilling Stories of the Railway*, 1912), Ernest Bramah (*Max Carrados*, 1914), A.E.W. Mason (*At the Villa Rose*, 1910), Melville Davisson Post (*Uncle Abner, Master of Mysteries*, 1918). The detectives still detected, and detected rationally, but none aspired to authorship of a treatise on The Science of Deduction and Analysis, or even a little monograph on the ashes of 140 different varieties of pipe, cigar and cigarette tobacco.

i

Dr. John Evelyn Thorndyke might have made such a claim, had he needed factitious confirmation of his scientific credentials. Unlike Mr. Sherlock Holmes, he did not need to. Freeman required no tactic of "John Thorndykitos" to persuade readers of his detective's analytic power. There can be no doubt about the justness of Thorndyke's reputation as the pre-eminent scientific detective. His M.D. and D.Sc. are not, like Professor Van Dusen's string of degrees, hollow (and half humorous) badges of authority; Thorndyke regularly employs the techniques and knowledge which those degrees represent. Thorndyke preaches and practices what passes, to a non-scientist at least, for exemplary normal science. Thorndyke's authentic method, combined with Freeman's excellence at story-telling, ought to have made him a central figure in the genre, or at a minimum have positioned him as a Marlowe to Holmes's Spade.[1] In the event, Thorndyke fulfilled the original promise of the detective story only to find writers and readers preferring tangential diversions in the form.

Though Thorndyke belongs to the post-Holmesian generation of detectives, his author was a near contemporary of Conan Doyle, and this may partly account for the sense that Dr. Thorndyke completes Holmes's reinterpretation of Dupin. Only three years younger than Conan Doyle, Richard Austin Freeman was raised in a similar world. He too was a doctor—a Victorian doctor—and he seems to have acquired the Victorian confidence in the power of science and the Victorian doubt about the verities of religion that Conan Doyle claimed for himself in his autobiography. But unlike Conan Doyle (or Edgar Allan Poe), Freeman was not driven to pursue new spiritualist truths; he remained, as a friend described him, "a healthy atheist" (Donaldson 7).[2] Though his early life had its share of adventure and disappointment, once Freeman settled into the character of detective story author, he seems to have led a more stable life than his major predecessors (with the exception of Anna Katharine Green). And his detective betrays a comparable stability: Dr. Thorndyke is a mature presence upon his first appearance, and with admirable steadiness, he maintains his temperate manner through a career of nearly 40 years.

In *Memories and Adventures*, Conan Doyle described how, as a 27-year-old marginally successful doctor and aspiring writer, he added the qualities of Dr. Bell to those of his boyhood heroes, Dupin and Lecoq, to invent a detective who "would surely reduce this fascinating but unorganized business to something nearer to an exact science" (75). In "Meet Dr. Thorndyke,"

Freeman describes how, as a marginally successful doctor and aspiring writer in his mid-40s, he took Holmes as his starting point and, in effect, proposed to reduce this fascinating but rather unorganized business to something nearer an exact science: "I asked myself whether it might not be possible to devise a detective story of a slightly different kind; one based on the science of Medical Jurisprudence, in which, by the sacrifice of a certain amount of dramatic effect, one could keep entirely within the facts of real life, with nothing fictitious excepting the persons and the events" ("Meet Dr. Thorndyke" x). Freeman's willingness to sacrifice drama to science enabled his detective to fulfill the ideal of the heroic knower, but it may also have been a major impediment to his popularity. Conan Doyle's inspiration had been to make the action of knowing an exciting as well as a moral one; Freeman's inspiration was to make it a plausible and moral one.

"Medical Jurisprudence" seems to have functioned as a talisman for Freeman; it is regularly invoked in the Thorndyke stories. It synthesizes two traditional professions of knowing: medicine studies the individual; law studies the individual in relation to society. "Traditional" and "profession" matter: it was Holmes's boast that he had invented a *trade of his own* (emphasis added), that of "consulting detective," and that he was its unique practitioner. Thorndyke is unique in his competence and rare in combining his two professions, but he explicitly depends for his authority upon his membership in these two established, long-institutionalized professions. There is nothing of the parvenu in the disciplines of inquiry that Thorndyke pursues.

Freeman, who was apparently acutely embarrassed by his own origins (his father was a tailor), idealized the individual who, by mastering these disciplines, acquired the status of epistemological aristocrat. A "medico-legal expert," he declares in "Meet Dr. Thorndyke," should be more than "a doctor and a fully trained lawyer." And the "more" includes, first of all, a superficial excellence: "On the physical side, I endowed him with every kind of natural advantage. He is exceptionally tall, strong, and athletic because those qualities are useful in his vocation. For the same reason he has acute eyesight and hearing and considerable general manual skill, as every doctor ought to have. In appearance he is handsome and of imposing presence, with a symmetrical face of the classical type and a Grecian nose" (xi-xii). All of this "on the physical side" is detailed before Freeman turns to the intellectual character of the medico-legal expert.

Lest anyone suspect that Thorndyke's symmetrical face of the classical type derives from the author's romantic infatuation, Freeman adduces an argument: "In real life a first-class man of any kind usually tends to be a good-looking man." The premise is unconvincing, but revealing in two respects. The psychology of detective story writers is not at issue here, but it might be observed that the three principal figures in the evolution of the detective as articulate hero—articulate man—of knowing suffered major embarrassments relating to their fathers. Poe's troubled relations with his actor-father and merchant-stepfather are well known; Conan Doyle's father, it now appears, ended his life in an asylum, a secret long protected by his family; and Freeman was so unhappy and so silent about his father's occupation and his own early life that his biographer has recovered only two paragraphs of information about Freeman's life prior to his entering into medical school and acquiring his own professional status. At one level, Freeman would seem to be sculpting in Dr. Thorndyke the wise and handsome (or, rather, the handsome and wise) *professional* father he would have preferred.

At another level, however, Freeman was contributing to the generic argument that the profession of knowing is not a monstrous one. There is not a maniacal Dr. Hyde drooling inside every handsome Dr. Jekyll. Conan Doyle had used Sherlock Holmes's bohemian qualities as a balance to his scientific qualities (and, remembering that Charles Doyle was an artist, perhaps as a bow to his father). His successors found it easiest to distinguish their detectives by their physical deformities (Max Carrados's blindness or, in milder form, the uncommonly large head of Professor Van Dusen) or eccentric habits. Dr. Thorndyke was designed, Freeman asserts, as "a protest against the monsters of ugliness whom some detective writers have evolved." The detective's genuine science requires no balancing extravagance. The first-class medico-legal expert, because he is a first-class medico-legal expert, is naturally an ideal specimen of humanity.

Having established Thorndyke's physical presence, Freeman turns to the mechanism of his investigative technique. He discusses two aspects: "imagination" and "method." The first recalls the nineteenth-century debate over the place of imagination in scientific inquiry. That debate had concluded that imagination, expressed in hypothesis and theory, was indeed an essential addition to the Baconian practice of gathering data and inducing generalizations. Thorndyke reflects this conclusion. He possesses no "supernormal mental qualities"; but to the Baconian virtues of thinking clearly ("exceptionally acute reasoning powers") and commanding his data ("great and varied knowledge") he adds fertility in conceiving hypotheses ("that invaluable asset, a scientific imagination").[3] The first two qualities are those which the early chapters of A Study in Scarlet so insistently assign to Sherlock Holmes. Holmes is not without imagination; it is certainly implicit in his bohemian inclinations; but it is not a featured element in his method. Thorndyke's aversion to eccentricities and oddities excludes him from stereotypical artistic imagination; he is no bohemian, and when the occasion arises (as in The Stoneware Monkey), he can be quite disparaging about modern art. But he does possess scientific imagination. "Hypothesis" is one of his favorite words, and he applies it accurately to describe a crucial part of his scientific thinking. Hypotheses are imaginative propositions which must be tested by inventive experiment.

The second aspect of the detective's intellect addressed in "Meet Dr. Thorndyke" is his method. "His methods are rather different from those of the detectives of the Sherlock Holmes school. They are more technical and more specialized.... He is a medico-legal expert, and his methods are those of medico-legal science" (xiii). The distinction becomes clearer when Freeman identifies the first method—that of the Holmes school and the police—as the accumulation of circumstantial detail: "inquiring into the movements of suspected and other persons; interrogating witnesses and checking their statements particularly as to times and places; tracing missing persons, and so forth." The second, medico-legal method, by contrast, "consists in the search for some fact of high evidential value which can be demonstrated by physical methods and which constitutes conclusive proof of some important point" (xiii). In short, the medico-legal method "consists in the interrogation of things rather than persons" (xiv).

The distinction is crucial, and it has important implications. Thorndyke never disfigures his symmetrical features with disguise. Several motives may restrain him. In part, it may offend his dignity, and though Thorndyke is very far from the humorless figure some critics have depicted, his humor is always verbal. His dignity matters, and Freeman never suffers it to be offended. Under extreme circumstances, Thorndyke may exercise admirable energy and dexterity, but he always sustains a superior, magisterial manner. Mature gentlemen do not paint their faces; more importantly, honest gentlemen do not pretend to be something other than they are. Thorndyke's refusal to exploit disguise in the pursuit of knowledge becomes a proof of his integrity. But his refusal also proves the sufficiency of his method. The interrogation of things yields truth; the interrogation of people is largely superogatory, and subtle practices in the interrogation of people are entirely unnecessary. By appearing always as himself, as a barrister-physician-gentleman, Thorndyke demonstrates the efficacy of purely objective, scientific inquiry.

In this regard, he fulfills what Edmund and Jules Goncourt saw as the essential character of the fictional detective. In their journal entry for 16 July 1856 they wrote: "After reading Edgar Allan Poe. Something the critics have not noticed: a new literary world pointing to the literature of the twentieth century. Scientific miracles, fables on the pattern A+B; a clear-sighted sickly literature. No more poetry, but analytic fantasy. Something monomaniacal. Things playing a more important part than people; love giving way to deductions and other sources of ideas, style, subject, and interest; the basis of the novel transferred from the heart to the head, from the passion to the idea, from the drama to the denouement" (Goncourt 19-20). There seems a large element of accurate prophecy in this description, though the healthy and broad-minded Dr. Thorndyke would seem to refute "sickly" and "monomaniacal," and despite the professed objections of Dorothy Sayers and others, love has never been banished from the detective story, and least of all from Austin Freeman's. But the detective story has indeed become the analytic fantasy of the age of science, and Dr. Thorndyke's interrogation of things seems the apotheosis of a literature dedicated to things, deductions, the head, the idea and the denouement.[4]

Thorndyke's devotion to interrogating things finds an interesting reflection in his origin. Both Conan Doyle and Freeman were inspired by hospital experiences. Conan Doyle observed the Edinburgh surgeon and brilliant diagnostician, Dr. Joseph Bell, infer a man's livelihood or domicile from his outward appearance. He recited one anecdote in *Memories and Adventures*; in it, Bell observes a sufferer from elephantiasis who is respectful, but does not remove his hat, who is obviously Scottish and has "an air of authority." Bell infers correctly that the man is a recently discharged, non-commissioned officer from a Highland regiment who has served in Barbados. Doyle—and other of Bell's students as well—recorded their amazement at

Bell's accuracy in these exercises. Freeman's inspiration, as reported in "Meet Dr. Thorndyke," was significantly different. While he was writing prescriptions for eyeglasses in the Westminster Ophthalmic Hospital, it occurred to him that each formula "furnished an infallible record of personal identity" and that a pair of spectacles discovered in, say, a railway carriage might constitute "practically conclusive evidence" regarding the identity of the individual who had travelled in that carriage. He composed the first Thorndyke story (*The Mystery of 31, New Inn*, not published until 1912) based on this realization. Conan Doyle was impressed by an interview in which an experienced diagnostician played with speculative inferences; Dr. Bell's little exercises became the prototype of the Sherlockholmitos demonstrations which Conan Doyle employed as incidental proofs of the power of Holmes's method. Freeman, on the other hand, was impressed by the human data which could be derived from examination of an inert object. And this became the paradigm of his detective stories. Invariably some object, some piece of detritus associated with a crime, passes into Thorndyke's possession, and from it he carefully, through physical scientific analysis, extracts a key to understanding the criminal action.

Freeman's second collection of short stories was entitled *The Singing Bone* (1912). The title derives from the title of part two of one of the stories, "The Echo of a Mutiny," and the meaning of this subtitle is explained by Thorndyke and his narrator, Jervis, at the end of the story. Thorndyke has exposed a murderer through an analysis of a pipe accidentally dropped by the victim. Jervis admiringly comments: "it spoke like the magic pipe—only that wasn't a tobacco-pipe—in the German folk-story of the 'Singing Bone.' Do you remember it? A peasant found the bone of a murderer and fashioned it into a pipe. But when he tried to play on it, it burst into a song of its own—'My brother slew me and buried my bones / Beneath the sand and under the stones' " Thorndyke then draws the "excellent moral": "The inanimate things around us have each of them a song to sing to us if we are but ready with attentive ears" (*Best* 108).

Thorndyke's moral applies to all of his investigations. He is a virtuoso at making inanimate things—a pipe, an overcoat, a hat, a half-smoked cigar—speak. Of course, Holmes and all detectives, as Freeman admits, interrogate things as well as persons, and Thorndyke can be a skillful interrogator of persons as well. But the examination of things is his special province. In a well-known comparison, Alfred Ward contrasted the information Sherlock Holmes derives from an abandoned hat to that which Thorndyke derives (223-26). Holmes makes more inferences (six to Thorndyke's three), and they are more spectacular (e.g. "that he was a man of foresight, but has suffered moral retrogression, probably due to drink," "that his wife has ceased to love him"). Thorndyke merely concludes that the hat's owner was Japanese, employed in a mother-of-pearl factory, and orderly in his habits. Holmes's deductions are wonderful, but examined individually, highly speculative and even improbable. The observations might justify the conclusions, but they might equally well justify a dozen other conclusions. Because the owner, when he appears, verifies each of Holmes's deductions, Holmes's method of knowing acquires the illusion of providing extensive, certain knowledge. Thorndyke's method is more modest in scope, but depends upon no tricks for verification. The man is Japanese because measurement of the hat's brim indicates that the head has the Japanese feature of being nearly as broad as it is long, and when a small piece of hair is examined under the microscope, it displays the distinctive characteristics of Japanese hair (and Thorndyke enumerates these characteristics: circular in section and wide in diameter). This is indeed "practically conclusive evidence" drawn from an inanimate object.

"Conclusiveness" was the key to Freeman's aesthetic of the detective story, and he returns to it in his essay, "The Art of the Detective Story." The essay is in most respects a typical Golden

Age document. S.S. Van Dine or Father Knox could take little exception. The author of the most scientific of detectives makes no mention of scientific method at all. He does insert two judgments that do reflect his own bias. The first is a warning against sensationalism, which is, after all, the most seductive alternative to rigorous methodology. This warning, however, reflects the common Golden Age assumption that the detective story is primarily an intellectual exercise—a puzzle—and would have been readily endorsed by the entire school. In his second judgment, however, Freeman does challenge much of the work of that school. Detective stories "most commonly fail," he asserts, when "the conclusion reached by the gifted investigator, and offered by him as inevitable, is seen by the reader to be merely one of a number of possible alternatives" (10).[5] Holmes's conclusions about Henry Baker's alcoholism and disaffected wife are exactly the sort of thing Freeman objects to.

Freeman wants certainty in the particular knowledge yielded by the detective's method. Although advanced science was already sliding toward relativity theories and uncertainty principles (which to a layman seem to imply relativity and uncertainty) and toward a general recognition of the provisional quality of all scientific interpretations, Freeman reasserted the ideal of scientific certainty. The conclusions of the scientist are incontrovertible because they are scientific. And to insure the incontrovertibility of Dr. Thorndyke's conclusions, Freeman laboriously verified every experiment he assigned to his detective. There is no sleight of hand to Dr. Thorndyke's science. Indeed, his entire world is verifiable. With rare exceptions, the topography of Thorndyke's world could be measured by any reader with the leisure to do so; the same physical and chemical laws applied to both worlds; and any reader who chose to repeat an investigation would achieve the same result and be compelled to the same conclusion.

The verifiability of Thorndyke's inquiries was a source of their strength; there was also a cost attached. Because his conclusions depended upon certain details, Thorndyke's investigations often turned on specialized knowledge—that this sort of mollusc is native to this particular location—and required highly technical processes of analysis. Readers sometimes were frustrated by the crucial role played by such minutiae. And Freeman's commitment to verisimilitude and plausibility rendered him immune to the appeal of extravagance as a literary device. In "The Art of the Detective Story," he specifically deplores the mind-reading episode in "Murders in the Rue Morgue" (and he might as well have included Holmes's imitation in "The Cardboard Box"). The playful use of excess was anathema to Freeman, and there is little playfulness in the action of his detective stories (and his flights into playfulness in the non-detective stories have generally been deemed unhappy). He compensates handsomely with verbal wit and Dickensian characterization, but the sobriety of his actions doubtless cost him readers.

ii

Freeman admitted that the example of Sherlock Holmes was in front of him when he introduced Dr. Thorndyke. (He even chose a crimson title—*The Red Thumb Mark*—to pair with *A Study in Scarlet*.) There is an interesting contrast between the scenes in which the reader first makes the acquaintance of the detective. Dr. Watson's introduction to Holmes occurs after hours in the chemical laboratory of St. Bartholomew's Hospital. Holmes appears as the "enthusiast in some branches of science," pursuing his irregular studies actively and in isolation. Dr. Jervis, Thorndyke's first and most frequent, but not sole narrator-companion, meets Dr. Thorndyke in the "old-world surroundings" of King's Bench Walk, an honorable precinct of the Inner Temple whose venerability is emphasized by Jervis's noticing an inscription relating a building's destruction and rebuilding in the seventeenth century. Watson sees the lone figure of Holmes bent over a laboratory table, examining the test-tube which contains confirmation of his discovery of a new test for the presence of blood. Jervis also sees a lone figure, but it is not the figure of an active enthusiast. In his first appearance, Thorndyke, returning from his day's routine labors in court, is, in fact, attired in the "wig and obsolete habiliments" of a certified barrister.

Over dinner, Thorndyke explains his own professional evolution to his old school fellow. He had remained at St. Margaret's Hospital after Jervis had left, "taking up any small appointments that were going—assistant demonstrator—or curatorships and such like—hung about the chemical and physical laboratories, the museum and post mortem room, and meanwhile took my M.D. and D.Sc" (*Red Thumb* 6). He began, then, exactly in the manner of Sherlock Holmes, hanging about the laboratories, but the two part ways in that final phrase— Sherlock Holmes was no taker of degrees. (Nor was he a taker of honors, declining a knighthood; though he never has the opportunity, Thorndyke would surely have welcomed the substitution of "Sir" for "Dr.") Even the M.D. and D.Sc. were not enough for Thorndyke, and, in hopes of getting a coronership, he pursued a call to the bar. His medical credentials enable him to function officially "in the character of that *bête noir* of judges and counsel—the scientific witness"; his legal credentials enable him to serve as an official consultant—"I do not appear at all; I merely direct investigations, arrange and analyse the results, and prime the counsel with facts and suggestions for cross-examination" (7). Thorndyke's practice is thus comparable to Holmes's, but with the crucial difference that his inquiries and consultations are formally sanctioned by the established medical and legal institutions and guided in their execution by the rules and technologies which those institutions sponsored.

Dr. Watson had discovered in Holmes "a good practical knowledge of British law" (I.156). Dr. Thorndyke's status as barrister represents more than the professionalization of this "practical knowledge." The law, especially in the common law tradition, is inherently conservative. Hanging about laboratories, museums, and post mortem rooms may inspire revolutionary theories, or, at least, the illusion that the scientific method may be successfully applied in all fields of inquiry; lawyers know that human problems are intractably complex and that a decent regard for precedent, not a new theory of right and wrong, is the best guarantee of justice. Freeman was explicit about the value of Thorndyke's synthesis of the two modes of thinking, the scientific and the legal. In what seems to be a version of the very first Thorndyke story, "31, New Inn," a solicitor makes the point to Jervis: "Thorndyke views things from a radically different standpoint and brings a new and totally different kind of knowledge into the case. He is a lawyer and a scientific specialist in one, and the combination of the two types of culture in one mind, let me tell you emphatically, is an altogether different thing from the same two types in separate minds" (*Best* 220). The solicitor's anticipation of C.P. Snow's famous formulation of the two cultures is fortuitous, but relevant. The solicitor intends a compliment to the efficacy of Thorndyke's method: the union of the two cultures, scientific and legal, produces a uniquely effective investigator. But there is a compliment to the ethic as well as the efficacy of the method which synthesizes the insights of both cultures: it produces an effective investigator who is safe as well as effective. A lawyer-scientist will not create a Frankenstein.

Thorndyke's dual profession provides him with several occasions to discourse on the two modes of thinking. In response to a question by the barrister, Anstey, in *The Cat's Eye* (1923), for example, Thorndyke analyzes "the difference between the legal and the scientific outlook": "The business of the man of science is impartially to acquire all the knowledge that is obtainable; the lawyer tends to concern himself only with that which is material to the issue" (82). Thorndyke cannot sustain the distinction; Anstey quickly compels him to admit that the scientist must select his facts, too. But the opposition between the dispositions toward impartiality and advocacy remains. In *A Certain Dr. Thorndyke* (1927), Thorndyke develops a different aspect of the contrast. The legal mind makes judgments based on sworn testimony—"according to evidence"; in scientific research, the investigator's knowledge "is first-hand, and hence he knows the exact value of his evidence. He can hold a suspended judgment. He can form alternative opinions and act upon both alternatives. He can construct hypotheses and try them out." He can, in short, use imagination, in a way the legal mind cannot. And, raising Freeman's own thesis, Thorndyke observes that, "Above all, he is able to interrogate things as well as persons" (*A Certain Dr. Thorndyke* 283-84). Expositions such as these occur regularly in the Thorndyke stories. They are more substantial than Holmes's injunctions (though Thorndyke practices injunction too: hardly a story passes without a reminder to collect all data and to record them accurately), and they are less fanciful and less didactic than Dupin's lectures.

Thorndyke makes the most straightforward statement of his basic scientific method in his first published case, *The Red Thumb Mark*: "I make it a rule, in all cases, to proceed on the strictly classical lines of inductive inquiry—collect facts, make hypotheses, test them and seek for verification. And I always endeavor to keep a perfectly open mind" (*Red Thumb* 29). Classical induction, if the induction of Mill is meant, had been less confident of the place and value of hypotheses, but Thorndyke's use of "strictly classical" as a commendation is typical: his is a method justified by its venerability. He instinctively appeals to a conservative standard; his scientific method must be effective because it is *not* new; it is certainly not revolutionary.

Freeman's great formal innovation, the "inverted" detective story (e.g. "The Case of Oscar Brodski"), makes the method openly the protagonist of story. The narrative first describes the commission of the crime, then the investigation. The reader's interest, then, must lie not in the solution, but in the solving. The narration of the crime moves simply forward; the investigation portion moves backward logically as it continues to move forward chronologically, and it is from the contrary motions of the second half that any tension is generated. How can Thorndyke's science take him another step forward in his progress backward to the criminal? The reader already knows the entire song of the crime; how can Thorndyke methodically tease another verse from the singing bone?

Freeman's decision to place his six "Inverted Stories" as "Group I" in the 1929 collection of 37 Thorndyke stories, *The Famous Cases of Dr. Thorndyke* indicates the high value that Freeman and his readers placed on this methodologically based form. In his short preface to *The Famous Cases*, Freeman specifically calls attention to his innovation. But although he claims the approbation of "excellent judges on both sides of the Atlantic," the inverted story remained something of a freak. Freeman employed it in two of the Thorndyke novels, *The Shadow of the Wolf* (1925) and *Mr. Pottermack's Oversight* (1930), and the second of these has often been regarded as one of his most successful. But though it expressed Freeman's notion that method was the sufficient as well as the essential quality of the detective story, the inverted form failed to persuade his readers or his fellow writers.[7] Critics who mention Freeman usually mention the Inverted Story, and usually accord it respect, but little enthusiasm.

iii

One of the obstacles science finally overcomes in the nineteenth century was the widespread social prejudice that scientific investigation was too much a low, mechanical occupation, beneath the dignity of the gentleman. Holmes's bohemian character immunized him from the prejudice, and he beat his corpses with his own stick. As his embarrassment over his origins suggests, Richard Austin Freeman was not immune, although paradoxically, he was quite proud of his own mechanical aptitude. Vincent Starrett, when he visited Freeman in 1924, had been most impressed by the author's own workshop: "a little world of test tubes, cameras, microscopes and all manner of medico-legal apparatus that would have caused a pseudo-scientific pretender like Craig Kennedy to stammer and retreat" (qtd. in Donaldson 134). Freeman could boast that every device employed by a criminal in the commission of a crime (such as the aluminium dagger fired from an air gun in "The Aluminium Dagger") or by Thorndyke in the investigation of a crime (such as the walking-stick-periscope in *Mr. Pottermack's Oversight*) had been fabricated and tested by himself.

And yet Starrett had to add a parenthesis to his compliment to the author: "Freeman was his own Thorndyke (and his own Polton)." Freeman divided his methodological protagonist into a patrician professor of knowing and a plebeian professor of making. Nathaniel Polton, with his ever "crinkly" eyes, is introduced in *The Red Thumb Mark* as Thorndyke's "mechanical factotum." A watchmaker and optician by training, Polton constructs the devices which Thorndyke applies to the investigation of crime. In the course of the Thorndyke saga, Polton's role expands; the first half of the penultimate Thorndyke novel, *Mr. Polton Explains* (1940), is cast as a biography of Polton's early life. Freeman has a clear affection for the character and a genuine admiration for his craftsmanship, but he also clearly distinguishes the craftsman from the scientist.

Again, this is part of the supporting argument of the Thorndyke series. The scientist is, for Freeman, an ideal type of the gentleman, and vice versa. And while some of its advocates may defend gentility as essentially a matter of morals, it is visibly a matter of manners, a matter of class. Thorndyke's manners are as impeccable as his morals. His professional credentials, his magisterial style of speech—his gravity and his wit, his irreproachable attire (even when not dressed in the barrister's "wig and obsolete habiliments"): all attest to his easy carriage of his class privileges. His absolute aversion to disguise fits this character. Nor is he embarrassed by his advantages. In "31 New Inn," Thorndyke explains to Dr. Jervis why he—Jervis—would make a welcome addition to Thorndyke's establishment. Polton, as a technician, is excellent in his kind ("my right hand") but "of course his education and social training do not allow of his taking my place excepting in a quite subordinate capacity" (*Best* 236). Thorndyke has, in fact, been "greatly pushed for want of a colleague of my own class," and Dr. Jervis, a doctor who eventually emulates Thorndyke by being called to the bar, qualifies nicely. The class consciousness is entirely natural, and it pervades Thorndyke's world. Polton embraces his subservience happily; Thorndyke plays the aristocrat with the magnanimity that, if anything does, justifies aristocracy.

Sherlock Holmes was an aristocrat of sorts, too, and the contrast of the two sorts is suggestive. Both heroes demonstrated their excellence essentially through their commitment to justice and their expertise in pursuing their commitment. But both authors used supplemental indications of the hero's distinction. Thus Conan Doyle dropped hints about Holmes's ancestors in the English squirearchy and in French artistic circles; he announces Sherlock's brother, Mycroft, "occasionally *is* the British Government" (II.433). Holmes, then, is explained partly as a natural aristocrat; he has to some degree inherited his genius. Freeman's much more conservative hero is a self-created aristocrat; Freeman is as reticent about Thorndyke's familial origins as about his own.

The result is that Holmes enjoys a freedom denied to Thorndyke. The contrast in their styles is evident in their first exchanges with their companions. Thorndyke makes his case that Jervis's profession would be of great practical use in a professional alliance. Holmes's negotiations with Watson, by contrast, took quite a different vein, with Holmes declaring his addiction to strong tobacco, chemical experiments and violin-playing; and Watson replying by confessing to laziness and a bull pup. Though Holmes and Watson have surely measured one another as gentlemen broadly defined—obviously neither is proletarian, both are university trained—there is none of the protocol of Thorndyke's interview with his old medical school fellow. Indeed, Thorndyke's instinct for protocol was present in his conception; this is the point of Freeman's assertion that *his* scientific detective would possess "the dignity of presence, appearance and manner appropriate to his high professional and social standing" (qtd. in Donaldson 65). Holmes accepts Watson as a roommate; Thorndyke selects Jervis as a "colleague."

Much should be made of Dr. Thorndyke's character as a gentleman-scientist, but there is a limit. Freeman makes very clear that his hero is not mechanic, but he also concedes that the empirical scientist must manipulate material objects. The interrogation of things, after all, requires contact with things. Polton is the primary doer in the Thorndyke stories; he manufactures the equipment; he develops the photographs. But then Thorndyke reaches his conclusions by using the equipment and interpreting the photographs in ways that leave Polton baffled. The most ubiquitous emblem of Thorndyke's reliance upon technological means is his "little green box," the case of miniature implements which he always carries with him. It is, as Jervis says, a "portable laboratory," containing "rows of little re-agent bottles, tiny test-tubes, diminutive spirit-lamp, dwarf microscope and assorted instruments on the same Lilliputan scale" (*Best* 17). Freeman is specific about the limitations and uses of this equipment, and all of Thorndyke's impressive work accomplished through it could doubtless be duplicated by any other possessor of such singular instruments. But the adjectives—"little," "tiny," "diminutive," "dwarf," "Lilliputian"—all suggest a toy-like quality. Even the larger devices which Polton constructs for single uses have this playful aspect, such as the walking-stick which can function as a periscope. In *The Red Thumb Mark*, Thorndyke commissions Polton to turn on his lathe two dozen objects resembling chess pawns. Neither Polton nor Jervis can imagine what these toys will be used for; in the event, they serve as handles for the fake thumb-prints Thorndyke will flourish in the court room. None of these items is, in fact, a toy, and Thorndyke's imperturbable maturity makes him the least puerile of heroes. Thorndyke is intensely serious in his use of all these tools, but there is, ever so slightly, the hint that he is, in an Emersonian sort of way, a Man Practicing Science (or even a Man Playing at Science), rather than a Scientist.

Much of Thorndyke's technology is the repetition of Holmes's, on a much higher plane. Holmes flourishes his lens; Thorndyke focuses his microscope. Thorndyke employs his tools diligently, and his operations and their results are consequential for the case he is working on. They actually provide tangible evidence which is used to identify victims and criminals. Moreover, the devices he employs are sometimes quite sophisticated. In *The Eye of Osiris* (1911) he arranges for an X-ray photograph to be taken of a mummy in the British Museum. The appearance of the X-ray machine is described by the narrator, Dr. Berkeley; the principle and the limits of its operation are described by Dr. Thorndyke; and the resulting "skiagraph" yields definitive information about the identity of the body inside the wrappings. Though he preserves his status as a gentleman by minimizing his physical exertions (Polton is at hand to develop the skiagraph), Thorndyke is master of whatever machinery modern science places at his disposal. The Thorndyke stories display an admiration of technology as an aid in the interrogation of things, but the methodological intelligence of the human interrogator is always the primary hero.

iv

Dr. Thorndyke's adventures occupy, in all, 21 novels and 42 short stories.[8] The short stories (and serializations of some of the novels) were first published in *Pearson's Magazine*, which had been founded in 1896 by a former *Strand* employee in direct competition with *The Strand*. Arthur Pearson recognized the contribution of the detective to *The Strand's* success, and secured imitations of his own. One of the earliest had been Matthias McDonnell Bodkin's "rule of thumb" detective who began appearing as Alfred Juggins in *Pearson's* in 1897 (and as *Paul Beck, the Rule of Thumb Detective* (1898) when collected in a volume). But it was not until the Christmas issue of 1908, with the publication of "The Blue Sequin," that Pearson finally found in Dr. Thorndyke his answer to Sherlock Holmes, who had recently been resurrected by Conan Doyle in *The Strand*. All of the Thorndyke stories (with one exception) would be published in *Pearson's*. And, beginning in 1911 with *The Eye of Osiris*, all of the Thorndyke novels and collections would be published in England by the firm of Hodder & Stoughton. Dr. Thorndyke's popularity, never as phenomenal as that of Holmes, was sufficient to insure access to these quite respectable venues.[9]

Freeman's success in America was less consistent. He seems to have had no regular outlet in periodicals, though *Argosy All-Story Weekly* reprinted a half dozen stories at intervals in the mid-1920s. Dodd, Mead was his usual American publisher; they discovered him in 1912, publishing an edition of *The Eye of Osiris*. *The Red Thumb Mark* (1907) had already been issued by Donald W. Newton of New York in 1911, and *The Mystery of 31 New Inn* would be issued by John C. Winston of Philadelphia in 1913. Dodd, Mead published the remaining Thorndyke volumes, sometimes a year or more following their English publication. In one instance, that of the longest Thorndyke novel, *Helen Vardon's Confession* (1922), they declined publication and Freeman could interest no other American publisher. Dr.

Thorndyke's American reputation was, it seems, adequate, but not extraordinary. In 1922, Freeman expressed his disappointment at his reception in America to Vincent Starrett: "I am rather puzzled by the very slight vogue that my work has had in the States. There seems to be a good demand for detective stories and the supply seems to be, as you remark, of a very poor quality. I cannot help thinking that editors must be somewhat lacking in critical judgement, or else that they take no trouble in looking for good-class work" (qtd. in Donaldson 137-38). American reviewers were generally kind to Freeman, praising Thorndyke as a model detective and, in the obvious comparison with Craig Kennedy, the American scientific detective, readily acknowledging Thorndyke's superiority.[10]

Before turning to the case of the American scientific detective, it may be useful to follow the scientific detective's further career in England. He becomes a much diminished thing. Freeman's excellence may have intimidated rather than inspired imitation, and his popularity was not of a magnitude to encourage rivals. The evolution of science and of the reading public, of course, played a major role by undermining a disposition toward naive awe at the works of science. And Dupin, Van Dusen and Thorndyke had already established the expectation that every detective detected methodically. Further demonstrations were superfluous. Explicit reminders of the scientific basis became ornaments, added to flavor the narrative rather than to justify it.[11]

Nineteen-twenty is frequently cited as beginning of the "Golden Age" of the detective story because three of the major Golden Age writers published their first volume in that year: H.C. Bailey, *Call Mr. Fortune*; Agatha Christie, *The Mysterious Affair at Styles*; and Freeman Wills Crofts, *The Cask*. All of their detectives found themselves engaged in complex intellectual puzzles, and all of them concluded their investigations with convincing expositions of the true pattern of events, demonstrating who the real villain was and how he or she committed his or her villainies.

The Great Detectives take care to offer logical conclusions; they are less careful about stipulating the model of their logic. It may be analysis, ratiocination, mathematics, observation and deduction, medico-legal reasoning, science, whatever. The Great Detectives are more concerned with reaching rational results than with prescribing the technique for achieving those results.

Sherlock Holmes had combined the method and the eccentric genius of Dupin with the energy of Lecoq, with method about evenly balanced with the combination of eccentricity and genius. Agatha Christie, by far the most successful heir of Conan Doyle, deleted the element of energy entirely from her formula, and greatly de-emphasized method, leaving eccentric genius as the soul and essence of Hercule Poirot. His researches into vegetable marrows represent Poirot's closest encounter with science; he is an excellent detective, but he makes no credible references to his method. He detects solely through his intellect—Poirot's prominent moustaches and egg-shaped head insure that he never slips into disguise—but he finds it unnecessary to explain the rules by which that intellect proceeds. Poirot might have said, "You know my little grey cells," but it would have been an assertion of genius rather than a call for imitation. Poirot's genius extemporarizes its tactics according to the circumstances Miss Christie arranges for him, and only in his retrospective account, as he reveals the true order of events, is there the implication that there was order to his inquiry as well.

Reggie Fortune does inherit a scientific mantle, but he wears it loosely. He is a practicing medical doctor who, like Holmes and Thorndyke, studied pathology in a London Hospital, though unlike Dr. Thorndyke, he prefers "Mr." He possesses a laboratory, in which he professes to be happy. But Mr. Fortune is not the deliberate scientist; his other affectations far outweigh his scientific claims. Eccentric genius is his primary character as well. He pays rhetorical tribute to science, but not practical. "The rest was merely obedience to the rule of scientific inquiry, that one ought to try everything": this passes for methodology in a Fortune story ("The Little House"). That he invokes the authority of science at all is significant, but the rule he cites—"one ought to try everything"—hardly qualifies its speaker as a methodical investigator. Reggie Fortune is clever enough, and he may be more methodical than his reputation as an intuitional detective allows, but his pretensions to science may actually have performed a disservice by setting expectations he was not, by his nature, prepared to fulfill.[12]

Though it was the first and most famous of Freeman Wills Crofts's novels, *The Cask* does not feature his most famous detective, Inspector French. Nonetheless, it illustrates the same virtues as the French stories, and these differ in degree from the Great Detective type that Poirot and Fortune represent. Inspector Burnley of Scotland Yard, Monsieur Lefarge of the Sûreté and the Anglo-French investigator, Georges La Touche, are genuinely methodical (and energetic) in their approach to the problem of the body discovered in the cask, but they make no boast of scientific principle. Burnley and Lefarge operate according to police procedure. By 1920, the police had not only adopted scientific techniques in their investigations, the corporate and bureaucratic nature of their methods more accurately reflected real science than did the individual researcher reflected in the practice of Dr. Thorndyke. Twentieth-century science has rarely celebrated the discoveries made by a quixotic researcher in his home laboratory. This reality is, of course, not necessarily binding upon fictional detectives; Dr. Thorndyke was a vigorous and thoroughly convincing individual scientist through the first 18 years of Inspector French's career. But Croft's disciplined, observant police detectives do embody a new method, and one that, in its methodicalness, is scientific second-hand. Inspector Burnley makes careful measurements of footprints and ladder marks, and he uses these measurements to move forward in his case, but he is quantitative by habit rather than by deliberation, and he utters no apothegms about accuracy. He assumes what Holmes and Thorndyke had to advocate.[13] (Of course, in *The Cask*, Burnley and LeFarge prove to be very competent and thorough, and also wrong; but Georges La Touche, "commonly regarded as the smartest private detective in London," proves their error only by repeating their same procedures under the special stimulus of a commission to prove a defendant innocent. La Touche never recites methodological imperatives either.)

Inspector Burnley's routine attention to detail reflects Freeman's insistence that the detective ought to proceed by the disciplined interrogation of things; Hercule Poirot and Reggie Fortune, both amateur detectives (though Poirot had been a professional in Belgium and Fortune maintains a connection with Scotland Yard), prefer the ad hoc interrogation of people—their conversations and their behaviors. There was, however, an emerging science of interrogation of people: psychology. The chief practitioners were American, and will be dealt with in the next chapter, but mention can be made here of the brief fame of Dr. Xavier Wycherley. Dr. Wycherley's creator was Max Rittenberg, an Australian-born writer who published the first of "The Strange Cases of Dr. Xavier Wycherley" in *The London Magazine* in March 1911. The series was popular enough to be reprinted in America in *Blue Book* beginning in June 1911. It was not, however, popular enough to justify preservation in book form.

Students of science fiction and pulp literature have found something admirable in the Dr. Wycherley stories,[13] but they have little to recommend them to students of the detective story. They belong to the category of Edwardian gothic, playing heavily on the uncanny. A London capitalist, a Ruritanian (actually, a Varovian) heir, a French peasant girl—all find themselves afflicted with mysterious afflictions. Dr. Wycherley intuits the mysterious source of the trouble and achieves a satisfactory resolution. There may be some historical interest in the doctor's sympathy for the workers in "The Sending" or in the exposition of a case of multiple personalities in "The Thrall of the Past," but what is relevant here is the doctor's claim to science. He is always identified as Dr. Wycherley, and there is occasional reference to him as "the foremost mental healer in Europe" and the founder of the "Annalen der Psychologischen Forschungen." But he shows no other symptom of a methodological mentality, and his strange cases and his island retreat (on Isola Salvatore) mark him more as a magus than a scientist; his superfluous claim to the latter title illustrates the cachet that it could still bestow. It would be the Americans who would exploit the potential of the new scientific psychology, and they would emphasize its methodological legitimacy by drawing upon its most reductive and material techniques.

Science still had some credit in 1925 when John Rhode introduced Dr. Priestley, one of the most reliable of the Golden Age detectives. Rhode published 72 Dr. Priestley novels (and scores of other detective novels) in a career which ended with his death in 1964. Dr. Priestley evolved over his long career, but he was consistently a model of the Great Detective. He is an amateur; police officials bring him cases and he disposes presumably scientific advice which they apply to their investigations. (In the beginning he demonstrates a good deal of energy; latterly he is more content merely to advise from his armchair.) Like Poirot and Reggie Fortune, he is inclined to interrogate persons rather than things, and he relies more on extemporized tactics than upon scientific strategies, but he also draws upon his character as a scientist to color his inquiries. He is a sort of missing link.

Until a disagreement with university authorities led to his resignation, Dr. Priestley had held a chair of applied mathematics at an English university. Now he is an independent researcher, world-renowned for his contentious defiance of "The Orthodox Scientific School." By 1947, in *Death in Harley Street*, it was enough to identify Priestley as "an eminent if somewhat eccentric scientist," but in the early novels, Rhode devoted a page or two to establishing Dr. Priestley's scientific credentials. In *The Ellerby Case* (1927), the first pages announce the recent publication of Dr. Priestley's book, *Fact And Fallacy*, the first sentence of which reads: "It is my settled conviction, a conviction based upon incontrovertible mathematical reasoning, that the majority of theories underlying so-called scientific knowledge are the result of a willful distortion of observed facts, or, alternatively, of an inability to distinguish between fact and fallacy" (*Ellerby* 1). Rhode thus assigns Priestley to the familiar type of the contentious scholar. "His almost mischievous delight in stirring up scientific strife" certainly affiliates Dr. Priestley with Professor Challenger (and even to Professor Van Dusen). Scientific detail is never as central to the problems faced by Dr. Priestley as it was to Dr. Thorndyke, but it is never absent. Technological developments are often part of the context of the cases which are brought to his contention. In *The Ellerby Case*, for example, a minor point turns on the process of manufacturing and smuggling saccharine, and the Professor's expertise in chemistry becomes relevant. He is also competent to identify the poison into which the quills of a hedgehog have been dipped. Nonetheless, although Dr. Priestley's science is genuine, it is, compared to the solid oak of Dr. Thorndyke, only a functional veneer.

There may be some allusions in Dr. Priestley's background that suggest his continuity with his methodical predecessors. His career as a mathematician may refer to the mathematical logic expounded by Dupin; to the university career of the similarly irascible Professor Van Dusen; and, most likely, in an inverted way, to the suspended career of another professor of mathematics at an English university, Dr. Moriarty. His chemical researches recall those of Holmes, and his delight in scientific strife may be a deliberate recollection of Dr. Challenger. When the narrator observes of Dr. Priestley's inquiring mind that "the nature of the problem was immaterial to him; it was as welcome if it concerned the precession of the Equinox as it was if it contained mere human interest" (*Ellerby* 2), there may be an allusion to Holmes's facility in discoursing on "the obliquity of ecliptic." The parallels should not be pressed too far. But clearly Rhode sought to position Dr. Priestley as the most direct Golden Age heir of the methodological Original Detectives.

Chapter 8

Arthur B. Reeve

At least two American detectives advertised themselves as "The American Sherlock Holmes" in the early twentieth century. Where Holmes's English heirs tended to subtract energy from the Holmes formula and to multiply his eccentric genius (the American Professor Van Dusen also took this route), both of these self-proclaimed American Holmes's multiplied the energy and subtracted the eccentricity: they were both active and abstemious examples of ideal young American manhood. But they took opposite positions on the ingredient of method. The first of the two, Nick Carter, was actually Sherlock Holmes's senior by a little over a year, his first adventure having appeared on 18 September 1886. A number of authors contributed episodes to his long career. Energy plus disguise (and, of course, pluck and clean living) seem to have been Nick's original virtues, though when necessary he could call upon intelligence and knowledge. In fact, he seems much more the offspring of Pinkerton than Holmes. In his long (and as yet unended) career, Nick has undergone a variety of transformations, but despite his persistence and his chameleon reflections of his times, he has never received much respect and has had little influence upon the history of the genre.

The second American claimant occupies a slightly more respectable position; the paternity of Craig Kennedy is at least certain: Arthur B. Reeve was his only begetter.[1] And Kennedy did, for a decade, actually epitomize the ideal of American detective. His success was far greater than that of Nick Carter or of Professor Van Dusen, and was enjoyed in several media. All the stories were first marketed to magazines in America and England, then collected in book form, eventually filling 25 volumes. By 1931, the Kennedy books boasted sales of two million in America and a further million in England. In addition, Kennedy was featured as the hero in one of the most successful and popular of the silent film serials, the Elaine movies of 1914-15, and he reappeared intermittently in film thereafter. He was in his time the ubiquitous model of the American detective. When Tom Finch, the untutored Hoosier narrator of Ring Lardner's *The Big Town* (1920), saw an inebriated jockey sitting with a highball and remarked that "It didn't take no Craig Kennedy to figure out that it wasn't his first one" (277), Lardner could be confident that the allusion would a natural one for an everyman like Tom, and that it would be readily grasped by every reader.

The degree of Craig Kennedy's fame is now hard to imagine, and the reasons for it even harder to understand. It is difficult to be fair to Arthur B. Reeve in this respect. His style was, at best, undistinguished; at times it was dreadful. His narratives were weak in all of the basic elements—plot, setting, characterization. One need not subscribe to a high-minded, Jamesian standard in the art of fiction to fault Reeve. The virtues of Erle Stanley Gardner's flat, efficient prose are cast into high relief by Reeve's inadequacies.[2] Reeve cannot even claim originality in the conception of his new type of scientific detective. What he can claim is the insight that this new type of detective could be developed into a hero whose technique of knowing spoke most forcefully to the popular audience in the decade 1910-20. And whatever his defects, Reeve had the literary talent sufficient to exploit this insight repeatedly to the satisfaction of that audience.

By the mid-1920s, Craig Kennedy degenerated into a parody of himself, but he had contributed a new dimension of the methodological detective to literature. His technique differed fundamentally from that adopted by Dupin, Holmes, or Thorndyke (or Lecoq, Pinkerton, Gryce, Hewitt, Van Dusen, etc.). Craig Kennedy's was not a method of thinking which might be enjoined upon, or at least demonstrated to admirers, but rather a method of using thought. Kennedy's thinking is rarely displayed; he does not imagine or hypothesize or test. Instead, he rushes to apply the physical products of other scientific thinkers' thoughts—the latest inventions—to the problem at hand. Kennedy's methods are always pre-invented; on the rare occasions when his technology is intellectual rather than physical—such as his precocious application of Freudian dream interpretation in "The Dream Doctor" (August 1913)—he emphasizes the preconceived, systematic quality of the ideas he adopts. Kennedy embodies the ideal of a culture that assumes that the securest knowledge is machine-generated knowledge; in this respect, he is the antithesis of Dr. Thorndyke, who certainly also uses tools and technologies, but who prefers to emphasize the opposite aspect by having his tools individually manufactured to his specifications by the craftsman, Polton.

Kennedy's addiction to prefabricated methods necessarily undermines any impression of his individuality as a hero. If method is the soul and essence of the detective, Craig Kennedy sold his soul to the machines that really constitute method in his stories. And he paid a further penalty. Character survives nicely in literature; Holmes's Victorian habits do not diminish him; on the contrary, they have lasted as a source of his appeal. Machines are less durable goods in the literary market. By investing his essential method in a variety of wonderful new machines that, 50 years later would seem quaint gadgets, Craig Kennedy helped to consign himself to the dustbin of detective fiction. Reeve's prose offered nothing that would make him immortal, and Kennedy's essence lay in technologies that were inevitably superseded.

Nonetheless, Arthur B. Reeve achieved something significant. His stories certainly speak to the American vision of science and technology at the beginning of the twentieth century, and this historical importance is worthy in itself. The Craig Kennedy stories are, in one respect, the most overtly didactic of all detective stories. Just as readers of James Michener derive palatable history lessons from his novels, readers of the Kennedy series had the sense of painlessly acquiring current information about developments in science and technology. Reeve was careful in his research; Kennedy's machines (physical and intellectual) were often of quite recent design, and Kennedy's exposition of their mechanisms and their powers was accurate.

And further, Reeve was an important figure in opening an important new arena for literature to depict the encounter between science and morality. It would, perhaps, be facile to see Kennedy's little black boxes as precursors for such later and much more problematic technological devices as the atomic bomb, but such leaps are not necessary. Two of Kennedy's most frequently conscripted machines are his variety of lie detectors and his variety of eavesdropping devices. And while the century has seen enormous advances in the efficacy of such devices, Kennedy was raising questions about the morality of their use during their infancy. His answer, to be sure, is a naive certainty that they serve justice and the commonweal; Craig Kennedy uses his devices with a blithe confidence in their innocence as well as in their accuracy. This confidence (or the desire for this confidence) was evidently shared by millions of readers; Kennedy's exploits reassured them that technology's swords were all single-edged. But Reeve did take the problem seriously, and more than a few readers must have conceived doubts as they followed his narratives. In fact, in his essays on his fiction, Reeve felt compelled to respond to such doubts, arguing that his popularization of scientific techniques, like the techniques themselves, did not assist criminals.[3] Neither Reeve nor his readers seem to have guessed the dimensions that the problem would acquire in the late twentieth century; but surely the technology of monitoring the private lives of individuals has become a major moral issue, and Reeve's simplistic fables of that technology's earliest victories are an untapped source in the history of that issue.

ii

Science at the beginning of the twentieth century occupied an ambivalent position in the popular imagination. It was no longer either wonderful or demonic; the great pulse of the nineteenth century—an outward, inclusive, reassuring movement followed by an inward, professionalizing movement—was virtually complete. Science was once again something of a mystery, but a mystery which might as readily generate a benefit as a monster. Craig Kennedy is the purest type of the new, professionalized scientist. He is unadulterated by any non-scientific culture; Kennedy cannot, as Holmes easily could, allude casually to Goethe or Carlyle, or, as Thorndyke could, to Agamemnon, Bacon and Dickens. The morality of Kennedy's science must, then, be the inherent morality of science rather than the accidental possession of the scientist, as it may have seemed to be in cases of Holmes and Thorndyke.

By 1910, when Craig Kennedy first appeared, "The great age of popular science generated by the controversy over evolutionary theory had passed.... The eruption of public anxiety over physical science in the 1920s was still to come" (Tobey 3). Science's success in securing support from universities and foundations (the Rockefeller and Carnegie Institutes were founded in 1901), industry and government had made appeals for popular understanding and popular support less necessary. The professionalization of science had actually rendered such appeals suspect within the world of science itself. *Real* scientists wrote for other scientists, not for laymen. "Even the name *popular science* was in disrepute" (Tobey 12). As a result, "By 1915, the nineteenth-century tradition of popular science had ended. Scientists were vaguely esteemed, though they complained of being misunderstood and not appreciated" (Tobey 11). The first American winner of a Nobel Prize in science illustrates the problem. There was great national pride in the award to Albert Michelson in 1907, but few Americans could claim to have followed closely his long career devoted to measuring the speed of light or to have comprehended the experiments through which Michelson and Edward Williams Morley disproved the existence of ether. Science was widely (and, increasingly, correctly) credited with the technological innovations that were clearly affecting and largely improving the daily lives of individuals, and the Progressive movement in American politics advocated the rationalized methods of scientific thought as central to its plan for the nation.[4] Reeve's intention was to give this vague esteem a local habitation and some very specific names (sphygmograph, dynameter, plethysmograph).

Reeve was not, however, as original in his conception of "the first purely scientific detective story" as he sometimes pretended to be. In his 1913 essay, "In Defense of the Detective Story," he devotes a paragraph to a survey of "the scientific detective story which just now seems to be popular." The subgenre began, he reports, when "several writers tried to apply psychology, as developed by Prof. Hugo Muensterberg of Harvard and Prof. Walter Dill Scott of Northwestern University, to either actual or hypothetical cases of crime." He credits Cleveland Moffet with a story along these lines, and then makes a peculiar acknowledgment: "and some years ago two writers collaborated in the creation of a psychological detective for a popular magazine" (92-93). The names of the "two writers," names which apparently slipped Reeve's mind, were Edwin Balmer (1883-1959) and William B. MacHarg (1872-1951); their psychological detective was Luther Trant; and the magazine was *Hampton's*.

Luther Trant is, undoubtedly, the prototype of Craig Kennedy. Reeve's debt is as unmistakable as it was unacknowledged. As Sam Moskowitz has observed, Reeve lifted a plot element and a mechanical device (a machine for registering reaction time in a word-association test) for the first Craig Kennedy story, "The Case of Helen Bond" (December 1910) directly from the first Luther Trant story, "The Man in the Room" (May 1909) (126). (Moskowitz also notes that Reeve had published an article in *Hampton's* in January 1909.) Kennedy's claim to importance cannot, therefore, be made on the basis of his originality; it must be made rather on the basis of his success and perseverance. Luther Trant appeared in only 12 short stories, appearing monthly from May 1909 to October 1910; the first nine were collected in *The Achievements of Luther Trant* (1910); and that marked the end of Mr. Trant. Balmer and MacHarg continued to write other collaborative works (*Surakarta*, 1913; *Blind Man's Eyes*, 1916; *Indian Drum*, 1917), so it was not the collapse of the partnership that terminated Trant. Whatever the reason, Trant's valediction in October 1910 provided the opportunity for Reeve to push Craig Kennedy forward as the model of the scientific detective.

The inventors of "Luther Trant, Psychological Detective" were a pair of Chicago journalists. If they followed the practice in Balmer's later collaborations with Philip Wylie, Balmer was chiefly responsible for the story lines and MacHarg for the writing. The editor of *Hampton's* proclaimed the thesis of the series in a headnote to the first story. Luther Trant, he declared, "is "a new sort of a detective—the psychological detective. To make a bold statement, this new detective theory is as important as Poe's deductive theory of 'ratiocination' and may be pursued even further than that brilliant method in the actual business of thief-catching" (qtd. in Moskowitz 124). Luther Trant's devices are, he asserted, not "mere dreams of the imagination"; they "are in use everyday in the psychology laboratories of our universities." The reference to Poe's ratiocination sets the new empirical method of the technologist directly against that of the armchair speculator. The assurance that the machines are genuine reinforces the contrast between the pseudo-Parisian pseudo-aristocrat Auguste Dupin and the straightforward Chicagoan Luther Trant. Finally, that the machines are used in universities makes the admission that scientific and technological advances had become largely the province of large dedicated institutions. Holmes and Thorndyke might pursue their individual researches; but real science in the twentieth century belongs to universities and corporations.

Luther Trant's place in this institutionalized scientific world is clearly described in the opening of "The Eleventh Hour" (February 1910). He establishes his credentials as a member of an established profession: he began his work in a university, as "a callow assistant in a psychological laboratory." But, like all American detective heroes, Trant must assert his individualism: he must defy the corporate orthodoxy in pressing his new, moral applications of the "new psychology." His professor laughed when he proposed to apply its techniques to crime detection, "But the delicate instruments of the laboratory—the chronoscopes, kynographs, plethysmographs, which made visible and recorded unerringly, unfalteringly, the most secret emotions of the heart and the hidden workings of the brain; the experimental investigations of Freund [sic] and Jung, of the German and French scientists, of Münsterberg and others in America—had fired him with a belief in them and in himself" (244).[5] As in Arthur B. Reeve's Craig Kennedy stories that would exploit the Trant model, the machines come first; in fact, the systematic theories of Freud, Jung and Münsterberg, though occasionally cited, are of considerably less practical significance than the machines. The delicate instruments which objectify the inner life are the primary means of detection. Luther Trant has an unlimited (and, in the event, a justified) confidence in the infallible operation of these devices, and their power to "make visible" the most secret emotions and thoughts is taken to be an unqualified good.

In his pursuit of this mechanical objectification of the subjective, Luther Trant unconsciously juxtaposes his practice in a revealing way to that of Dr. Thorndyke. Trant has dedicated himself tracing "the criminal not by the world-old method of the marks the evil-doer had left on *things*, but by the evidences which the crime had left of the mind of the criminal himself." Dr. Thorndyke used science to interrogate things, hence his insistence upon attention to the physical details of the circumstantial evidence. Luther Trant uses science to interrogate people, but in a peculiar way: he interrogates persons *through* things. Trant's science creates things (the unerring, unfaltering recordings from his machines) which expose persons. But in both forms of interrogation, things must be interrogated: the right questions must be posed, and the answers must be correctly interpreted. This stage of interrogation is more or less finessed in the Trant stories. Where Thorndyke painstakingly expounds each line of investigation, often supplementing what seems to be a sufficient indication of guilt with another and yet another corroborating line of evidence, Trant (and Craig Kennedy after him) takes pains to expound the operation of his machine, but seems content to take its visible recordings as virtually self-evident.

Trant himself is a featureless figure; he has no substantial life other than as the operator of his machines. Occasionally he is described—"a red-haired, blue-eyed young man of medium height" ("Man Higher Up" 471), but usually he is simply "the young psychologist," sufficiently identified by his age (implying vigor and novelty) and his profession (implying scientific discipline). He possesses energy and courage and knowledge; he never submits to disguise; and he always has a device for the occasion: an "electric psychometer—or 'the soul machine'," ("probably the most delicate and efficient instrument contrived for detecting and registering human emotion," "The Eleventh

Hour"), the sphygmograph ("Every thought you have, every feeling, every sensation—taste touch, smell—changes the beating of your heart and shows upon this little record," "The Hammering Man"), the plethysmograph and the pneumograph ("The Man Higher Up"). Trant explains how each of his machines works, and in each case, its work does result in the revelation of the criminal.

The problems Trant faces are interesting—a mother suffers from "hyperæsthesia" and becomes extremely suggestible ("The Red Dress"); a woman with an "anæsthetic spot" falls into a divided consciousness, half of which can only be recovered through hypnosis (the researches of Charcot are cited in corroboration). Though they suppress the personality of their detective in order to enhance the focus upon his method, Balmer and MacHarg do take the time to give some flesh to their other puppets and to their scenes. In some cases, social issues are raised. In "The Man Higher Up," for instance, a murder is the by-product of a smuggling operation; Trant is not satisfied to capture the actual murderer; as the title suggests, he wants, this time, to also make a case against the usually insulated capitalist, the president of the American Commodities Company who has been behind the operation. "It's some advance, isn't it," Trant asks an ally at the end, "not to have to try such poor devils alone; but at last, with the man who makes the millions and pays them the pennies—the man higher up?" (483). And the writing in the Trant stories is always competent. The favorable reception which critics gave to the 1910 collection seems justified.[6] But for whatever reason, Balmer and MacHarg abandoned their "new sort of detective" following the publication of his twelfth adventure in October 1910. Two months later, Arthur B. Reeve introduced Craig Kennedy, and by July 1913 Balmer and MacHarg had become what Reeve could only recall as "two writers collaborated in the creation of a psychological detective for a popular magazine."

iii

Although Craig Kennedy is unquestionably derived from Luther Trant, Reeve did make changes which may help to explain why his facsimile enjoyed such phenomenal success. The crude simplicity of his style had at least this virtue: it gave the reader his action and his machinery straight. There was no veneer: no distracting atmospherics, no incidental insights or extraneous details. Reeve was not a Dashiell Hammett or even a Carroll John Daly; but his original readers must have found some energy in his bare prose. Looking backward in the detective story tradition, Reeve restored the convention of narrating the story through an associate of the detective, aligning Kennedy with his great predecessors—Dupin, Holmes, Hewitt, Van Dusen and Thorndyke. Craig Kennedy, Professor of Chemistry, has his Walter Jameson, newspaperman. Kennedy's discipline—chemistry—also signals a shift. Again, he is returning to the detective's roots, claiming the authority of a hard science (with Holmes, Van Dusen and Thorndyke, and as opposed to Trant's semi-soft psychology). In fact, Kennedy is an omni-disciplinary scientist, competent in chemistry, psychology, physics, medicine, electricity—whatever the occasion calls for. His versatility may have made him a more interesting figure to a non-specialist audience eager for the latest developments in any science, and it certainly gave his author the broadest field of innovation to select his machinery from.

Perhaps his biggest advantage lay in the vehicle of his introduction, *Cosmopolitan* magazine. *Cosmopolitan* had been a prosperous monthly when William Randolph Hearst purchased it as his first important experiment in magazines. By 1914 he had more than doubled its circulation, to something over one million, with most of the increase coming in the period 1910-14 when Craig Kennedy was a featured performer in its pages. (Fifty Kennedy stories or episodes appeared in *Cosmopolitan* between December 1910 and June 1915.) *Cosmopolitan* dominated the important category of serious, general interest periodicals between 1891 and 1918: "It was the most complex and the most interesting, borrowing features from its rivals but going beyond them in exploiting ideas" (Tebbel and Zuckerman 77).[7] The historians who make this judgment illustrate it with *Cosmopolitan's* more picturesque travel articles and more complete "reports of scientific and technological advances," but it applies precisely to the genesis of Craig Kennedy. *Hampton's* was, in 1910, making a challenge to *Cosmopolitan*, rising from a circulation of 13,000 in 1907 to over 400,000 in 1911. In 1910, as Luther Trant was completing his run in *Hampton's*, *Cosmopolitan* was shifting its emphasis from muckraking articles to fiction, and Reeve's submission of a fictional scientific detective who "went beyond" the *Hampton's* hero came at an opportune moment.

The imprimatur of *Cosmopolitan*, and its massive circulation, certainly assisted the fame of Craig Kennedy. Coincidentally, William Randolph Hearst was making tentative steps into the new medium of film, and Reeve benefitted when, in 1914, Hearst joined with Pathé to produce a 14-episode Pearl White serial, *The Exploits of Elaine*. Pearl White reprised her *Perils of Pauline* plucky-girl-in-danger; Arnold Daly played Craig Kennedy, Scientific Rescuer. Two sequels followed, and Reeve novelized the scripts into two (or, in Britain, three) Craig Kennedy books. Hearst mobilized his publicity machine on behalf of the film, insuring that Craig Kennedy became a household name.

When he made his fortunate break into *Cosmopolitan* in December 1910, Arthur B. Reeve had been working as a journeyman journalist for several years, publishing articles in serious journals such as *The World's Work*, *Everybody's Magazine* or *The American Review of Reviews*. His articles are generally competent descriptions, nicely illustrated, of a particular industry or technology—or sport ("Our Industrial Juggernaut," "The Potash Industry and the American Farmer," "New York's Water System," "What America Spends on Sport") or they are plausibly argued calls for humanitarian changes in social policy ("Capital and Labor Agree on Workmen's Compensation," "Why Not a 'Red Cross' for the Army of Industry?"). The two elements reflected here—an interest in how things work in the new industrial America and an inclination to moralize about the effects of industrialization upon common citizens—served Reeve in developing his detective.

Reeve maintained that he had the inspiration to write "the first purely scientific detective story" in 1909. His desire to usurp Balmer and MacHarg's claim to originality may render the year suspect, but his admission that the first Craig Kennedy story, "The Silent Bullet"—his first effort in fiction since his college days—was turned down by every editor may be credited. "That story was a commuter. It had the highest mileage of any story ever written."[8] When it finally reached its home in *Cosmopolitan*, it found itself in the company of stories by Jack London, George Ade and Booth Tarkington. Craig Kennedy's monthly appearances made him a regular feature; his nearest rival was George Randolph Chester's very popular and also now-forgotten hero, "Get-Rich-Quick Wallingford." *Cosmopolitan* promoted Kennedy and Reeve in the headnotes to the series, drawing comparisons to Conan Doyle ("Arthur Reeve begins where Conan Doyle leaves off," February 1911: 434), Poe (June 1911: 117), Thomas Alva Edison and Nicola Tesla ("Craig Kennedy, scientific detective, is Edison and Tesla rolled into one," August 1911: 376), Thomas DeQuincey (October 1911: 665), and even, on the occasion of his twelfth appearance, to Get-Rich-Quick Wallingford (Kennedy "is running Wallingford a close second as a Cosmopolitan favorite," November 1911: 737). *Cosmopolitan* reported Edison's endorsement of the tales as "great" (May 1912: 835) and anointed Craig Kennedy, Scientific Detective, as "The American Sherlock Holmes."

And the American accent which distinguished the transatlantic claimant was most apparent when he spoke the language of technology. The crucial importance of scientific machinery in the Craig Kennedy series can be demonstrated negatively through the paucity of other attractions. Even such scientific methodologists as Dupin, Holmes and Thorndyke inhabited fully realized places. Dupin's unusual mansion at au troisième, No. 33 Rue Dunôt Faubourg St. Germain is part of his character; Holmes's lodgings at 221B Baker Street are, for many, more real than many real London sites; and one of the first critical treatments of Dr. Thorndyke was P.M. Stone's essay on "5A King's Bench Walk." There is, by contrast, a vacant quality about the "neat bachelor apartment" which Craig Kennedy shares with Walter Jameson somewhere in New York City: it has no character—no precise address, no definite furniture, no patriotic TRs shot into the walls. And the scenes of the crimes are equally insubstantial. They may be unusual—an airfield, a slum district, a nightclub, a munitions factory, a hunting lodge—but Reeve spends little space on non-functional details. The places are not imagined; they are bare stages with a minimum of shopworn props to facilitate the action. Craig Kennedy does not search for identifiable cigarette ashes in rooms with twisted carpets, half empty wine glasses, torn bell pulls and French doors slightly ajar.

Kennedy and Jameson have their professions—Kennedy as a professor at, apparently, Columbia University, and Jameson as a reporter for the New York *Star*. But neither, even after dozens of appearances, acquires a personality. Kennedy's romance with Elaine, developed over two book-length collections of episodes, has no consequence; she simply vanishes without explanation. Though they share dozens of adventures, Kennedy and Jameson do not accumulate biographies. They do not even have distinguishing physical features. As portrayed in Will Foster's illustrations in *Cosmopolitan*, Kennedy appears as a generic magazine hero.[9] His clean cut features are indistinguishable from those of the manly men drawn for other stories. Kennedy is a vector of action rather than a character.[10]

Though most of the stories are painfully bereft of human interest, there are occasional incidental pleasures. *The Film Mystery* (1921), for example, provides an insider's view of the early New York motion picture industry; 13 of the 14 stories in *The Fourteen Points* (1925) are painfully bad, but "The Sixth Sense" offers the gratuitous and interesting spectacle of Kennedy and Jameson returning to their (and Reeve's) alma mater, Princeton. *Pandora* (1926)—with its extended accounts of an international conspiracy of industrialists who are subverting America with Jazz, pacifism and birth control—casts a fascinating sidelight on American popular opinion in the 1920s. But these pleasures are exceptional. When a tale like "The Artificial Paradise" features exiled South American revolutionaries who spend their evenings consuming hallucinogenic mescal buttons, Reeve's interest lies neither in the political nor the exotic dimensions of the situation. The revolution provides a motivation for a murder, and the mescal provides the opportunity for Kennedy to lecture on current research into alkaloid hallucinogens (by "Dr. Weir Mitchell and Dr. Harvey Wiley and several German scientists...") and then to employ a "special induction-coil" (developed by "professor Leduc of the Nantes Ecole de Medicin") to revive a man who had apparently died of a drug overdose. The Kennedy stories focus on technique, on how a crime is committed or a criminal is discovered. Moral questions—why a crime was committed or how it ought to be judged—are evaded with undeveloped, thoroughly conventional formulas.

The crudity of Reeve's moral sense is illustrated in the initial Kennedy story, "The Scientific Cracksman" (reprinted as the second story in *The Silent Bullet*). The villain here is a young heiress who, rather than see the bulk of her inheritance pass to "a great school of preventative medicine" which would sponsor the research of her lover, breaks into her uncle's safe and steals his will. Surprising her in the act, the uncle dies of a heart attack. She explains to Kennedy and Jameson: "I need a fortune, for then I could have the town house, the country house, the yacht, the motors, the clothes, the servants that I need—they are as much a part of my life as your profession is of yours" (61-62). Later, she adds, "What difference, I said, did thirty millions or fifty millions make to an impersonal school, a school not yet in existence?" (63). Kennedy and Jameson are, appallingly, moved by this appeal, and though they insist on recovering the original will, they agree to conceal her entire involvement in the matter. In the other stories, Kennedy plays a fairly even hand; though he frequently acts on behalf of the wealthy elite, he never becomes an uncritical tool of the establishment. He is, of course, a gentleman in his dealings with women and a patriot in his dealings with espionage. But Reeve was more interested in arranging the occasion for an exercise in practical technology than in moral or ideological analysis.

The plotting of the stories can be complex; Reeve was required to develop situations in which a new device could be employed either to commit a crime or, preferably, to detect one, and this requirement often led to conveniently revealing but highly improbable conversations in conveniently accessible but highly improbable locations. Functional aspects of character— those which caused or facilitated the crime, such as motives, habits, and susceptibilities—were distributed arbitrarily according to the exigencies of the plot; non-functional idiosyncrasies were almost completely absent. The contrast to Freeman's sometimes Dickensian portraits or to the effective sketches of Conan Doyle works dramatically to Reeve's disadvantage. The chief virtue of Reeve's prose was its efficiency; it rushed straightforwardly to the intersection of action and technology, undistracted by the peripheral texture of experience.

And the intersection of action and technology was, of course, the place Reeve's readers wanted to reach. The literary pleasures of fiction were secondary. Craig Kennedy's appeal lay in the argument that the impersonal, *non*-fictional advances in science and technology in the twentieth century were inexorably rendering successful crime obsolete.[11] The individual qualities of the crime or of the criminal or of the detective are precisely what Reeve's formula abhors. It is not Craig Kennedy's peculiar bohemian genius which solves the moral dilemmas caused by crime in modern American society, or even his peculiar scientific genius; it is the objectified, mechanical result of scientific thinking that will retire the criminal. The thrust of the stories is exactly that the human idiosyncrasies of the situation—those of the detective, the criminal, and the environment—are irrelevant; what matters is the inhuman accuracy of the applied science.

Craig Kennedy proclaims his new approach in the first paragraphs of the first published story, "The Case of Helen Bond" (subtitled, "The first of a series of unusual detective stories in which the professor of criminal science adopts the new method of making the criminal discover himself," *Cosmopolitan* December 1911). The paragraphs were extracted and printed as a three-page preface, "Craig Kennedy's Theories," to the first volume of collected stories, *The Silent Bullet*. Once again, the methodological detective proclaims his method first and then appends a detective narrative. "I am," Kennedy declares, "going to apply science to the detection of crime, the same sort of methods by which you trace out the presence of a chemical or run an unknown germ to earth" (3).[12] And significantly, he claims an institutional authority for his application: he proposes to become the first "professor of criminal science."

This proposal is, explicitly, a claim that the proven research techniques of the scientist—the professional scientist—hitherto practiced in pursuit of abstract laws governing natural phenomena can now be applied to the particular, pragmatic problems that offend the established social and moral order. Kennedy informs Jameson: "It's only within the past ten years or so that we have had the really practical college professor who could do it. The silk-stockinged variety is out of date. Today it is the college professor who is the third arbitrator in labor disputes, who reforms the currency in the Far East, who heads our tariff commissions and conserves our farms" (2). He continues: "Colleges have gone a long way from the old ideal of pure culture, and they have got down to solving the hard facts of life—all except one. They still treat crime the old way, study its statistics, and pore over its causes and the theories by which it can be prevented. But as for running the criminal down scientifically, relentlessly—bah!" (2). The old humbug of "pure culture" must yield to the demonstrably greater effectiveness of the hard-nosed practice of the new scientific movement.

And it is thematically important that Kennedy advocates "an endowed professorship in criminal science," that he presents himself as a "professor of crime," and not as a detective. Holmes invented himself as a consulting detective; Dr. Thorndyke justified his method by identifying his profession as a very rare but not entirely unprecedented synthesis of two familiar professions, medicine and law. Kennedy moves further toward the commonplace. His occupation is still exceptional, but the university professor, especially in America, is not an exotic or even a very prestigious creature (though perhaps more so in 1910 than today). Though fully possessed of the chivalrous instincts which American readers preferred in their young male heroes at the turn of the century, Kennedy is a representative American man, not a gentleman in the English—Thorndykian—sense. He is an everyman who studied hard at night and now commands the accumulated power of the knowledge produced by thousands of other hard-studying everymen. There is nothing of the genius in Craig Kennedy. He is the embodiment—a rather disembodied embodiment, to be sure—of a scientific, systematic analysis.

The complex problems and methodologies of twentieth-century science preclude the isolated, idiosyncratic investigator. Kennedy belongs to a research organization—the university (and, as the stories emphasize, to the larger international organization of scientific knowledge).[13] Kennedy's professorship is largely nominal; his academic duties almost never intrude in a story and even his discipline seems ambiguous: he is a professor of chemistry, but he aspires to be a professor of criminal science, and Edwin Markham, in an editorial note ("Shop-Talk") in *Cosmopolitan,* actually calls him "a professor of experimental psychology" (February 1911: 434). (Markham presumably confused Kennedy with Luther Trant.)

Further, Kennedy readily accepts the authority of the organized guardians of public safety, the police. He makes a point in the first stories of distinguishing himself from his idiosyncratic predecessors by repeatedly emphasizing his high estimation of the police insofar as they represent an established, systematic approach to crime detection, though he does deplore their ignorance of technological advances. He opens "The Silent Bullet" by criticizing the "detectives in fiction" who "nearly always make a great mistake": "They almost invariably antagonize the regular detective force." Kennedy has no temptation to usurp the role of the police (or of the judge and jury, as both Dupin, Holmes, Thorndyke sometimes do). His own power derives from his application of other men's innovations; he is content to allow the police credit for exercising their corporate power. "My idea of the thing...is that the professor of criminal science ought to work with, not against the regular detectives....Half the secret of success nowadays is organisation" (5). Half is science, half is organization, nowadays at least. None is genius, or moral insight or hard-boiled persistence. Again, in "The Seismograph Adventure," the fifth story of the first collection, Kennedy observes, "Science is all right, but organisation enables science to work quickly" (137-38).[14] Craig Kennedy presents himself as an inherently establishment detective.

In practice, Kennedy's devotion to organization is little more than rhetoric, and as Reeve retreated toward what he acknowledged to be his roots in the dime novel,[15] even the rhetoric vanishes. The organized police force functions in the Kennedy stories exactly as it does in the Dupin or Holmes stories: it follows the detective's leads and, in the end, it makes the arrest. Nonetheless, Reeve does, in a way, continue to honor organization. Inspector G—— or a Lestrade or Gregson may have more substance than Reeve's colorless functionaries, Inspector Barney O'Connor (later promoted to First Deputy) and "our friend Burke, of the Secret Service," but the individualizing substance of the Parisian or London police emphasizes their limitations. Poe and Conan Doyle sought exactly this effect; Reeve repudiates it. His faceless officials are simply a necessary part of the impersonal system of the modern crime detection team: Science & Organization.

Science & Organization, not Scientist and Organization Man: and just as O'Connor and Burke are merely personifications of Organization, so Kennedy is merely the personification of Science. But whereas Organization can remain an airy nothing, Science, as the primary force in the investigation of crime, must be a real presence in the stories. And if the insubstantial person and office of Craig Kennedy offer little in the way of a local habitation, then it must be found in the much more tangible machinery of twentieth-century science: in the glass and wire and black boxes of the electrical and pneumatic technology that represent the real body of the detective in the Craig Kennedy stories. Hence the plenitude of devices in the stories. In the first volume (*The Silent Bullet*) alone, these include: the standard microscope, slides, bunsen-burners and test-tubes; pressure-sensitive chair arms (a sort of lie detector); a dynameter (44); a "plethysmograph" (used by "experimental psychologists" to measure blood pressure, 53); a "stereopticon" (to view fingerprints and handwriting, 84); "a little instrument called a microphone" (120); a seismograph; a selenium light-sensitive switch (187); an ondometer ("a little instrument" which detects energy radiated from a Tesla coil, 281); a dictograph with which he can eavesdrop on a gang of kidnappers (314); a "special induction-coil" with which he re-animates a man who has apparently died from an overdose of mescal buttons (351); and an acetylene torch (383).

Science and technology have progressed considerably since 1910. Some of Craig Kennedy's expectations have proven justified, such as his study of ballistics; others have proven unwarranted—his variety of infallible lie detectors, for instance; and there is certainly something quaint about Kennedy astonishing Jameson in *The Dream Doctor* (1913) with a new device—"my scientific sledgehammer"—that can pry open steel doors. The device, a hydraulic jack, astonishes no more, yet Reeve is so impressed with it that he repeats its use in a non-Kennedy novel *Guy Garrick* (1914) (*Dream Doctor* 276-77; *Guy Garrick* 108). But this wonder at the new technologies should only add to the appeal of the stories. The modern reader can recover a bit of the surprise which accompanied the introduction of ideas and devices which everyone now takes for granted. Some of Sigmund Freud's earliest appearances in American popular literature occur in the Kennedy stories. In "The Dream Doctor" (*Cosmopolitan*, August 1913, reprinted in the first two chapters of *The Dream Doctor*) Kennedy expounds "the new and remarkable theories of Dr. Sigmund Freud, of Vienna" concerning the interpretation of dreams, and then applies the theories to the troubled dreams of Mrs. Maitland (*Dream Doctor* 33-36). Four years later, in "The Soul-Analysis," Kennedy draws upon the psychoanalytic view of hysteria ("perhaps you are not aware of the fact that Freud's contribution to the study of insanity is of even greater scientific value than his dream theories taken by themselves") (*Treasure Train* 65-66). In both instances, the application is perfunctory, but the exposition is serious and unsensational.

Kennedy's optimism regarding the validity of his lie detectors and his other systematic devices and methods is always justified in the economical world of Reeve's fiction. As Kennedy draws upon an apparently endless sequence of technological innovations, the reader obtains the impression that *all* technological innovations *always* work. There are no mechanical failures in the Kennedy stories, and no unintended side effects. This unqualified affirmation of technological infallibility complements the moral uses to which Kennedy puts his machines. Reeve finesses the problem of the operator's interpretation of his machine's output. The indications which Kennedy draws from his experiments seem to point transparently and incontrovertibly toward conclusions about innocence and guilt. The machine always works, and the machine (not the operator) seems to make the moral judgment.

Whether they now appear outdated or revolutionary or overly optimistic, the scientific and technological innovations compose the core around which each of the Kennedy stories is constructed and therefore they must have been the basis of his appeal. Certainly they comprise the one element to which Reeve does devote detailed attention. Here, at least, there is verisimilitude. Jameson's untutored description of each apparatus is amplified by Kennedy's account of its operation and of its origins, usually traced to some European source. Kennedy's citation of their originators emphasizes the universality of modern science: in the first volume alone, Kennedy calls upon the expertise of Frenchmen—Professor Leduc of the Nantes Ecole de Medicin, who developed a "process of electric resuscitation" (351) and the famous Alphonse Bertillon, who devised the dynameter Kennedy employs in "The Case of Helen Bond" (44); Englishmen—Dr. Lindsey Johnson, who demonstrated that handwriting may be as sensitive as a sphymograph in detecting irregularities in a human pulse (88) and the great Charles Darwin, who discussed the effects of curare (215); Germans—Dr. Uhlenhuth, who invented a test for blood (245), Professor Robert of Rostock, who isolated the poison ricin, and the chemist

Goldschmidt of Essen, who invented thermite (163-64); an Anglo-German—Sir Robert Schomburgk, who also wrote about curare; and a Russian—Prince Galitzin of St Petersburg, who designed a more sensitive seismograph.[16] This roster of actual European scientists verifies the authenticity of Kennedy's science—they are not alumni of imaginary universities like the Camford visited by Holmes or the Yarvard visited by Van Dusen. References to these actual, contemporary scientists implies the international validity of the modern scientific endeavor: Kennedy's methods are not eccentric or parochial.

The mission of the all-American, practical, un-silk-stockinged professor is to apply these discoveries and inventions to the detection of crime. A Prince Galitzin might develop a new, more sensitive seismograph, but it takes a Craig Kennedy to use the device to detect and identify the distinctive footsteps of a woman who sneaks up hallways to rap on a wall in a plot to deceive an aging spiritualist.[17] In later volumes, Kennedy also cites the work of American scientists, such as Dr Walter Cannon of Harvard (*The Social Gangster* 23), but the real American talent—Craig Kennedy's talent—is not for research, but for technology. It lies in realizing the applications of scientific discoveries, and especially the moral applications. The machine which measures earthquakes for a Russian Prince measures innocence and guilt for a "really practical"—really American—"college professor."

Reeve's citation of authorities may recall the strategy by which Conan Doyle validated Dr. Challenger's scientific credentials, but there is this significant difference between Craig Kennedy and Dr. Challenger: Kennedy does not expect Jameson (or the common reader) to be satisfied with the citation. It is important—it does provide a cheap access to the authority of science; but Kennedy, like Dupin and Holmes and Thorndyke, also expects Jameson to know his methods. Dr. Challenger (and Professor Van Dusen as well) embodied the arrogance as well as the power which science had acquired in the course of the nineteenth century. The detective's function is to demonstrate, one, that the power may be moral in its application, and two, that its nature may be understood by any Watson, Jervis or Jameson who attends to the thinker's expositions and aphorisms. The detective is an epistemological democrat.

Craig Kennedy is conscientious to a fault in accounting for his devices. He enthusiastically describes the powers and limitations of his devices, and in terms comprehensible to a layman. That he strives to communicate the operations of methodical machines rather than of methodical minds should not obscure his admirable diligence; his problem, however, is precisely that whereas "methodical" thinking is a peculiar mental distinction, it is the universal quality of machines. The excellence of methodical thinker is exceptional, and the average reader is disposed to admire it. Machines may be more or less efficient; but they are inherently methodical, and nothing but methodical. Imagination never enters into their operations; machines never hypothesize. The machine is, indeed, the aptest metaphor for a merely methodical process of acting or thinking.

A detective who acquires a method of thinking and applies it with genius to a particular problem always has an interesting story: how did these rules lead this mind to this result? Dupin, Holmes, and Thorndyke modelled methodo-logical ways of thinking, advocating them in aphorism and exposition, and applying them concretely to the irregular phenomena of human experience which constituted the given case. Craig Kennedy applied the method of his machines to similar phenomena, but too often it was apparent that to permit this application, Reeve had been compelled to schematize improbably mechanical moral problems. The reader might wonder at how the systematic method of Dupin solved a specific murder mystery or retrieved a specific compromising letter. In the Craig Kennedy stories, there is no wonderful discrepancy between the effective, universal method and the concrete phenomena of the case. Both are equally mechanical; Reeve's men and women are as mechanical as his machines.

The intrinsic flaw in Reeve's conception, however, lay not so much in his fleshless and contrived plots, but in the fact that expositions of chemical reactions and electrical transmissions lose their fascination sooner than expositions of methodical inference. The inferences of a Dupin, Holmes, or Thorndyke (or of any of the less overtly methodical Great Detectives of the Golden Age) are necessarily concrete and germane to the case at hand. That case, if successfully depicted, has been fleshed in human terms and has engaged the reader's sympathies; he wants to know what really happened, and the detective supplies the "what" as he supplies the "how." Chemical reactions and electrical transmissions are inanimate and universal; they operate identically in all places and all times; given the same input, the machine or the chemical will produce the same result. There is no character to their operation, only mechanism. And the detective who relies upon machines must present the "how" of his method—how the device works, how the chemical reacts— separately from presenting the "what" of crime. Kennedy either explains the technology, then uses it to single out the villain, or he uses a black box to single out the villain and then explains the technology involved. Even the strained strategy of gathering the suspects in his laboratory, connecting them to a device, and then working the device as he explicates its function does not repair the defect. The method and the result remain radically divorced from one another when the one is a mechanical operation and the other is a human situation.

Still, Arthur B. Reeve's brilliant stroke lay in recognizing that a tool might—even if only for a historical moment—function as a hero; or, more precisely, that a sequence of new tools—tools still invested with the aura of the new sciences of chemistry, electricity, psychology— manipulated by the colorless hand of the scientist, could be accepted as a popular hero in the early twentieth century. These technological tools offered appealing virtues to a generation which had on the one hand to assimilate the proven power of modern science and, on the other, to admit that crime and corruption remained endemic human problems. Technological tools seemed to function without prejudice; they were incorruptible; their power over the world—to penetrate secrets and to control events—was seemingly unlimited. The American Sherlock Holmes would not be an American individual; it would be American technology.

The transparency of Craig Kennedy's personality and the reductive schematizing of the action of his cases allow Reeve's narratives to feature the machines. The technician supplies the energy—he places them where they can work, and he plugs them in—but the machines produce the certain result. The power of scientific technique, as embodied in its electrical/chemical/etc. machinery, does not depend upon the character—the personality or the integrity—of the technician; it is, on the contrary, an autonomous mechanism that can indisputably expose the specific cause of a social disorder. It does, of course, depend upon the technician's intelligence, on his knowing his machine, but Reeve plays down this aspect. He does not assign Kennedy any peculiar mastery of any particular machine (and given the number and variety of Kennedy's machines, he could not). Kennedy's power lies simply in his knowing where to place the machine; reading its result is always presented as simple and straightforward: the machine answers the moral question with an entirely unambiguous sign of innocence or guilt. Reeve emphasizes Kennedy's knowledge of how his machines work and what their limits are. He might have emphasized the other forms of knowing, and had he done so, he might have created a character of more lasting interest. But his infatuation with machines made Kennedy instantly popular—and ultimately obsolete.

The high point of Craig Kennedy's career came in 1919, when Harper & Brothers published a 12-volume standard edition of "The Craig Kennedy Stories." *The New York Times Book Review* consistently rated Reeve's books "entertaining" until the 1920s, and was still praising him as late as *The Film Mystery* (1921) and *Atavar* (1924), but by the mid-twenties the Craig Kennedy adventures were being rated "manufactured" and "wildly impossible." Most of Reeve's books of the late 1920s and the 1930s went unreviewed, another measure of his decline.[18] Reeve's later books have their occasional incidental merits, but, having little else to offer his readers, Reeve declined largely into mechanically repeating his formula. His work ceased to find a place in *Cosmopolitan*, appearing instead in *Detective Story Magazine, Flynn's, Popular Detective*, and *Scientific Detective Monthly*. The last of these was a production of the famous editor of science fiction, Hugo Gernsback. Its first issue appeared in January 1930, and Reeve was advertised as its "editorial commissioner." Reeve had no responsibilities; his status evidently reflected Gernsback's confidence that it retained an appeal. It did not. Though it reprinted old Luther Trant and Dr. Thorndyke stories as well as old Craig Kennedy stories (and changed its name to *Amazing Detective Tales*), the magazine failed after ten issues. The scientific detective's moment had passed.

iv

Craig Kennedy virtually exhausted the possibilities of the technologically scientific detective. Kennedy-manqués were few and transient; several predeceased their original.[19] One whose magazine appearances were preserved in book form was Francis Lynde's Scientific Sprague (*Scientific Sprague* 1912). Lynde had already published fiction about western railroads, and while young Calvin Sprague is a scientist ("I'm down on the Department of Agriculture pay-rolls as a chemistry satrap" 9) and while he does investigate problems plaguing the Short-Line Railroad in Nevada, the interest of the stories lies in the railroad adventures, not in the science or in detection.

Stoddard Goodhue's adventures of Dr. Daniel Goodrich, published in *Everybody's Magazine* between December 1921 and June 1922, much more clearly imitate the Craig Kennedy model, but enjoyed correspondingly less success. *Everybody's* promoted him as the "Detective of the Future, Whose Startling Achievements Are Accomplished by Practical Application of Newly Discovered Methods in Science" (December 1921: 51). Dr. Goodrich is, like Craig Kennedy, a student of new technologies. The second story, "Test-tube Necromancy" (January 1922), opens with a question: "whether the microscope or the laboratory test-tube had proved in his experience, the more valuable implement in the performance of those feats of scientific sleuthing with which his name is associated" (145). The case at hand turns on the analysis of dried blood on a knife. Dr. Goodrich describes in copious detail the chemical tests which he applies to the blood, even explaining, in good Craig Kennedy style, that his last test "had not originated with him but had been developed by a distinguished American biologist, Dr. G.H.F. Nuttall, of Cambridge University, England" (151). The blood proves to be that of a kangaroo, and thus convicts the one suspect who happened to originate in Australia. In matters of setting and characterization, the Goodhue stories are considerably more generous than the Kennedy stories, but the detail slows the action without improving the texture or the insight of the story, and Dr. Goodhue's career was short. *Everybody's* terminated him after six adventures. (In its continuing quest for talent, the magazine actually turned to Craig Kennedy himself for a brief period in 1923.)

It may be useful finally to make a brief comparison between the very popular Scientific Detective and his very popular contemporary, the Boy Scientist. Arthur B. Reeve certainly designed Craig Kennedy for an adult audience. The crimes Kennedy confronted and especially the technological means with which he combatted were sophisticated; but Reeve's emphasis upon action at the expense of character and setting suggested a style well-suited for a more juvenile audience. As early as 1919 he was aware that he had "quite a large number of readers among boys," and as the general interest market for his stories disappeared in the early 1920s, Reeve was compelled to appeal to more specialized audiences. The detective magazines became his primary vehicle, but he also found it easy enough to sell Craig Kennedy stories to *Boy's Life*. These were collected to yield *The Boy Scouts' Craig Kennedy* (1925) and *The Radio Detective* (1926).

Tom Swift, whose preference for the technological side of science paralleled Kennedy's, was from the beginning a boy's scientist.[20] The Swift stories also first appeared in 1910, and in the five novels published that year, young Tom and his father Barton emerge as scientist-inventors whose innovations—motor cycle, motor boat, airship, submarine boat and electric runabout—are employed to rescue (or enrich) the good and defeat the bad. Though authorship was assigned to "Victor Appleton," the series concept belonged to Edward Stratemeyer and most of the novels were written by Howard Garis. The series extended to 40 volumes, but, as the final two were published under special circumstances in 1939 and 1940, the series run of 1910 to 1935 is almost exactly that of Craig Kennedy's 1910-36.

Though they are also simplistic in characterization and style, the Swift novels are in fact rather better written than the Kennedy books. In them, Tom Swift, boy inventor, is a genuine hero. The reader can identify with Tom and with his relationships to the various recurring characters, and is not required to marvel at the scientific details of his inventions, which in the first years are only improvements to existing technologies. The machinery is essential, but secondary; in the Craig Kennedy stories it is essential and primary. Tom and his father Barton are basement tinkerers, not university professors. They are ingenious individuals who expand man's control of his world in their workshop beside a lake in western New York state. Craig Kennedy is an active member of an international scientific community, and he is conscientiously dedicated to applying that community's discoveries to the solution of moral problems.

In the Tom Swift stories, science is not directly related to morality; a character's moral status is immediately identifiable through literary stereotyping: the decent lad, the bully, the eccentric old man, the good girl. A person's character determines how he or she uses the various devices and machines which shape the action of a given novel. In the Craig Kennedy stories, this formula is, in a sense, reversed: the various devices and machines are employed to determine the person's character. For Tom Swift, science is power because it enables him to go farther or faster or deeper; for Craig Kennedy, science is power because it enables him to know, to penetrate to the truth of virtue and vice. The Tom Swift series argues that new technologies are fun and adventurous and profitable and sometimes dangerous; the Craig Kennedy series argues that they are effective and good. As new technologies became old technologies, both arguments lost their force, and with it, much of their interest.

The Kennedy series lost the most. The premise that machines yield adventures could be revived: new machines permitted new adventures; Tom Swift, Jr. began a multi-volume career in 1954, employing Flying Labs and Atomic Earth Blasters and 3-D Telejectors. And an entire line of science fiction has pursued the same idea. But the premise that machines yield moral truth was always more dubious. It counted upon the reader's wonder at the power of the new machines to suppress his doubts about the improbable contrivances in plot and scene that enabled that power to work effectively. When readers stopped being amazed—stupified—by the things the machines could do, they began to realize that the mechanical things that the machines did were not, in fact, so simply and so happily applicable to the concrete complexities of moral affairs. They were actually rather blunt instruments, and, from the perspective of the late twentieth century, two-edged.

Nor could a Craig Kennedy, Jr. prosper by simply turning to the new generation of more sophisticated machines. It often took Kennedy too many paragraphs to explain his sphygmographs and dynameters; an exposition of DNA analysis would make much greater demands, and its results would still remain debatable. Even more problematic, the debate could be entered only by experts. The novelist may report such a debate, but he can no longer convincingly conclude it by having his detective dramatize its certain results. Technology has become too commonplace to inspire wonder and too complex to sustain interest; this, plus our increasing mistrust of the intrusions of technology into our own entirely non-criminal lives, makes the Craig Kennedy type of scientific detective an unlikely candidate for revival.[21]

Still, there remains an appetite for technological fiction. The very popular James Bond novels and, even more, the James Bond movies demonstrated as much, and the vogue for the novels of Tom Clancy indicate that far from being sated, the appetite has grown. But Jack Ryan is an adventurer, not a detective; he is closer to Tom Swift than to Craig Kennedy. His complex and powerful machines are more adapted to changing the world—threatening or preserving it—than knowing it. But in one respect—in his extensive accounts of modern intelligence-gathering technologies—Clancy appeals to exactly the same appetite for Knowing How to Know that Reeve appealed to more than half a century earlier. Reeve's readers were impressed by a detectaphone's power to eavesdrop on gangsters; Clancy's readers may be impressed by a satellite's power to monitor enemy actions and intercept enemy communications. In either case, modern science and technology seem to promise an enhancement of safety through knowing.

Chapter 9

Conclusion

In the 1840s, as method was becoming the defining characteristic of scientific enterprise, Poe invented the detective as a hero whose soul and essence lay in methodical knowing. The succeeding generation of writers largely ignored Poe's invention. It did make an important contribution by introducing the new phenomena, the policeman and the detective, into popular literature and by making criminal affairs a major literary topic. But it was not until Conan Doyle that the detective as hero of methodical knowing captured the popular imagination. Conan Doyle substituted Method (Scientific) for Method (Ratiocinative) as the whole character of the detective, thus creating the paradigm for what would become the supreme genre in popular literature for more than a century. The two most significant developments in the type to follow Holmes were those of R. Austin Freeman, whose detective pursued Method (Really Scientific), and Arthur B. Reeve, whose detective pursued Method (Scientifically Technological). But coincident with the First World War, the scientific paradigm began to lose its appeal. Method (Miscellaneous) and, even more, Method (Implied) became the sufficient soul of the detective. The success of Conan Doyle's formula attracted less scientifically oriented writers whose detectives were satisfied with the implication of method and compensated their readers with other appeals. And although science retained its authority as undoubtedly the best secular means of knowing or doing anything, the distance between "best" and "perfect" was widening. The First World War clearly contributed to the shift, demonstrating graphically the inhumane side of scientific and technological advance. The utopian visions of nineteenth-century defenders of science gave way to a sense that science's answers were questionable as to their morality as well as to their certainty.

As early as 1913, G.K. Chesterton, who was probably the greatest writer of detective fiction in the immediate post-Holmes period—the period of Dr. Thorndyke and Craig Kennedy—composed a pair of detective stories that amount to radical criticisms of both the Method (Really Scientific) and the Method (Scientifically Technological). They were collected in his second book of Father Brown stories, *The Wisdom of Father Brown* (1914). The little Catholic priest was, of course, intended as the antithesis of the scientific detective. Catholic orthodoxy, as a crucial moment in his first adventure makes clear, commanded Father Brown to be a rationalist; but his basic method of detection was intuitional. Because he could sympathize with others, including criminals, Father Brown could sense those who had sinned.[1] In "The Absence of Mr. Glass," (first published March 1913) Chesterton sets Father Brown's empathy against the "deductive" method of the "man of science," Dr. Orion Hood, "the eminent criminologist and specialist in moral disorders." Dr. Hood and Father Brown together visit the scene of a crime. There are signs of disorder and a man gagged and bound with ropes. Dr. Hood examines the scene generally, then focuses upon a hat, and like Sherlock Holmes and Dr. Thorndyke before him, proceeds to draw extensive conclusions about the missing victim, Mr. Glass, to whom it evidently belonged: "tall, elderly, fashionable, but somewhat frayed, certainly fond of play and strong waters, and perhaps rather too fond of them" (Chesterton, *The Father Brown Stories* 177).[2] But, as Father Brown realizes from attending not to the appearances in the room but to the expression on the bound man's face, there was no crime and there was no Mr. Glass. Had the hat belonged to an individual, Dr. Hood's inferences might have been valid, but in fact it is a magician's prop, and the bound man, whom Dr. Hood had identified as the villain, is an altogether non-homicidal magician. The scientific interrogation of things can be misleading.

But if a chain of deductions can fabricate a non-existent crime, a "delicate instrument of the laboratory" can be equally erroneous. In "The Mistake of the Machine," (October 1913) a scientific "ex-detective"—an *American* scientific ex-detective, Mr. Greywood Usher, relies upon the infallibility of his Psychometric Machine, which functions exactly like the sphygmograph of Luther Trant and Craig Kennedy. Flambeau explains its operation to Father Brown, a good deal more succinctly than Craig Kennedy would have done, but adequately ("they put a pulsometer on a man's wrist and judge by how his heart goes at the pronunciation of certain words" 221). Father Brown declares this device as valueless as the medieval technology that put a man's hand on a corpse and judged by whether its blood flowed. "Who but a Yankee would think of proving anything from heart-throbs? Why, they must be as sentimental as a man who thinks a woman is in love with him if she blushes. That's a test from the circulation of the blood, discovered by the immortal Harvey; and a jolly rotten test, too." The mock citation of Harvey seems a palpable hit at Craig Kennedy.

And, of course, "The Mistake of the Machine" justifies Father Brown's skepticism. Greywood Usher attaches a disreputable-looking man discovered in the vicinity of an apparent murder to his Psychometric Machine and discovers with satisfaction that the needle jumps when the name of Lord Falconroy—the presumed victim—is pronounced. But, as Father Brown observes, "the reliable machine always has to be worked by an unreliable machine," that is, by a fallible man. The disreputable-looking man's pulse jumped, not because he had killed Lord Falconroy, but because he was Lord Falconroy. Once again science has manufactured the crime and the criminal.

ii

Father Brown did not single-handedly retire the scientific detective, but he represents the more skeptical attitude which undermined science's claim to be the sole authority for intelligent criminal investigations. Detective story writers began to emphasize other aspects of its formula, such as the personality of the detective and the peculiarities of the plot. The Golden Age authors certainly moved in these directions: Agatha Christie's Hercule Poirot (debuted in 1920) and Dorothy Sayers's Lord Peter Wimsey (1923) amply illustrate the tendency. Both men are thoroughly intellectual; neither lectures on methodology. Their authority is derived from their imposing personalities rather than from demonstrable adherence to any technique. They assert their authority rather than explain it. Wimsey is especially interesting. He is not, for example, above using disguise as a technique; his role as Death Bredon in *Murder Must Advertise* constitutes a central element of his investigation on that occasion. And by a neat sleight of hand Sayers substitutes expertise in elegant living for expertise in criminal investigation; Wimsey acquires intellectual authority from his knowledge of old books and fine wines.

A third important Golden Age detective, pre-eminent in his time, S.S. Van Dine's Philo Vance, offers a useful bridge between the original Scientific Detective and new Great Detective. Vance is no more a scientist than Poirot or Wimsey, but he pays an eccentric tribute to the scientific method. From Poe to Reeve, two professions lay behind the best writers of detective fiction: journalism (Poe, Gaboriau, Morrison, Futrelle, Balmer and MacHarg, Reeve) and medicine (Conan Doyle, Freeman). The next generation drew from a much wider range of backgrounds. S.S. Van Dine (Willard Huntington Wright), with his connections to *The Smart Set* and *International Studio* and his books on modern art, was a professional intellectual. When, in 1925, he wrote a detective story, he intended to move it in a new direction. Van Dine admired Austin Freeman, ranking the Thorndyke books "among the very best of modern detective fiction," and disparaged Agatha Christie specifically for her want of a credible method: Poirot's "methods are...intuitional to the point of clairvoyance"; as a result of Miss Christie's preference for "artificial," "far-fetched" plots, "the interest in the solution is vitiated" ("Introduction" 17, 20). Van Dine proposed a compromise between the demanding rigor of a Thorndyke and the entertaining artificiality of Poirot. Philo Vance would combine the frivolous dilettante with a sober methodist. His method would be a non-mechanical, intellectualized version of the science embraced wholly by Luther Trant and opportunistically by Craig Kennedy: Philo Vance declares himself an advocate of "the science of individual character and the psychology of human nature" (*The Benson Case* 106).[3]

Vance waits until the middle of his first adventure, *The Benson Murder Case* (1926), to make his statement of method—another sign of method's diminished status—but he at least develops it in some detail. In Chapter Four, he expresses his disdain for pedestrian (Thorndykian) interrogation of things, asking District Attorney Markham, "Won't you ever learn that crimes can't be solved by deductions based merely on material clues and circumstantial evidence?" (72). In Chapter Six, he elaborates his own, psychological/aesthetic science: "Just as an expert aesthetician can analyze a picture and tell you who painted it, or the personality and temp'rament of the person who painted it, so can the expert psychologist analyze a crime and tell you who committed it—that is, if he happens to be acquainted with the person—, or else can describe to you, with almost mathematical surety, the criminal's nature and character....And that, my dear Markham, is the only sure and inevitable means of determining human guilt. All others are mere guess-work, unscientific, uncertain, and—perilous" (107). "Mathe-matical" method versus unscientific guess-work: Vance thus seeks to claim legitimate descent from Poe. But the chief appeals of the Philo Vance cases lie elsewhere—in the artificial precision of the plots and above all, in the character of the detective, with his erudition and his Nietschean postures. Still, although Vance's technique may be more method-and-water than straight method, and his practices may fall short of his preachments, the roots of the genre are still visibly alive in his approach to the investigation of crime.[4]

iii

The most radical shift in the history of the detective story genre—the revolt of the American hard-boiled detectives in the 1930s—may seem to have put the quietus to the scientific detective. Even the thesis-ridden scholar would seem to be hard put to discover a scientific method—or any intellectualized method—in the practice of private investigators like Sam Spade or Phillip Marlowe. They know how to *do*, not how to know. Persistence, not intelligence, seems the key to their success. They endure (with a resilience that gives their subgenre its name) rather than outwit. Detection is a job, not a profession. Knowledge, observation and deduction are rarely central to their pursuit of moral truth, and their pursuit rarely ends with neatly conclusive demonstrations; the villain is eliminated, but the whole story argues that pervasive villainy survives. Toughness is their soul and essence.

And yet, without straining the idea too far, they can be called masters of a technique. *Knowing* how to do is still knowing. The hard-boiled detectives are street-smart. They do not know how to precipitate a red stain indicating the presence of blood, but they do know how to negotiate the mean streets of modern urban life. They can walk with confidence into tenements and mansions and talk with self-assurance to punks and millionaires. They know how cops' minds work, and how gangsters' minds work, and they know how to use this practical knowledge. This is not a "science of individual character and the psychology of human nature," and certainly not a mathematical/poetical program for investigating, but it is a way of knowing how to interpret and manipulate the world.

Sherlock Holmes offered the possibility that if Dr. Watson (or any reader) did heed his injunction and did come to know his method, he too could solve problems through knowledge, observation and deduction. Sam Spade significantly has no companion. The hard-boiled detective's aloneness testifies, primarily, to his alienation in a corrupt society; there is no moral community to which he can belong. But it also testifies to the absence of an intellectual community. Spade had a partner, Miles Archer, but Archer's death precipitates the action of *The Maltese Falcon*, and even were Archer alive, he would still be "as dumb as any man ought to be." (Spade also has a secretary, Effie, but she too is intellectually defective, blinded by her romantic sentiments.) The hard-boiled detective must abandon the overt didactic impulse that the first detectives had made central to their mission. The Great Detective, for all the eccentricities of his genius, is a clubbable man; he invites others to join him, and it is only their incompetence that precludes their full membership. The Hard-boiled Detective mistrusts clubs; his survival depends upon his inviting no one—neither Watson nor wife—to share intimately in his affairs. Even if he had an effective, ratiocinative or scientific method, the hard-boiled detective would have no one to enjoin it upon.

At the end of *The Maltese Falcon*, in the famous passage in which he recites for Brigid O'Shaugnessy the reasons why he must turn her in, Spade offers as his final and main reason, "I won't play the sap for you." "Playing the sap" means committing himself to a significant moral action (here helping Brigid escape punishment for having murdered Miles Archer) without knowing certainly the basis for that action. The Great Detective, with his air of certain knowledge, can make authoritative judgments, and these judgments constitute his principal form of action; the heroic acts of the hero of knowing are, naturally enough, acts of knowing. Poirot or Wimsey or Vance reach intellectual conclusions; they assign to the cruder powers of society—the police and courts—the physical actions of apprehending, imprisoning and executing the villain. The hard-boiled detective also concludes with a judgment, but he reaches it principally through action, not thought; through personal encounters, often violent, with a sequence of clients, suspects, witnesses, policemen. Action thus precedes judgment; judgment, indeed, comes from action. The hard-boiled detective knows because he does, not because he thinks.

This is Spade's valedictory point: he knows, based on his interactions with Brigid and the others, that she killed Miles Archer; but, as he tells her, he doesn't *know* whether he loves her or she loves him. And only saps make choices based on uncertainties. The technique of the Great Detective is presumed to be omni-applicable; the thrust of his fable is that he can apply it to any problem and derive a certain answer. He often does, for example, in passing inform an obtuse lover that his suit will be rewarded. The fable of the Hard-boiled Detective is one of limitations. He cannot solve his society's gross problems, and can barely protect his own integrity, even his own life. His technique is very limited; it cannot, for example, prove that Sam loves Brigid or that Brigid loves Sam. It cannot prove whether Brigid's behavior has been motivated by cold-blooded calculations or deeply-felt emotions. And even the minimalist hero of knowing refuses to base a crucial moral judgment on unproven, unprovable appeals to sentiment. The hard-boiled detective can never know much in his half-lit world, but he need never be a sap.

Yet if there is much that he must leave unknown and unaltered, still the hard-boiled detective does know and does change something. In this, at least, he is the heir of the original detectives. Toughness, cynicism, wit: these instruments are less scientific than the lens or the microscope, but they still represent a technique of sorts: they must be applied with some intelligence. Even the hard-boiled detective does not happen upon the right answer. His method may seem improvised, but his ability to apply it consistently in a sequence of adventures argues that it must have some coherent basis. He conducts his experiments in an open field, without controls, and he relies upon hunches even more than the scientist relies upon hypotheses, but he drives toward empirically verifiable conclusions. He has moved a distance from the original scientific detective, but not much further than the Great Detective, who also uses the demonstrable correctness of his conclusion as the principal proof that his investigation has, all along, been governed by a methodical intelligence.

And the hard-boiled detective is not without incidental signs of technique in the more traditional sense. There are frequently allusions to the detective's mastery of specific techniques that demonstrate his capacity to control some aspects of his world. These may be related to his investigation, as he offers advice on tailing a suspect, or on escaping a tail, or on sneaking into off-shore gambling ships. Or they may be purely incidental demonstrations, as Spade rolls his cigarette or Marlowe works out his chess problems. These asides are the hard-boiled equivalents of Sherlockholmitos: non-essential miniatures of the power of the hero's technique. From a different perspective, they can also be compared to the Hemingway ethos. Precision in technique— fishing for trout the right way; killing the bull the right way— acquires an inherent value in a disordered, apparently valueless world. The hard-boiled detective may know little, but he knows how to do things. John D. MacDonald has exploited this hard-boiled version of Sherlockholmitos most effectively: his protagonists rarely declare themselves as methodical investigators, but they almost always demonstrate a command of incidental technologies: from road paving and machine tooling to hotel keeping and stock manipulation to restoring traumatized women and repairing bilge pumps. Elmore Leonard employs a researcher to insure that the scenes which his characters inhabit and the techniques which his characters employ are accurately represented. The reader of detective stories can acquire an incidental education in techniques as diverse as orchidology and haute cuisine (Rex Stout), gambling (Ian Fleming), banking (Emma Lathen) and horse-racing (Dick Francis).[5]

The emergence of the female private investigator in detective novel series by writers such as Marcia Mullen, Sue Grafton and Sara Paretsky may raise the interesting and complex question of whether heroines of knowing differ in their ways of knowing from the heroes. These detectives are self-consciously female; the problems they encounter and their responses to the problems are often presented as in some degree different from those of the male detectives who defined the formulas which they now exploit and perhaps subvert. It is not, however, clear that they have radically altered the epistemological premises which the patriarchs of the genre established. Sara Paretsky, as much as John D. MacDonald or Elmore Leonard, is concerned with getting the techniques right. The acknowledgments pages of her novels imply this concern: in *Deadlock* (1984) she thanks those who helped her get right the routines of a Great Lakes freighter; in *Bitter Medicine* (1987), it is the workings of a hospital; in *Burn Marks* (1990), contracting and construction. The sex of the detective does not alter the imperative that his or her narrative assure the reader that the writer and the detective know the way that things are done.[6]

It might be observed that the jargon of the American scientific detective—sphygmographs, dynameters, plethysmographs—finds its parallel in the jargon of the American hard-boiled detective, with his gooseberry lays and his gunsels. The tough, underworld slang is as much a proof of his mastery of the technology of modern violence and crime, as Craig Kennedy's invocations of his machines and their inventors was proof of his mastery of science and technology. Interestingly, Reeve himself seems to have recognized the parallel. By the 1930s, Reeve had exhausted the scientific appeal of his detective; in an effort to revive him as a popular hero, he attempted to move Kennedy toward the hard-boiled style which Hammett had just moved into the mainstream with *Red Harvest* (1929), *The Dain Curse* (1929), *The Maltese Falcon* (1930) and *The Glass Key* (1931). In *The Kidnap Club* (1932), Kennedy begins to talk about "grifts," "rods" "bulls" and "mouthpieces." Instead of an electric device with coils and wires, Jameson reports: "Kennedy packed a mean gat and it was in his hand now."[7] Reeve was less convincing in his depiction of the discourse of gangsters than in that of science, but his effort indicates the analogy between the two languages of power. Knowing how to speak is another facet of knowing how to know.

Finally, it might be noted that by far the most popular hero to emerge directly from the hard-boiled tradition was the one whose whole character was methodical to a degree that Sherlock Holmes himself never imagined. Perry Mason, the lawyer-detective, enjoyed an 82-novel career that was a continuous argument that mastery of a special method was a sure (and exciting) way to investigate crime and to convict the criminal. Mason's highly formalized legal inquiries are the epitome of methodical knowing. Like the scientist and the hard-boiled dick, he too demonstrates mastery of an esoteric jargon, here the English and Latin formulae of courtroom procedure. And he practices a consistent technique of inquiry. Mason's dialectical encounters with victims, witnesses and prosecutors have their hard-boiled aspects, as he rushes from scene to scene in southern California, and their intellectual aspects, as he cleverly cross-examines witnesses in the courtroom. Further: Mason is an interrogator of things as well as people. The Mason novels are full of the testimony of forensic experts; Mason inquires into ballistics, post-mortem lividity, and, on occasion, into the science of detergents, the technology of constructing cosmetic glass eyeballs or intricacies of sidereal time. Because the principal virtue of Gardner's narrative technique is its fast pace, achieved through short sentences and short paragraphs, much conversation and little description, Gardner's willingness to pause for detailed explications of these topics makes clear the premium that even a hard-boiled hero places on knowing how to know.

One of the prominent subgenres of the detective story in the second half of the twentieth century has been the police procedural.[8] Jack Webb's television series *Dragnet* (1951-59; 1967-70), J.J. Marric's Gideon series (1955-76) and Ed McBain's 87th Precinct series (1956-) are the best-known representatives of the type. Its debut is usually dated to 1945, with the publication of Lawrence Treat's *V as in Victim*. The police procedural, simply defined, narrates the progress of a team of police as they use actual police methods to investigate one or more crimes. There are, then, two distinctions. "Team of police" excludes such earlier police detectives as Lecoq, Sgt. Cuff, or Ebenezer Gryce. And "actual police methods" means that well-done routine replaces brilliant deduction as the basic technique of inquiry. Method thus returns, in a pedestrian form, to the center of the detective narrative. The routines may include such mundane bureaucratic matters as filling out forms (McBain even provides facsimiles), but however mundane, these routines are quintessentially methodical. The original detective proved that the detective might bend the proven techniques of science to incisive applications in criminal investigation; the procedural detectives prove that the time-tested, systematized practices of police work will inexorably operate to distinguish guilt from innocence.

Though knowing how to know—having a method for knowing how to know—has remained the basis of the character of the detective, it has ceased to be a self-conscious, purely intellectual discipline. Instead of explicitly advocating a science of knowing, with aphoristic laws and discursive lessons, the detective begins to adopt a more pragmatic program. His techniques prove themselves by their results rather than by their principles. And he is pragmatic in the root sense as well: he knows more by doing than by thinking; methodical work, more than methodical thought, becomes his primary tool for investigation. But the work always leads to thought: knowing is still the goal and the justification for his action. It is what makes him a hero. And this continuity provides the essential link between Sherlock Holmes, Hercule Poirot, Sam Spade and Joe Leaphorn.

Notes

Introduction

[1]Despite its title, Régis Messac's study, *Le "Detective Novel" et l'Influence de la Pensée Scientifique* (Paris 1929), has little to say about the aspect of the relations between scientific and detective methods which are discussed here. His massive work has much to recommend it; it covers a broad range of literature, providing a useful survey of the literary context—especially the French literary context—of the emergence of the detective story. He discusses many authors who are not part of the history of the genre narrowly defined—Voltaire, Ann Radcliffe, Fenimore Cooper, Bulwer Lytton, Balzac, Eugéne Sue—as well as extended discussions of Poe, Gaboriau and Conan Doyle. Of the other authors central to my argument, Pinkerton, Anna Katharine Green and Reeve receive only passing notices; Morrison, Futrelle and Austin Freeman are entirely overlooked. On the other hand, Old Sleuth and Nick Carter do receive much more substantial attention from Messac. Though he makes some interesting and relevant comments about Cuvier (and, as well, Huxley's admiration of Cuvier, 34 ff.), Messac is not much interested in method as the soul and essence of the detective. Only a few pages of his treatment of Holmes take up the methodological question, and these are mainly devoted to disparaging Holmes's scientific pretensions: "Bien mieux, l'attitude de Holmes à l'égard de la science en général est extrêmement critiquable" (615). In his remarks on Gaboriau's Lecoq, Messac does raise the much debated question of "deduction" versus "induction."

[2]See e.g. Bruce, *The Launching of American Science*, 128, and Tobey, *The American Ideology of National Science*, 81-82.

[3]Edward Malone, the young narrator of Conan Doyle's Dr. Challenger stories, speaks for this common view in *The Poison Belt*

(1913): " 'I don't profess to be a scientific man,' said I, 'though I have heard somewhere that the science of one generation is usually the fallacy of the next' " (189).

⁴The playful egotism of a Poirot is obviously far from Byronic; and even though Mike Hammer sometimes seems a Byronic solipsist, he identifies himself as the voice of the the common man. The great exception is S.S. Van Dine's Nietzschean Philo Vance, who does presume to find his standards solely within his exceptional self.

⁵Oedipus, though he inquires into a murder mystery and is sometimes cited as an antecedent of the detective, seems less so in this regard. He is willful in the pursuit of answers to riddles, but his pursuits are not notably methodical.

Literature offers few precedents to Dupin and Holmes; men who devote themselves entirely to any naturalistic, rationalistic method of investigation were much more likely to be objects of abhorrence than of praise. Chaucer's *Canterbury Tales* provides a panorama of medieval heroes: true knights, humble parsons, patient Griselda's, prosperous Merchants. But his knowers, other than those pious knowers whose knowledge was derived from faith, were villains like the Pardoner, practiced in the technologies of deception, or, in the most pertinent example, the alchemical Canon of *The Canon Yeoman's Tale*, whose devotion to his materialist science was directly related to his capacity for fraud. The great Renaissance knower was Dr. Faustus; and though a hero of sorts, his science procured him damnation. (The heroism of Faustian knowing, if it is admitted, lies in its ambition: Faust aspires to universal knowledge, universal experience. The detective's power to know is also unlimited, but only within a severely limited sphere: he can know everything about moral relations between men; all other knowledge and experience he disclaims (hence Sherlock Holmes's blithe ignorance of the Copernican system).

The seventeenth century saw English science move toward the center of intellectual culture with the founding of the Royal Society, but the most popular image of the scientist was Sir Nicholas Gimcrack, the would-be astronomer, would-be areonaut, would-be all-round natural philosopher and actual utter fool in Thomas Shadwell's *The Virtuouso* (1676). Alexander Pope might celebrate the achievements of Sir Isaac

Newton ("Nature, and Nature's Laws lay hid in Night. / God said, *Let Newton be!* and All was *Light,*" Epitaph Intended for Sir Isaac Newton, 1730), but his scientist for the popular stage, "Fossile" in *Three Hours after Marriage* (1717, with John Gay), was another misguided object of satire.

⁶The nineteenth century was, according to George Orwell, "our great period in murder, our Elizabethan period, so to speak" ("No Orchids for Miss Blandish"). Richard D. Altick, in *Victorian Studies in Scarlet,* argues that "It was in, or just before, the early Victorian era that homicide first became institutionalized as a popular entertainment, a spectator sport" (10). Altick discusses 15 notorious English murderers who committed their crimes between 1849 and 1903. The Glasgow case of Jessie M'Lachlan is one of them. It was indeed sensational: Jess M'Pherson's body was found semi-nude in the basement, stabbed 40 times; there was a narrow circle of suspects (actually only two, Jessie and a lecherous 87-year-old grandfather, toward whom much circumstantial evidence pointed); there were clues (a stolen plate, blood-stained clothing, slips in the testimony of witnesses); the judge pressed the case against Jessie and, after her conviction, sentenced her to death; public sentiment erupted in her favor; and her sentence was finally commuted to 15 years in prison. The Glasgow press apparently increased its circulation fivefold during the case. Its conclusion illustrated dramatically the imperfections of the judicial system, imperfections which the detective, with his scientific method, worked to eliminate.

The most famous killer of the century was, of course, Jack the Ripper, who operated in the Whitechapel district of London between 31 August and 9 November 1888. Jack's atrocities do not coincide with any author's birth, but they did occur between Sherlock Holmes's first appearance (December 1887) and his debut in *The Strand* (July 1891).

The sensational actions of western outlaws like Jesse James (1847-82) and Billy the Kid (1859-81) provided Americans with an exotic alternative to domestic crime, but in Lizzie Borden, who, in 1892, was accused of giving her mother 40 whacks and her father 41, America could claim its own Elizabethan murderess. The celebrated murder and mutilation of the prostitute, "Old Shakespeare," in New York in 1891 led journalists to proclaim an American Jack the Ripper. James Fulcher, in

"Murder Reports: Formulaic Narrative and Cultural Context," discusses one aspect of the rising American fascination with domestic murder.

[7]These are the values Jacques Ellul assigns to "technique" in *The Technological Society*: "*technique* is the *totality of methods rationally arrived at and having absolute efficiency*" (xxv). Though I have not burdened this study with much theoretical framework, I must acknowledge the influence of Ellul's work. He makes the clearest argument for the pervasive influence of "technique" in the modern world; one need not share what has been called his pessimism to be impressed with his exposition of the dimensions of the influence. The fictional detective provides, I think, a literary footnote to his argument. He embodies, in a formulaic drama, some of the tensions which Ellul describes.

[8]In 1815 there were 11 scientific journals (other than medical journals) published in the United States; by 1825, the number had more than doubled to 24. The most prominent of these, Benjamin Silliman's *American Journal of Arts and Sciences*, was founded in 1818 and had a European circulation (Daniels 15, 17). Poe added verisimilitude to his hoax, "Von Kempelen's Discovery," with a reference to Silliman's quarterly.

[9]Most commentators follow their citation of Darwin's dismissal of theory by observing that he was, in practice, less theory-free than he admitted. See Irvine 90-91.

[10]On naive Baconism, see Bozeman 3, Daniels 65. Robert V. Bruce writes, "The more explicit American preachers of Baconianism (few of whom were active scientists) often seemed more grudging of hypotheses than Bacon himself had been. With American facts accumulating in quantities undreamed by Bacon and no end in sight, they despaired of final generalizations and spoke as though classification alone should be the goal" (68).

[11]"I frame [or feign] no hypotheses." The famous phrase appears in the "General Scholium" of the second edition of *Principia Mathematica* (1713). Sophisticated discussions of Newton's methods and statements on method can be found in *The Methodological Heritage of Newton*, eds. Robert E. Butts and John W. Davis, Toronto: University of Toronto Press, 1970.

[12]For Newton's patience and humility and the contrasts with Kepler and Descartes, see Yeo, "Scientific Method and the Rhetoric of Science" 265, 275

[13]According to Bozeman, the Baconian method "evoked a cluster of related ideas: a strenuously empiricist approach to all forms of knowledge, a declared greed for the objective fact, and a corresponding distrust of "hypotheses," of "imagination," and, indeed, of reason itself" (3); see also Daniels 65.

[14]"All these writers on the philosophy of science [i.e. Hershel, Mill, and Whewell] "were attracted to his [i.e. Bacon's] vision of an extension of the method of science to the study of politics and society." Yeo, "Scientific Method and the Rhetoric of Science," 263.

[15]"From about the 1850s, it was commonplace for scientific commentators to stress the role of genius in science in contrast with the earlier emphasis on careful empirical observation" (Yeo, "Scientific Method and the Rhetoric of Science" 271). The *Encyclopedia Britannica* admitted the folly of naive Baconism in 1875: "The inductive formation of axioms by a gradually ascending scale is a route which no science has ever followed, and by which no science could ever make progress. The true scientific procedure is by hypothesis followed up and tested by verification; the most powerful instrument is the deductive method, which Bacon can hardly be said to have recognized" (R. Adamson, "Bacon," 9th ed. III.216).

[16]Huxley's persistence had motives beyond his lifelong commitment to the belief that workingmen were also entitled to know science. His preference for describing the scientific method as "trained and organized common sense" derived in part from his dedication to seeing the biological sciences rated as scientific as the physical sciences, despite their differing techniques of hypothesis and experimentation.

[17]Bruce, in *The Launching of American Science*, offers a very useful survey of the process of the professionalization of science in America, and dates it to the period 1846-76.

[18]Shapin and Thackray, in their survey of writings about science 1700-1900, observe: "A speculation as to the dating of the ultimate divorce between natural knowledge and general culture in Britain would seem to place it between 1870 and 1900" (11). In "Science" Yeo

discusses the early Victorian address to a wide audience which was followed, after 1870, by the narrowing address to specialists (9). In "Scientific Method and the Image of Science 1831-1891," Yeo explains that after 1870 scientists became aware that 1. in light of the Darwinian debates, discussions of method were more likely to become points of controversy than of consesus, and 2. the proposition "that scientific method could be explained to any intelligent reader, even one lacking in scientific experience" was no longer tenable (80). Dale, reading the history of scientific debate from a literary perspective, finds that "By the late 1870s there began to emerge a distinctly negative reading of the meaning of science for the future of man" (221).

[19]In the narrow sense, of course, scientific method only alters perceptions of the world: it introduces new concepts; technology introduces new things. Twentieth-century thinkers have severed the causal connection between science and technology. Most of the very visible technological advances of the first half of the nineteenth century were, it seems, not directly endebted to prior scientific discoveries, and even later, as science has come to play a larger role, it is often difficult to determine whether new technology has led to new science or vice versa. But the assumption that scientific innovation causes technological innovation is widespread. The assumption was encouraged by scientists in the nineteenth century. Writing about mid nineteenth-century America, Bruce notes the prevalence of "the dubious but spreading popular assumption that *everything* in technology was rooted in science. Professional scientists and technologists, who surely knew better, heartily endorsed the delusion, presumably because they wished it were true, hoped it might be some day, and in any case knew it to be in their best interest" (128).

[20]"By the late 1880s and 1890s the cult of science was on the decline as scientists themselves began to doubt that they alone could lead mankind to truth and happiness. Their doubts, when added to the earlier criticism of religious faith, contributed to the feeling of despair so prevalent in the final years of the century" (Bassalla 20).

[21]"Men of science themselves recognized by the end of the century that they were not dealing in certainties.... If indeed the criteria in science are pragmatism and coherence, then 'truths' are provisional and

will change with our notions of what we want from it, and of what it must cohere with.... Maxwell in his statistical interpretation of the Second Law of Thermodynamics had gone deeper. He seemed to have shown that physics itself rested upon uncertainty, and that predictions and explanations are based on probability—overwhelming in most ordinary cases" (Knight 207).

Chapter 2
[1]Poe's contemporaries also acknowledged method and air of method as the source of the stories' unusual appeal. *Graham's Magazine* cited "The Gold-Bug" as "quite remarkable as an instance of intellectual acuteness and subtlety of reasoning" and then observed, " 'The Murders in the Rue Morgue,' and 'The Mystery of Marie Roget,' are fine instances of the interest which may be given to subtle speculations and reasonings, when they are exercised to penetrate mysteries which the mind aches to know" (Sept. 1845, *Log* 567). Poe's friend Duykinck drew a comparison between the method of the detective and of the backwoodsman, a comparison which some historians of the detective story genre have advanced further: "The murders of the Rue Morgue [sic], the History of Marie Roget and the Purloined Letter turn upon matters of police, and would do credit either to the sagacity of an Indian hunter or the civilized skill of a Fouché for their ingenuity and keeness of scent" (New York *Morning News*, 28 June 1845; Log 543). The Boston *Morning Post* (8 July), the New York *Evening Post* (9 July), the New York *Daily Tribune* (review by Margaret Fuller, 11 July 1845) all specifically praised the tales of detection. In London, the *Spectator* added to the chorus: "To unfold the wonderful, to show that what seems miraculous is amenable to almost mathematical reasoning, is a real delight of Mr. Poe: and though he may probably contrive the mystery he is about to unravel, this is not always the case—as in the tale of Marie Roget; and in all cases he exhibits great analytic skill in seizing upon the points of circumstantial evidence and connecting them together" (2 August, *Log* 557).

[2]The search for Dupin's precursors has been pursued with more or less seriousness and with various results. It began almost immediately. A reviewer of the first volume to collect Poe's detective tales in 1845 was

already citing *Zadig* as the prototype of his detective: "The records of every court of criminal justice furnish, in doubtful and perplexing cases, or conflicting testimony and contradictions, much more curious tales than those which Mr. Poe has invented, and the type of which is [Voltaire's] *Zadig*" (*Tait's Edinburgh Magazine*, September 1845, quoted in *Poe Log* 567). The Edinburgh reviewer's purpose was to diminish the detective's originality; most of the seekers of prototypes Senecas have undertaken their searches to improve the detective's bloodline.

[3]The subtitle of Huxley's lecture (reprinted in *Science and the Hebrew Tradition* 1-23) is, in fact, "Retrospective Prophecy as a Function of Science." The essay's epigraph, taken from "one of the most important chapters of Cuvier's greatest work" (i.e. *Recherches sur les Ossemans Fossile*), reveals Huxley's inspiration. Cuvier, the taxonomist, was for Huxley the model scientist; Zadig's method the model method. As I have suggested in the introduction, Cuvier occupied a special status as scientist in the early nineteenth century: his genius was recognized by all, his method seemed most clearly Baconian, and his conclusions were not threatening to any orthodoxy.

[4]The appeal of the detective stories was evident during Poe's lifetime. Poe had the opportunity to publish his stories in book form three times during his life. The first occasion, *Tales of the Grotesque and Arabesque* (1839), predated his detective stories. The second, *The Prose Romances of Edgar A. Poe*, was published in July 1843. It was an abortive attempt to reprint Poe's tales in a series of pamphlet editions. Only the first number appeared, but what is significant is that first story chosen for the series was "The Murders in the Rue Morgue" (the other was "The Man That Was Used Up," which has sometimes been read as a quasi-detective story). The third and final collection of his stories, *Tales* (June 1845) selected 12 from the over 50 short stories Poe had published. Of these 12, three were the Dupin tales, and a fourth was "The Gold-Bug." Reviewers of *Tales* made clear what they took to be its principal strength. The detective stories were singled out for praise, and the critics invariably noticed the importance of the methodical character of the protagonist's intelligence.

[5]Poe was naturally disposed toward imagining worlds as issuing from individuals. He was inclined to the view that the world was

pregnant with hidden meanings. (His cosmological "prose poem," *Eureka*, suggests a metaphysical basis for the inclination.) His fiction tended usually to assume that these meanings were accessible only to sensitive—often deranged—natures. Only they could intuit, and then only momentarily and often madly, the transcendent meaning that lies beyond the distracting phenomena of mundane life. Most of Poe's heroes and heroines make their own worlds and, as well, the meaning of their worlds. They create their own Houses and their own Falls. Roderick Usher projects a world and an interpretation—the only world and the only interpretation imaginable for a Roderick Usher.

The detective stories operate on a different principle. Here Poe— the external author—makes the world and mixes in the meaning; the detective makes the meaning visible. His projection lies in his application of a rational, orderly method of knowing to the world that confronts him, whether it be the world of a murdered widow, a missing grisette, or a scheming minister. And the judicial knowledge that the detective derives is concrete and certain, not eccentric and transcendent. The significance of events to the mind of the detective is immanent in the empirical phenomena of everyday life—in, for example, the prosaic report that, listening to the same strange voice, an Englishman heard German, a Spaniard heard English, and an Italian heard Russian. When a rational, generalizable method of inquiry is applied to such surface details, they can be made to yield an irrefutable conclusion with a practical significance: the voice must be that of an orangutan.

⁶J. Lasley Dameron has made the point that Dupin was the first hero in western literature and culture "to use methodical thinking in solving crimes," "America's first fictional hero as thinker" (165, 169).

⁷Unless otherwise indicated, all references to Poe's works are to the two volume Library of America edition: I, *Poetry and Tales*; II, *Essays and Reviews*.

⁸"Analysis" (and its variants: "analyst," "analytic," and "analytical") is repeated 13 times in the Discourse.

⁹"Method" (and "methodical," "methodically," and "methods") appears eight times in the first half of the story. When "Rue Morgue" was reprinted in *Prose Romances* in 1843, Poe made a point of having "acumen" italicized.

[10]Poe himself blurred this distinction when, in a letter referring to the second Dupin tale, he made precisely the error he has the narrator of "Rue Morgue" warn against, confounding "analytical power" and "simple ingenuity" by describing the *theme* of "Marie Rogêt," as "the exercise of ingenuity in detection" (Letter to George Robert, 4 June 1842; Mabbott 718).

[11]More sophisticated readers may detect lessons in logic (see Harrowitz) or in politics (Irwin).

[12]"Analysis" recurs only twice in "Marie Rogêt" and three times in "Purloined Letter." And similarly, "Method" appears only twice in "Marie Rogêt," and twice in "Purloined Letter." "Acumen"does not appear in "Marie Rogêt" at all and in "Purloined Letter" only once.

[13]"Mathematical" (and "mathematician," "mathematicians" and "mathematics") occurs four times in "Marie Rogêt" and 14 times in "Purloined Letter." (If the related terms, "algebra" and "algebraists," are included, the number in "Purloined Letter" rises to 19). The increase in reference is geometrical.

[14]The source of Dupin's name is usually taken to be the prominent French politician André-Marie-Jean-Jacques Dupin (1783-1865), but André-Marie-Jean-Jacques had a brother, Baron Charles Dupin (1784-1873), who enters dictionaries of scientific biography as a major mathematician. Baron Charles may be the secret (so secret as to have been unknown possibly to Poe) patron of the first detective.

It may not be irrelevant that mathematics was the only scientific pursuit that enjoyed any success in the antebellum South. According to Robert V. Bruce, "the field of science in which the South most nearly approached its population quota was mathematics. Of all sciences, mathematics is freest of physical effort" (63).

[15]A similar perversity can be found in Poe's other statements on artistic method. In "The Philosophy of Composition," for example, he criticizes those who accept the more common association of imagination with spontaneous overflows of emotion: "Most writers—poets in especial—prefer having it understood that they compose by a species of fine frenzy—an ecstatic intuition" (II.14). Poe, on the other hand, asserts that his creative imagination proceeds methodically, "step by step, to its

completion with the precision and rigid consequence of a mathematical problem" (II.15).

For a different view of the implications of the first pages of "Murders in the Rue Morgue," see Terry J. Martin, "Detection, Imagination, and the Introduction to 'The Murders in the Rue Morgue'," *Modern Language Studies* 19:4 (1989): 31-45. Martin sees Dupin as an "arch-positivist" in "Rue Morgue," condemned by Poe for the failure of his method. Martin argues that Dupin actually practices "ingenuity" rather than "analysis."

[16]Quoted in Daniels 63 and Bozeman 3.

Joel Barlow could rhapsodize that Bacon informs men "what to learn and how to know":

Bacon with every power of genius fraught,
Spreads over worlds his mantling wings of thought,
Draws in firm lines and tells in nervous tone
All that is yet and all that shall be known,
        ....
Bids men their unproved systems all forgo,
    Informs them what to learn and how to know.
        (*The Columbiad* [1825] IX. 617-20, 623-24)

[17]This bias was evident in the work of the pre-eminent American scientist, Louis Agassiz. Agassiz's public lectures around the country made him by far the best known of the serious American scientists. Agassiz's masterwork was to have been a ten-volume taxonomy of American flora and fauna, *Contributions to the Natural History of the United States of America*. Only three volumes (two on turtles, 1857, and one on jellyfish, 1860) appeared before the Darwinian revolution rendered taxonomic science passe. "Even specialists found it of limited value because of its sterile Cuvierianism" (Bruce 233).

[18]Poe was paid to compose a preface and introduction, to translate some passages from Cuvier, and, most importantly, to lend his name to the title-page of what was, in fact, a cheap, authorized reprint of Thomas Wyatt's *Manual of Conchology*. Poe alludes to Cuvier in "Murders in the Rue Morgue"; Conan Doyle has Holmes allude to him in "The Five Orange Pips."

[19]They are: "MS. Found in a Bottle," "The Unparalleled Adventures of One Hans Pfall," "The Conversation of Eiros and Charmion," "A

Descent into the Maelström," "The Colloquy of Monos and Una," "A Tale of the Ragged Mountains," "The Balloon-Hoax," "Mesmeric Revelation," "The Thousand-and-Second Tale of Scheherazade," "Some Words with a Mummy," "The Power of Words," "The System of Dr. Tarr and Prof. Feather," "The Facts in the Case of M. Valdemar," "Eureka," "Mellonta Tauta," "Von Kempelen and His Discovery."

[20]Harold Beaver identifies three serious "scientific premises" as central to the argument of *Eureka*: the physics of elliptical orbits (Kepler), the laws of gravity and motion (Newton), and the wave theory of light and the nebular hypothesis (Laplace). On these matters, Poe acquits himself honorably.

[21]Dupin's version: "But it is by these deviations from the plane of the ordinary, that reason feels its way, if at all, in its search for the true" (I.414).

Chapter 3

[1]What is known of Forrester and his bibliography is summarized in E.F. Bleiler's introduction to *Three Victorian Detective Novels* (New York: Dover, 1978).

[2]An adapted translation of "The Purloined Letter" had appeared in a French journal in August 1845 (and was immediately reprinted in another journal). A translation of "The Murders in the Rue Morgue" appeared in June 1846, and then in October, publication of an abridged translation lead to a minor Parisian cause célèbre, with charges of plagiarism and a court case. Another abridged translation appeared in February 1847. (The first of Poe's tales to be fully translated into any language was the methodical detective story, "The Gold-Bug," which appeared in *Revue britannique* in November 1845.)

The Poe Log reports on all of the contemporary translations. The affair of "Rue Morgue" is covered on 666-68, 672.

[3]All information regarding Gaboriau is derived from E.F. Bleiler's introduction to the Dover translation of *Monsieur Lecoq*.

[4]Little is known of Waters, other than that his real name seems to have been William Russell. He began publishing his police detective stories in magazines in 1849; they were first collected in the American volume, *Recollections of a Policeman* (1852).

[5]Tabaret comes close to the ratiocinative model. He is too old to expend himself on other methods, such as disguise or eavesdropping. He is an amateur who, upon receiving a inheritance, devoted himself to mastering the literature of crime. His vicarious expertise (his "platonic investigations") eventually led him to offer his advisory services to the Prefecture de Police. In his first consultation, "he proved by A plus B— by a mathematical deduction, so to speak" the identity of the villain (*Monsieur Lecoq* 236-37). And in *Monsieur Lecoq*, he reasons elegantly and accurately. In all these respects he is a worthy heir of Dupin. The crucial difference between his character and Dupin is that he only exercises his ratiocinative method; he does not expound it. Method is not the centerpiece of the fiction.

[6]In *The Champdoce Mystery* (a translation of the second half of *Les Esclaves de Paris*), for example, the intellectual process by which Lecoq arrived at his conclusions is neither presented directly nor recapitulated by the detective. The only method seen in practice is his use of disguise.

[7]Frank Morn provides a review of Pinkerton's literary career in *The Eye That Never Sleeps*, 82-88.

[8]One indirect confirmation of the centrality of method in the Pinkertonian vision of the detective's soul and essence can be found in the anti-Pinkertonian burlesques of Mark Twain. Twain was offended by the unjustifiable arrogance he discovered in the Pinkerton narratives; the methodological busy-ness was, to him, all smoke and mirrors. The Pinkertonian detectives in Twain's short story, "The Stolen White Elephant" (1882), prove incapable of distinguishing fence post holes from elephant footprints. In the end, they find that the stolen elephant has been rotting in the basement of their Jersey City headquarters. Twain's Simon Wheeler manuscripts (1870-98), representing several abortive efforts to write a comic detective story in the form of a play and then a fragmentary novel, also contain explicit parodies of Pinkertonian operatives. In 1901, in "A Double-Barrelled Detective Story," Twain would burlesque Holmesian model of the detective. And yet twice, in *Pudd'nhead Wilson* (1894) and in *Tom Sawyer, Detective* (1896), Twain would himself propose detective heroes. Neither Pudd'nhead Wilson nor Tom Sawyer could, to be sure, be regarded as in the least Pinkertonian. *Tom Sawyer, Detective* is a potboiler, and Tom's detective

skills are as factitious as any other element of the narrative. But Pudd'nhead Wilson is a more interesting and relevant case, and had he been more fully fleshed in the novel, he would have occupied a more prominent place in the history of the detective genre. He is certainly a technological detective. With great precocity, he collects on plates of glass the fingerprints of the citizenry of Dawson's Landing, a village in antebellum Missouri. In the climactic trial at the novel's end, he uses these prints to expose a confusion of identities and thus to single out a murderer. Mark Twain was ambivalent about the progress of technology in the nineteenth century, but here a manifestation of that technology proves decisive in achieving what passed for justice in a slave-holding town. *Pudd'nhead Wilson* is, finally, much more interested in the social and moral implications of the confusion of racial identities than in the somewhat abrupt detective exposure of the confusion required to bring the narrative to a neat conclusion, but Pudd'nhead Wilson's confidence in his fingerprints—an anachronistic confidence which Twain derived from reading the seminal work, *Finger Prints* (1892), by Darwin's cousin, Francis Galton—reflects the faith that even a burlesquer of detectives might place in a scientific method.

⁹All three are practically unreadable: three titles by Gaboriau, seven by Pinkerton, and five by Green are in print in America in 1993, and nearly all of these are library editions. Only two books by Anna Katharine Green (*The Leavenworth Case* and *A Difficult Problem*) are available in popular editions.

¹⁰The greatest practitioner of what Van Dine labeled "to-day's technic" was Agatha Christie. In a late novel, *The Clocks* (1963), Miss Christie inserted in the mouth of Hercule Poirot, a brief, gratuitous compliment to Miss Green, praising her for exactly that quality of "romantic material and humanistic considerations" that Van Dine declared superseded. Referring specifically to *The Leavenworth Case* (which the narrator of *The Clocks* recalls his father having read as a boy), Poirot declares: "It is admirable.... One savours its period atmosphere, its studied and deliberate melodrama. Those rich and lavish descriptions of the golden beauty of Eleanor and the moonlight beauty of Mary" (Chapter 14). Poirot continues to praise the "psychological study" of the murderer. Poirot's kindness to his forebear contrasts with

the unkindness of Holmes to Dupin and Lecoq, but then Holmes was in his first adventure, struggling to achieve an independent identity, and Poirot spoke with 40 years of bestsellerdom behind him. Perhaps the most notable point is that Poirot doesn't mention Ebenezer Gryce's name. The story, the suspects, and the villain: these last, but Miss Green's detective, even to a sympathetic successor, has vanished.

[11]Van Dine also commends, with some justice, the "excellent style" of her books. Later critics have been less generous, but despite a degree of rhetorical excess which was conventional to the time (and which, it may be argued, effectively served to communicate subversive messages), Miss Green's prose remains quite readable.

[12]Barrie Hayne, whose article on Green in *10 Women of Mystery* presents the most persuasive argument for her rehabilitation, offers as one of his two main points "her consolidation of the detective novel as a *realistic* art form" (154). He is quite right. His other main point—"her contribution to the development of the detective hero"—carries some weight, though more, it would seem, with regard to her female detectives than to Ebenezer Gryce.

[13]This is true of all of the best detectives, and of many of the less than best. Unhappy experiments at updating the great detectives— Sherlock Holmes fighting the Nazis and Philip Marlowe going down the un-mean streets of seventies Los Angeles (or, worse, of seventies London) provide sufficient instances—illustrate the point.

[14]See A.E. Murch's comparison of Miss Green's work to that of Dickens, Collins, and Le Fanu: "in none of these does the detective theme monopolize the reader's attention so completely as in Miss Green's novels" (159). *The Stillwater Tragedy* (Boston: Houghton Mifflin, 1880) by the New England poet and novelist, Thomas Bailey Aldrich, offers an interesting comparison with *The Leavenworth Case*. Instead of Romance, Aldrich supplements his detective story with Social Concern (labor agitation). But the detective story itself holds interest: his detective, Mr. Taggert, resembles a young Pinkerton agent in his confidence and his use of disguise, but like Mr. Gryce, he builds his case largely on circumstantial evidence. Unlike Gryce or the Pinkertonians, however, he is completely wrong in his identification of the murderer. The falsely accused hero of the novel, having easily demonstrated his

innocence, declares, "The Lord was on my side." Mr. Taggert replies: "He was on your side, as you remark; and when the Lord is on a man's side a detective necessarily comes out second best" (313). This is a radical criticism of the premise of the detective story, restoring to the Lord the power to know which the secular detective was claiming. It has been suggested that Aldrich may actually have written the detective frame of his novel as a response to the optimistic moral epistemology of *The Leavenworth Case*; if so, his rearguard action must be judged a failure in its influence. Miss Green's vision would prevail.

[15]The reason for her preference, however, had nothing to do with modesty about the methodicalness of the detecting done, but rather with the connotations of "detective." Barrie Haynes reports her comment to a reporter: "Please do not call my books 'detective stories'...I abhor the word detective. It is too often applied to atrocities. I choose crime as a basic subject because from it arise dramatic situations" (160).

Chapter Four

[1]Conan Doyle held to this view. In his autobiography, *Memories and Adventures* (1924), he writes of Holmes, "If I have sometimes been inclined to weary of him it is because his character admits of no light or shade. He is a calculating machine, and anything you add to that simply weakens the effect" (108). One need only look at a character who openly aspires to the condition of "calculating machine"—Jacques Futrelle's Professor Van Dusen, The Thinking Machine (see Chapter Six)—to perceive Conan Doyle's misjudgment. Had he been merely a machine, Holmes could not have been the hero for his age; he might, at best, have been a curiosity of the proportions of Professor Van Dusen.

[2]The chapter, "The Chemical Corner," by Charles O. Ellison in Trevor Hall's *Sherlock Holmes and his Creator*, covers this aspect of Holmes's scientific credentials. Ellison observes that Conan Doyle assigns actual chemical research to Holmes in the first two novels and in the first three collections of stories (twice in the *Adventures* and the *Memoirs*, once in *The Return*); there are no such assignments in the second two novels or the last two collections (36).

[3]Though it has no bearing on Holmes's character as a scientist, there is an interesting connection between coal tar and the late

nineteenth-century science and technology. As Ronald C. Tobey points out in *The American Ideology of Science, 1919-1930*, the history of coal-tar applications made a contribution to the debate over whether scientific advance depended upon technological advance, or vice versa. Technologists (engineers) had viewed coal tar as a waste by-product of the manufacturing of coal gas and coke. It was a scientist, pursuing research into artificial quinine, who happened to observe that mixed with alcohol, coal tar produced a purple dye. Science, the example proved, created the new technology of synthetic dies.

[4]Holmes did not limit himself to chemistry, geology, botany and anatomy. In Appendix E (377-78) of their comprehensive study, *The Medical Casebook of Sherlock Holmes*, Alvin E. Rodin and Jack D. Key tabulate references to specific scientific disciplines in the Sherlock Holmes stories. These disciplines include: anatomy (references in 5 stories), anesthesia (3), ancient anthropology (3), physical anthropology (3), chemistry (11), dentistry (1), dermatology (1), forensic medicine (2), genetics (9), mental disease (2), neurology (1), ophthalmology (1), pathology (3). Rodin and Key provide many useful insights. Pasquale Accardo, in *Diagnosis and Detection: The Medical Iconography of Sherlock Holmes*, provides some provocative comments on the same topic.

[5]A similarly subversive allusion appears in the second Holmes novel as well. In the second chapter of *The Sign of Four*, Holmes recommends as "one of the most remarkable [books] ever penned" Winwood Reade's *The Martyrdom of Man* (I.619). Reade's book, strongly influenced by Victorian science, comprised a polemic against the pernicious influence of religion in human affairs.

And in "The Greek Interpreter," the same Holmes who professed ignorance of Copernicus discourses on "the causes of the change in the obliquity of ecliptic" (I.590). Holmes is, first of all, a safe, moral scientist; but he is no eunuch.

[6]Contemporary detective fiction provides one small sign of Tyndall's popularity: In a passing allusion, the hero (not the detective) of Thomas Bailey Aldrich's *The Stillwater Tragedy* (1880) advises his girlfriend, when she asks for a scientific explanation of a pins and needles sensation: "Tyndall's your man—Tyndall on Heat" (103).

[7]Many critics have attacked the shoddiness as well as the irrelevance of Holmes's scientific demonstrations. See Ousby 152-54; see also Accardo 91, Rodin and Key 285-86.

On the other hand, criminologists since Bertillon have found cause to praise the Holmes stories (Berg quotes Bertillon: "I love detective stories. I would like to see Sherlock Holmes methods of reasoning adopted by all professional police" 447).

[8]Owen Dudley Edwards proposes that Holmes's neglect of his laboratory (and, as well, the similar aversion to verifying experimentation found in Mycroft Holmes and Professor Challenger) may represent "affectionate satire" of the academic world Conan Doyle found in Edinburgh (*The Quest for Sherlock Holmes* 199).

[9]The invocation of Euclid may recall Poe's elevation of mathematics as a methodological paradigm. In part, both Poe and Conan Doyle may be repeating Thomas Hobbes's famous infatuation with the unique certainty of mathematical demonstration. But Holmes's admiration for mathematical reasoning, expressed here and elsewhere, also reflects the growing awareness of the importance of quantification in scientific thinking. The clearest development in the definition of the scientific method in the course of the nineteenth century lay in this increasing acceptance that mere Baconian accumulation of facts was insufficient and that mathematical rigor and sophistication was essential to effective scientific methodology. By the end of the century, mathematics had become essential in many disciplines, but it was the math of statistical probability, not the "mathematical certainty" of cliche.

It might also be noted that Holmes, in other places, invoked the importance of imagination in detective investigation (cf. "The Retired Colourman," "Silver Blaze"), and so he too might have endorsed a version of Poe's mathematician-poet. (He could also exclaim, "Cut out the poetry, Watson" ["Retired Colourman" II.547]). But Holmes clearly was not a Platonic inquirer; his actual methods were unquestionably empirical and scientific.

[10]A passage from the *Encyclopedia Briticannica* may be cited in defense of Conan Doyle and Holmes: "The inductive formation of axioms by a gradually ascending scale is a route which no science has

ever followed, and by which no science could ever make progress. The true scientific procedure is by hypothesis followed up by verification; the most powerful instrument is the deductive method, which Bacon can hardly be said to have recognized" ("Bacon" III.216; cited in Yeo, "Rhetoric" 269). "Hypothesis" is one of Holmes's favorite terms. And while it cannot be said that the "deductive method" Holmes employs functions in the verifying process in exactly the way the *Britannica* would have it, Holmes's "Science of Deduction" does acquire some authority from the connection.

[11]Marcello Truzzi's contribution to *The Sign of Three*, "Sherlock Holmes: Applied Social Psychologist," contains an especially relevant account of Holmes's method (59-71).

[12]"When you have eliminated": *Sign* (I.613), "Beryl Coronet" (II.299), "Blanched" (II.720), "Bruce-Partington" (II.446); "It is a capital mistake": *Study* (I.166), "Scandal" (I.349), "Second" (I.311); "It is an error": "Wisteria" (II.246), "Scandal" (I.349-50).

[13]"The only hypothesis" (*Sign* I.647); "test after test" ("Blanched" II.720); "one forms" ("Sussex" II.467-68).

[14]In *Bloodhounds of Heaven* (151-75), Ian Ousby charts a three-stage progress in Holmes's romance with science: an initial period of inhumane dedication to science (tinged with Decadence), a middle period of moderation in which Holmes is "moved as much by a passion for justice and a sense of noblesse oblige as by a love of scientific truth or artistic form" (151), and third, dark period in which Conan Doyle seems more interested in "the exotic and macabre.... the cruel, the gruesome, and the physically repulsive" (171). Ousby's scheme is a perceptive one, but behind this progress toward and then away from a cultural normalcy, Holmes's identity as a methodical investigator remains constant. The scientific aura may receive less emphasis, but it remains Holmes's inextinguishable soul and essence.

[15]That Huxley was far from alone in his advocacy of the common sense essence of the scientific method can be indicated by an excerpt from the prominent Victorian novelist and controversialist, Charles Kingsley, who defined the method: "It is simply the exercise of common sense. It is not a peculiar, unique, professional, or mysterious process of the understanding: but the same which all men employ, from the cradle

to the grave, in forming correct conclusions" ("Science," in *Scientific Lectures and Essays*, London, 1890: 210).

[16]Beatrice Webb, *My Apprenticeship*, New York: Longmans, 1926. Richard Yeo's section on "The Transferability of Scientific Method" in his essay "Method and the Rhetoric of Science" discusses at length the Victorian confidence that science's demonstrable successes in geology, chemistry, etc. should be repeatable in all other disciplines as well.

[17]For Dr. Bell, see Ely Liebow, *Dr. Joe Bell: Model for Sherlock Holmes*.

[18]Holmes makes these independent judgments at least four times, in "Blue Carbuncle," "Devil's Foot," "Charles Augustus Milverton," "Abbey Grange" and "Priory School." Significantly, Holmes's extra-legal judgments are always for mercy; he never undertakes vigilante justice (though he once comes close, in "Speckled Band").

[19]Conan Doyle himself came to see the destructive side of the mid-century scientific revolutions. Immediately after his acknowledgment of Huxley, Tyndall, Darwin, et al. as his chief philosophers, Conan Doyle wrote: "I know now [1924] that their negative attitude was even more mistaken, and very much more dangerous, than the positive positions which they attacked with such destructive criticism" (*Memories* 32).

See also Basalla's comment on the late-century disappointment in science: "By the late 1880s and 1890s the cult of science was on the decline as scientists themselves began to doubt that they alone could lead mankind to truth and happiness. Their doubts, when added to the earlier criticism of religious faith, contributed to the feeling of despair so prevalent in the final years of the century" (20). Holmes embodies Conan Doyle's optimism that science might after all lead mankind to at least one kind of truth and happiness.

[20]It might be noted that Holmes's adversary in what is generally regarded as his best novel-length adventurer, *The Hound of the Baskervilles*, is also a scientist: the entomologist, Stapleton.

[21]Moriarty's passion for mathematics and his prominent dome-like forehead both recall Poe. Perhaps the drama at Reichenbach Falls should be read as Holmes clasped in a death struggle with the author of his own great original.

[22]Ian Ousby, again, in *Bloodhounds of Heaven* (1976), provides the most perceptive account of the significance of Holmes's early association with Decadence and its place in his evolution as a character (see 156-62). Among the notions Samuel Rosenberg plays with provocatively in *Naked Is the Best Disguise* (1974) is the connection between Sherlock Holmes and Oscar Wilde. Paul Barolsky surveys some Aesthetic sources of Holmes in "The Case of the Domesticated Aesthete" (1984).

Chapter Five
[1]For Pinkerton, see *The Spiritualists and the Detectives* (1877). Pinkerton denies harboring an anti-Spiritualist bias, but declares, "my experience with these people, which has been large, has invariably been against their honesty or social purity" (xi). Only the "weak-minded" or "weak-moraled" are attracted by Spiritualism. For Craig Kennedy's anti-psychic forays, see, e.g. "The Seismograph Adventure" (*The Silent Bullet*, 1911) or *The Exploits of Elaine*, Chapter 13 (1914). The Thinking Machine also exposes a fake psychic ("The Crystal Gazer") and a fake ghost ("The Flaming Phantom"). Arthur Morrison's first book, *The Shadows Around Us* (1891), published two years before the debut of his detective, Martin Hewitt, presented stories which seemed soberly to argue for the reality of supernatural powers (though later Morrison wished to disavow the volume).

[2]The historical sources indicated in the appendices to *Land of Mist* illustrate the spectrum of approaches to spiritualist phenomena. Violet Tweedale's *Ghosts I Have Seen* (London 1919) is an informal, anecdotal narrative, which, in its apparent sincerity, speaks as much to the temper of the time as to the psychic phenomena themselves. The specific anecdote which Conan Doyle lifted is far removed from direct evidence: Conan Doyle has it from Violet Tweedale who had it from Lady Wynford who overheard her husband having the experience at Glamis Castle. Dr. Gustave Geley's *L'Ectoplasmie et la Clairvoyance* (1924, *Clairvoyance and Materialisation*, London 1927), by contrast, is a large, impressively scientific tome, very current (the English translation followed publication of *The Land of Mist*), full of statements of method, transcripts of reports, and authenticating photographs (including some of

paraffin molds and one of the materialized bird which Conan Doyle describes in the novel). That Conan Doyle inserts Dr. Geley and his Parisian institute directly into the narrative (as Dr. Maupuis and the Institute Métapsychique) indicates the special weight he placed on the evidence of the very scientific Dr. Geley. Dr. Carl Wickland of Los Angeles comes somewhere between Violet Tweedale and Dr. Geley. In his *Thirty Years Among the Dead* (London, n.d.), he too provides a theoretical apparatus and an abundance of documentary transcripts, but there is about him an air of charlatanry, to a non-Spiritualist at least.

[3]Conan Doyle, despite his lifelong commitment to social justice in life as well as in fiction (the Edalji, Slater, and Casement cases being often cited examples), never made much of the potential relevance of Spiritual revelation to criminal investigation. He never proposed a psychic detective (though, in Moris Klaw, *The Dream Detective* [1920], Sax Rohmer did). In an article, "A New Light on Old Crimes" (reprinted in *The Edge of the Unknown*, 1930), Conan Doyle does suggest that "psychic science" may offer solutions to old crimes which have baffled ordinary detective science, and he offers several examples, but even here he insists that all "normal" avenues of investigation must first be exhausted.

[4]As he makes clear in his autobiography, Conan Doyle's interest in Spiritualism was longstanding. As early as 1886, at the time he was writing the first Holmes novel, he had begun to attend séances. In 1887 he was corresponding with the psychic weekly, *Light*, and in 1892 he joined the British Society for Psychical Research. It was not, however, until the catastrophe of the First World War, in which his household suffered many losses, including his brother and his first son, that he confirmed himself a Spiritualist and set about the evangelical career which consumed the last decade and a half of his life. Kelvin I. Jones provides an excellent, sympathetic account of *Conan Doyle and the Spirits*.

Chapter Six

[1]Reginald Pound, in *The Strand Magazine 1891-1950*, discusses the magazine's first issue (30) and describes the importance of Sherlock Holmes (41 ff.). See also Jack Adrian's introduction to *Detective Stories from The Strand*.

Conan Doyle contributed a story, "The Voice of Science," to the inaugural issue of *The Strand*, and its subject matter justifies a brief comment. The substance of the story is slight: a brother uses a phonograph recording to dissuade his sister from marrying an adventurer. But the attitude toward science expressed in the story has some interest. The sister and her mother have discovered a new use of science in late nineteenth century England: it can underwrite social pretensions. Mrs. Esdaile and Rose base their social calendar upon "scientific conversatione," inviting local intellects to tea and lectures on "The Perigenesis of the Plasidule." They are, of course, dilletantes; but Conan Doyle writes of Mrs. Esdaile, "she supported Darwin, laughed at Mivart, doubted Haeckel, and shook her head at Weissmann" (Conan Doyle, *Uncollected Stories* 310). Even if it is derived, as her detractors charge, from "encyclopedias and text-books," such a range of reference is impressive. Twenty-five years later, Conan Doyle's professional scientist, Dr. Challenger, would support Darwin and shake his head at Weismann; he would not mention Mivart or Haeckel at all. Mrs. Esdaile's coterie, with its admiration of a table laid out with "specimens of the flora and fauna of the Philippines, a ten-foot turtle carapace from the Gallapagos, the os frontis of the Bos montis as shot by Captain Charles Beesly in the Thibetan Himalayas, the bacillus of Koch cultivated on gelatine" (311), may be something of a joke, but it was a joke that, even a half century earlier, would only have been made about a group of eccentric virtuosos, all men.

[2]Meade's other collaborations with Hallifax were *This Troublesome World* (1893), *Dr. Ramsey's Patient* (1896), *Where the Shoe Pinches* (1900), and *A Race with the Sun* (1901).

[3]Dorothy Sayers treated *Stories from the Diary of a Doctor* first in her discussion of "The Scientific Detective" in her introduction to *The Omnibus of Crime* (1929), describing it as the "fruitful" beginning of Meade's series of stories "in which the solution has a scientific or medical foundation" (31). Ellery Queen, in *Queen's Quorum* (1948), cites *Stories from the Diary of a Doctor* as the classic example of the "pseudo-scientific," "so-called 'medical mysteries" that became popular in the 1890s (241). Finally, Jacques Barzun and Wendell Taylor, in *A Catalog of Crime*, describe *Stories from the Diary of a Doctor* as "semi-

scientific"; they praise its management of locale and assert that "readers with a sense of period will find their interest sustained" (651).

⁴For the scientific knots, see "The Mysterious Death in Percy Street" and "The Lisson Grove Mystery" in *The Old Man in the Corner* (41, 106).

⁵In *Four Realist Novelists*, Vincent Brome makes an argument for Morrison's naturalistic fiction (*Tales of Mean Streets*, 1984; *A Child of the Jago*, 1896). For a review of Morrison's reputation, see Robert Calder, "Arthur Morrison, A Commentary." P.J. Kennedy's biographical sketch, which prefaces his edition of *A Child of the Jago*, provides the best account of Morrison's life.

⁶Too much ought not to be made of the Huxlean significance of "common sense." As Freud seems to have said, sometimes a cigar is just a cigar. Still, it is interesting that another of Sherlock Holmes's earliest rivals makes the same disclaimer as Martin Hewitt. "Never have I brought to my aid other weapon than a certain measure of common sense," declares Bernard Sutton, jewel dealer and detective, in "The Ripening Rubies." Sutton was the protagonist of ten stories by Sir Max Pemberton, collected in *Jewel Mysteries I Have Known: From a Dealer's Note Book* (1894).

⁷In the first Father Brown story, the very anti-mechanical G.K. Chesterton makes a point of distinguishing the intellectual French detective, Valentin, from a thinking machine: "He was not a 'thinking machine'; for that is a brainless phrase of modern fatalism and materialism. A machine only is a machine because it cannot think" ("The Blue Cross" 11). See Chapter Nine.

⁸Professor Stangerson is another example of the revolutionary scientist, the scientist who proves his excellence by disproving the orthodoxy of his fellow scientists (Professor Challenger, Professor Van Dusen, and, later, Dr. Priestley [see Chapter Nine] all exploit the type). Professor Stangerson's work made the discoveries of the Curie's possible, and his theory of "Dissociation of Matter by Electric Action" will "overthrow from its base the whole of official science, which based itself on the principle of the Conservation of Energy" (2). Stangerson's science has no functional bearing on the mystery at hand, but it does contribute a scientific atmosphere to the story. (In *The Perfume of the*

Lady in Black, Professor Stangerson and his physics are replaced by "Uncle Bob" and his pursuit of archaic anthropology.)

Stangerson's name may be an allusion to the villain of the first Holmes novel, Joseph Strangerson.

Chapter Seven
[1]The excellence of Austin Freeman's story-telling seems self-evident to me. For a contrary view, see Eric Routley, *The Puritan Pleasures of the Detective Story*, 64-72.

[2]The lives and opinions of Poe and Conan Doyle have been amply explored by admirers and scholars. Freeman has been less well served, though Norman Donaldson's biography provides a fine beginning.

[3]In the first published Thorndyke story, *The Red Thumb Mark*, Thorndyke himself praises "scientific imagination" (110).

[4]Ernest Mandel's observation that death itself is reified in the detective story seems relevant here. "Death in the crime story is not treated as a human fate, or as a tragedy. It becomes an object of enquiry. It is not lived, suffered, feared or fought against. It becomes a corpse, a thing to be analyzed" (*Delightful Murder* 41). Mandel, as a Marxist, sees this as a consequence of bourgeois ideology. But it also points to the way that a scientific ideology naturally treats death. The detective's exercise to neutralize death by objectifying it may be as much in the service of science as of capitalism.

[5]For yet another discussion of legal versus scientific methodology, see *The Eye of Osiris* (1911), chapter nine.

[6]The most notable influence of the Inverted Story was upon Roy Vickers, who employed a version of the form in his nearly 40 Department of Dead Ends stories, which he began in the 1930s. Vickers does not, however, use the form to accent Inspector Rason's method; there is no science at all.

[7]Two of the short stories were expanded into novels: "The Mystery of 31, New Inn" into the novel of the same title (1912) and "The Dead Hand" into *The Shadow of the Wolf* (1925).

[8]Access was not guaranteed to Freeman's non-Thorndyke works; Hodder & Stoughton evidently demurred at *The Uttermost Farthing* (1914) and *The Exploits of Danby Croker* (1916).

[9]Between 1924 and 1942 the *Saturday Review of Literature* published over 40 consistently favorable notices of his books (sometimes multiple notices of single publications), identifying Thorndyke as "one of our very favorite detectives" (28 Feb. 1931: 638) and Freeman as the "G.O.M. of mystery writers" (25 Feb. 1939: 16). The brief comments usually accented Freeman's strengths in what had become the generic virtues: plotting, characterization, atmosphere. Comparisons with Sherlock Holmes appeared several times, and usually to Thorndyke's advantage. Occasionally reference was made to Thorndyke's scientific orientation and empirical methods, but the character was not emphasized. *The New York Times Book Review,* which published some of the earliest reviews of Freeman, did attend to the science. Of the 1912 American edition of *The Mystery of 31 New Inn,* the *Times* reviewer wrote: "Mr. Freeman has been careful to extract the full effect of reality from the jargon of scientific proceeding" (26 Oct. 1913: 584); and the reviewer of *A Silent Witness,* after praising the novel as "unusually clever and interesting," noted that its developments "depend a good deal upon scientific theories and facts for their solution" (2 May 1915: 170). In comparisons with Craig Kennedy, the American scientific detective, Freeman was invariably rated superior—usually vastly superior—by all critics, and yet Kennedy enjoyed a triumphant popularity, Dr. Thorndyke remained the "favorite detective story writer" of a discerning few.

[10]In his characteristic profession of a "simple faith in facts" and his claim of "no imagination," Reggie Fortune does affirm a naive Baconianism, though a half century after such an ideology had been discredited by professional scientists.

[11]John Dickson Carr's second-string detective, Sir Henry Merrivale (introduced in 1934), does claim the same competencies as Dr. Thorndyke. He is certified in the law and in medicine, but he makes no practical use of these competencies in his detection.

[12]Constable Walker, who plays a minor role in *The Cask,* comes to the police profession with a revealing motive: "He had read Conan Doyle, Austin Freeman, and other masters of detective fiction, and their tales had stimulated his imagination" (New York: Dover, 1977: 29). The desire to emulate Holmes and Thorndyke led him to enter the force and

inspired him to practice the "observation and deduction" which caused him to notice the dray that was bearing the cask. Though his principal detectives do not claim science as their preceptor, Crofts does thus insert, through a young would-be detective, a bow to the scientific deans of detection.

[13]Samson calls them period pieces, but "interesting" (47-49); Moskowitz finds them "quite good" (128).

Chapter Eight
[1]Though even Reeve, toward the end, apparently found it possible to license his creature to other writers. Moskowitz reports that in 1934 Reeve, "having great difficulty writing," accepted a "token fee" to permit a ghostwriter (A.T. Locke) the stories that would be collected as *Craig Kennedy Returns* (*Strange Horizons* 152).

Moskowitz and Samson in *Yesterday's Faces*, Vol 2 ("Wilemite Fluorescing," 3-68; 23-46 are devoted to Kennedy) provide the best commentary on Craig Kennedy. The articles by Cox and Harwood in *The Armchair Detective* provide most of what is known about Reeve's life and his bibliography.

Briefly: Arthur Benjamin Reeve was born in Patchague, Long Island on 15 October 1880. He graduated from Princeton University in 1903. He attended New York Law School, but moved into journalism, writing science articles while serving as an assistant editor at *Public Opinion*. Reeve served as editor of *Our Own Times* from 1906-10, and worked on the staff of *Survey* in 1907. He married Margaret Wilson in 1906 and had three children. The family lived on Long Island, and Reeve maintained an office in New York City.

In *Who's Who 1914-15*, he identified himself as a Progressive and a Presbyterian. In the 1916-17 edition, he changed his political affiliation to Republican; in 1926 he, his wife, and two of his children (the third having died?) converted to Catholicism. He claimed membership in four clubs.

Harwood reports that Reeve was asked to help establish a scientific spy and crime detection laboratory in Washington during World War I. Between 1914 and 1929, Reeve worked on scripts for films (seven of them featuring Craig Kennedy). In February 1928 he sued Harry K.

Thaw, the notorious murderer of Stanford White, for breach of contract over screenplays which Reeve and John R. Lopez had written for a production company operated by Thaw and Stewart Mack.

In September 1928, Reeve filed for bankruptcy in Brooklyn, listing assets of $600 (a $100 royalty contract with Harpers, $300 in household effects, and $200 due him from his attorneys) and liabilities of $39,271.82 (which included debts for plumbing, carpentering and medical and dental work).

In the summer of 1930, Reeve began a crime prevention hour for NBC radio. *The Golden Age of Crime* (1931), Reeve's journalistic but quite competent history of gangsters and racketeering in the 1920s, was a by-product of this radio program.

In 1932 he moved to Trenton, NJ. There, in 1935, he served as a supervisor for the Federal Writer's Project, reported on the Lindbergh kidnapping, and raised prize-winning dahlias. He died of an asthmatic bronchial condition on 9 August 1936.

[2]Having said this, I will not much further belabor the poverty of Reeve's imagination. In preparation for this study I read through 15 of Reeve's books, and the work of reading consistently defeated my intention of championing him as an undeservedly neglected author. The only strong judgment I arrived at occurred as I read *The Master Mystery* (not, to be sure, a Kennedy story; it bills itself as a "novelization" of a screenplay and assigns co-authorship to Charles Logue): I have never read a worse piece of fictional narrative; it is, in my experience, an absolute against which all else can be measured. The two Elaine books, also novelizations but featuring Kennedy, are also very bad, and difficult to complete. I think one can enjoy the first half dozen Kennedy short stories one reads; and I think some of the later novels contain interesting social views (eg. *Pandora* 1926) or background information (*The Film Mystery* 1 921).

[3]See "In Defense of the Detective Story," *Independent* 75 (10 July 1913): 93-94 and "When the Criminal Takes to Science," *Forum* 62 (July 1919): 34-35.

[4]"When the Progressive spoke of the scientist, his primary reference was to the impartial expert who had the practical knowledge and ability to manipulate the environment, to make democracy work. In the new

urban age, the function of science was to generate methods or rules which would guide successful and efficient adjustment of conflicting claims to privilege.... As one historian has said, 'The sense of science not simply as a means of organizing knowledge or wisely viewing the universe but as a method for getting things done, exploring the practical problems of human experience, was central to progressive thought' "(Tobey 18).

Hearst's Magazine, which had in fact published at least four Craig Kennedy stories in 1912 and 1913, reflected this sentiment in a short piece, "The Age of Science," by Elbert Hubbard in October 1914: "This is the age of science. The demand of the world to-day is for facts, demonstrable truth, useful information. Business is not scientific....Theology, politics, medicine, and law are being classed with alchemy, astrology, palmistry, poetry, and all are passing away. They are being replaced by fact, knowledge demonstrable....In the year Nineteen Hundred Fourteen, we are demanding that our politics shall be operated according to business methods....Science rules" (434).

[5]All citations are to the original publication in *Hampton's*.

[6]"With one or two exceptions, these stories are far above the ordinary run of this type of fiction" (*Nation* 14 Apr. 1910: 377). *The New York Times* commended their literary quality (23 Apr. 1910: 230).

[7]See also Mott, *History of American Magazines, 1885-1905*, Chapter 10.

[8]Reeve, "When the Criminal Takes to Science" 36. As Moskowitz (132) observes, Reeve grew increasingly committed to asserting his priority to "the first purely scientific detective," even to the point of claiming to have introduced Craig Kennedy in 1901, and thus to have beaten Balmer and MacHarg by eight years. But while "Craig Kennedy" does appear in Reeve's college story in *The Nassau Literary Magazine*, that Craig Kennedy is a football hero and golfer, not a scientific detective. Reeve's claim to 1909 for the first true Kennedy story may also be suspect.

[9]Foster drew three or four illustrations for each of the *Cosmopolitan* tales, and one of these would be chosen for the frontispiece of the collected volume. Although he might well have supplemented Reeve's narrative emphasis upon the explication of

scientific principles and technological processes, Foster did not do so. Few of his drawings for the first 12 stories show Kennedy engaged in his research. The third drawing for "The Silent Bullet" (Jan. 1911) depicts a dramatic moment in Kennedy's laboratory in which he demonstrates the silencing device which the murderer used. For "The Diamond Maker" (May 1911) Foster drew a purely technological moment in which Kennedy prepares a device which will save his life ("Kennedy was winding two strands of platinum carefully about a piece of porcelain..." 839), and for "The Azure Ring" (June 1911) he depicts another distinctly scientific pose in which Kennedy holds a test-tube in front of a laboratory table ("Craig shook his head as he stared at the black precipitate" 119). These are the exceptions, however. In the facing-page drawing that opens "Spontaneous Combustion" (July 1911) he depicts Kennedy performing an experiment that helped decide the case, but with its gowned women and dinner-jacketed men, the scene is a parlor, not a laboratory, and only the caption makes the scientific occasion explicit. Most of the drawings emphasize the active or meditative or social aspects of the cases, and omit the scientific and technological entirely. The drawing which was selected for the frontispiece when the 12 stories were collected in *The Silent Bullet* was the one which showed Kennedy using an ax to destroy a crooked roulette wheel, the action of Kennedy the manly adversary of vice rather than of Kennedy the scientist. (To be sure, the small drawing which graced every title page of the collected edition does show Kennedy, dressed in jacket, high collar, and tie, sitting with a firm profile and a clenched fist at his laboratory table, surrounded by various chemical and electrical apparatus.)

[10]*The Fourteen Points* (1925) is often used to illustrate Reeve's weakness as a writer, especially in his later career; the stories are generally poorly conceived and written, but there is, in some of the details, an apparent late effort to embody Craig Kennedy as a character. In "Water," Kennedy and Jameson return to their alma mater, Princeton, and find the Nassau Club "so full of Princeton memories." Kennedy is so "gripped" by the experience that he actually utters a nostalgic remark: "Great to be back, Walter, great, isn't it" (188). In "Earth," Jameson speculates on Kennedy's celibacy. Kennedy plows a

field and observes it has been a long time since he "walked back one of those things," and Kennedy even sings "a ribald ditty" which he and Jameson had learned "over there" (220, 226, 229). Kennedy's emergence as an ex-farm boy and bawdy yet celibate ex-dough-boy seems, however, improbably sudden; it only emphasizes how little biography he had in the volumes which preceded *The Fourteen Points*.

Ironically, the man usually identified as the model for Craig Kennedy had a highly visible character. Dr. Otto Schultze was a prominent medical assistant to the New York District Attorney. His 30-year career gained him a reputation for, as his *New York Times* obituary put it, "skillful autopsies and scientific deductions." He was, in his practice, much closer to Dr. Thorndyke than Craig Kennedy (he even occupied a chair of Medical Jurisprudence at Cornell University). Asked about his relationship to Kennedy, he said, "I might have dropped the seed of fact, but Arthur made it flower into fiction." Schultze's career ended dramatically. His manner at the inquest into the murder of a yachtsman in September 1931 was so erratic that it forced the cancellation of the inquest. In December, his wife had him committed to an asylum. In March 1932 he was declared sane and released; he died in July 1934 (*New York Times* 5 July 1934: 18).

[11]An odd dimension of Reeve's attitude toward technology emerges in the non-Kennedy book, *The Master Mystery* (co-authored by John W. Grey; New York: Grosset & Dunlap, 1919). A key element of *The Master Mystery* is the so-called "Graveyard of Genius," the basement storeroom of "International Patents, Incorporated." There the dastardly corporation stores the models of revolutionary new inventions which might upset the economic status quo. It purchases the patent rights from the inventors, and then suppresses them—"For, when inventions threaten to render useless already existing patents, necessitating the scrapping of millions of dollars worth of machinery, vested interests must be protected" (2). And one of the guardians of this graveyard is the Automaton, described as a terrifyingly powerful robot (and pictured, to a late twentieth-century eye, as a silly man-dressed-up-in-tin-foil-tubes). Though the novel achieves a sort of nadir in the art of narrative, there is a suggestive fable in this account of vested interests employing technology to suppress technological advances.

[12]Unless otherwise noted, all references are to the Kennedy books.

[13]Kennedy's professorship and his preference for organization may have a historical dimension. As Nathan Reingold points out in "American Indifference to Basic Research" (60-61) whereas European academic science tended to be structured around individual, highly esteemed professors (with their assistants), American universities tended to prefer departments with two or more faculty. The American system thus expressed a structural bias toward cooperative research projects, a bias which the nature of advanced modern science has rewarded. Some European universities did not move toward the departmental model until after the second world war.

Kennedy's rhetorical advocacy of "organization" may reflect the American bias (Reeve would presumably have encountered it at Princeton and elsewhere). Dr. Thorndyke, with his preference for a private laboratory and private inquiries, would reflect the European tradition. Of course, Kennedy is, in practice, as individualistic as Thorndyke. The major example of an organizational, cooperative hero of knowing comes in the special genre of the Police Procedural (see Chapter 9).

[14]Reeve repeats this argument in an article written under his own name "In Defense of the Detective Story," *Independent* 75 (10 July 1913): 91-94. He cites the view of the famous detective William J. Burns (some of whose adventures Reeve had narrated for *McClure's Magazine* in 1912): "He says that it is a good thing to tell people how hard it is nowadays in the face of modern organization and modern science to "get away with the goods" (93). The article argues that the modern detective story, so far from inspiring criminals, actually benefits society.

[15]Reeve specifically identifies the pulp heroes Old Sleuth, Nick Carter and King Brady as his immediate models. He credits these detectives with supplanting the prior vogue for the Wild West. The new vogue, he observes, is science ("Our boys read scientific stories now"— he also expresses surprise at the number of women who are reading science), and so the detective-plus-science, Craig Kennedy, is the logical result ("When the Criminal Takes to Science," *Forum* 62 (1919): 38-39).

[16]Most of these scientists can be identified: Bertillon (1853-1914) and Darwin (1809-82) require no comment; others include the

bacteriologist Paul Theodore Uhlenhuth (1870-1954), the chemist Hans Goldschmidt (1861-1923), the traveller Robert Schomburgk (1804-65), and the physicist Prince Boris Borisovitch Golitzin [sic] (1826-1916); I have not identified Sir Lindsey Johnson, or Professors Robert and Leduc.

[17]The currency of Craig Kennedy's science (and an instance of its source) can be given. In September 1912 *Cosmopolitan* printed a pair of illustrated articles on Professor Elie Metchnikoff's research at the Pasteur Institute into microbiology and the aging process (436-46). The July 1913 *Cosmopolitan* contained the Kennedy story, "The Elixir of Life" (rpt. in *The Dream Doctor*). There Kennedy refers to "the theory of Metchnikoff, who says that old age is an infectious chronic disease" (*Dream Doctor* 142), and in the end he discovers that a husband has been prematurely aged by doses of indol, a toxin which "the Metchnikoff germs" could not neutralize. Readers who skipped the report of the scientist in September were caught by Reeve's dramatized exposition in July. (In this instance, unfortunately, both sets of readers were misinformed: Metchnikoff's hypothesis of a connection between intestinal microbiology and arteriosclerosis did not survive later research.)

[18]*The Times* applied "entertaining" to *The War Terror* (25 Apr. 1915: 162), *The Gold of the Gods* (30 Jan. 1916: 39) and *The Treasure Train* (24 June 1917: 238).

"Manufactured" was applied to *The Fourteen Points* (17 June 1925: 24) and "wildly impossible" to both *The Clutching Hand* (29 Apr. 1934: 3) and *Enter Craig Kennedy* (3 Nov. 1935: 2).

In an early review (of *The Dream Doctor*), *The Times* observed that Craig Kennedy was "a cross between Sherlock Holmes...and Luther Trant, with his marvellous machines for measuring mental conditions" (24 May 1914: 246). The review also noted that "The detective, especially the scientific detective, with his array of unpronounceable instruments for his emotional clinics, is becoming a little too pervasive nowadays."

The *Saturday Review of Literature*, an influential judge of mystery fiction from the mid-1920s into the 1950s, never cared for Craig Kennedy, calling him "one of the feeblest and least attractive of

238 You Know My Method

imaginary detectives" (Review of *Pandora* [30 Oct. 1926: 261]). Its comments on one of the weakest Kennedy collections, *The Fourteen Points*, is revealing. It attacks much—the stories are "flatly mechanical," Craig Kennedy is "absurd," his devices are "puerile"—but it still admits that some interest adheres to the detective's ingenuity (Apr. 1925: 714). Even at their worst, Kennedy and his machines retain some power to impress readers.

The London *Times Literary Supplement* (2 Nov. 1922: 708) found *The Film Mystery* "an unusually interesting crime story." "Unusually" is perhaps the key word; *The Film Mystery* is one of Reeve's better efforts. Still, the comment is a further testimony to Craig Kennedy's prestige at the time.

[19]See Moskowitz, 128-59, and Sampson, 49-68, for discussions of figures such as Michael White's Proteus Raymond, Charles S. Wolfe's Joe Fenner, or David H. Keller's Taine.

[20]John T. Dizer provides a commentary on the Swift series and a full bibliography.

[21]The Craig Kennedy television series lasted only one season in 1954. On the other hand, it might be argued that the quite successful *Quincey M.E.* series, which ran on NBC from 1977 to 1983, appealed to the same notion that a scientifically trained investigator might most convincingly interrogate things in his laboratory.

Conclusion
[1]In the prologue to *The Secret of Father Brown* (1927), Father Brown explains that his ability to detect the perpetrators of crime lies in his success in placing himself in the minds of others. "I had thought out exactly how a thing like that could be done, and in what style or state of mind a man could really do it. And when I was quite sure that I felt exactly like the murderer myself, of course I knew who he was."

[2]All references are to this omnibus edition.

[3]All further references to this edition.

[4]A good corrective to the monolithic construction that I may seem to be engaged in can be found in LeRoy Panek's *Watteau's Shepherds*. Panek sees the Poe-Gaboriau-Conan Dolye-Austin Freeman-G.K.Chesterton tradition as one of two lines of development which led

to the Great Detectives of the Golden Age; the other, he argues, is the Stevenson-Haggard-Hope/Edgar Wallace-Oppenheim-Rohmer-LeQueux-Buchan line of "vigorous literature for adolescents and the working class." He sees Play as a central merit in the Great Detectives, and he makes an excellent case, but I continue to think Method as the soul and essence. (There are, of course, many other correctives.)

[5]Ernest Mandel, in *Delightful Murder*, sees these incidental "crash courses" as the authors' attempts "to get an edge over competitors" by endowing "one's commodities with additional use-value (78-79)." This seems to me to be a usefully wrong theory. I doubt anyone buys an Emma Lathen novel to learn about banking, and I doubt Mary Latsis and Martha Hennisart thought anyone would when they joined to create Emma Lathen and her banker-detective. Rather, I suspect both writer and reader sensed the appropriate analogy between knowing high finance and knowing how to detect innocence and guilt. The well-researched undertakings of the Sloan Guaranty Trust are the expansive and often impressive equivalents of the "Sherlockholmitos" exercises that Conan Doyle exploited; the well-earned impression of technical competence in financial matters transfers, by literary sleight of hand, to the detective competence of the hero. The crash courses, then, are not supplemental "use-values," but rather versions of a basic device in the genre, a device whose specific purpose is to confirm the methodological competence of the hero.

[6]The phenomenon of the very popular female private eye has been a topic of discussion among scholars of the detective story genre and of popular culture generally. If the detective is indeed essentially a hero of knowing, it would seem that the emergence of a new class of essentially female heroes of knowing might have significant implications for the larger question raised by the proposition that there are peculiar "women's ways of knowing." I cannot, however, pursue these implications here.

[7]*The Kidnap Club* (New York: Macauley, 1932): 82. The novel is interesting for its reflection of Reeve's own life: Leslie Hunter, Chairman of the Crime Prevention Campaign, whose daughter is kidnapped, runs a radio program much like Reeve's own crime prevention hour that ran on NBC in 1931. Kennedy declares that "we live in a golden age of

crime": *The Golden Age of Crime* was Reeves's 1931 account of gangsters and racketeers.

[8]George Dove's *The Police Procedural* (1982) is the standard study of the subgenre.

Works Cited

I. Primary Texts

A. Major Authors

Poe

Dupin stories:

"The Murders in the Rue Morgue," 1841.
"The Mystery of Marie Rogêt," 1842-43.
"The Purloined Letter," 1844.

Editions cited:

Poetry and Tales Vol I. New York: Library of America, 1984.
Essays and Reviews Vol II. New York: Library of America, 1984.

Gaboriau

Lecoq novels:

L'Affaire Lerouge, 1866.
Le Dossier No. 113, 1867.
Le Crime d'Orcival, 1867.
Les Esclaves de Paris, 1868.
Monsieur Lecoq, 1869.

Editions cited:

The Champdoce Mystery. New York: Scribner's, 1913.
Monsieur Lecoq. Intro. E.F. Bleiler. New York: Dover, 1975.

Pinkerton

In addition to the following narratives of his agency's detective investigations, Allan Pinkerton is credited with the authorship of four other historical accounts: *General Principles of Pinkerton's National Police Agency*, 1867; *History and Evidence of the Passage of Abraham Lincoln from Harrisburgh, PA to Washington, D.C. on the 22nd and 23rd of February 1861*, 1868; *Bankers, Their Vaults, and the Burglers*, 1873; *The Spy of the Rebellion*, 1883.

The Expressman and the Detectives, 1875.
Claude Menotte as a Detective and Other Stories, 1875.
The Somnambulist and the Detective, 1875.
The Model Town and the Detectives, 1876.
The Molly Maguires and the Detectives, 1877.
The Spiritualists and the Detectives, 1877.
Criminal Reminiscences and Detective Sketches, 1878.
Strikers, Communists, Tramps and Detectives, 1878.
Gypsies and the Detectives, 1879.
Mississippi Outlaws and the Detectives, 1879.
Bucholz and the Detectives, 1880.
Professional Thieves and the Detective, 1880.
The Rail-road Forger and the Detectives, 1881.
Bank-robbers and the Detectives, 1882.
The Burgler's Fate and the Detectives, 1883.
A Double Life and the Detectives, 1884.
Thirty Years a Detective, 1884.

Edition cited:

Professional Thieves and the Detective. New York: G.W. Carleton, 1880.

Green

Ebenezer Gryce novels:

The Leavenworth Case, 1878.
Hand and Ring, 1883.

Behind Closed Doors, 1888.
A Matter of Millions, 1890.
The Doctor, His Wife, and the Clock, 1895.
That Affair Next Door, 1897.
Lost Man's Lane, 1898.
"The Staircase at the Heart's Delight." *A Difficult Problem*, 1900.
The Circular Study, 1900.
One of My Sons, 1901.
Initials Only, 1911.
The Mystery of the Hasty Arrow, 1917.

Edition cited:

The Leavenworth Case. Intro. Michelle Slung. New York: Dover, 1981.

Doyle

Sherlock Holmes novels and stories:

A Study in Scarlet, 1887.
The Sign of Four, 1890.
The Adventures of Sherlock Holmes, 1892.
The Memoirs of Sherlock Holmes, 1894.
The Hound of the Baskervilles, 1902.
The Return of Sherlock Holmes, 1905.
The Valley of Fear, 1915.
His Last Bow, 1917.
The Casebook of Sherlock Holmes, 1927.

Professor Challenger novels and stories:

The Lost World, 1912.
The Poison Belt, 1913.
The Land of Mist, 1926.

Editions cited:

The Annotated Sherlock Holmes. Ed. W.S. Baring-Gould. Two volumes.
    New York: Clarkson Potter, 1967.

The Lost World and The Poisoned Belt. San Francisco: Chronicle
    Books, 1989.
When the World Screamed and Other Stories. San Francisco: Chronicle
    Books, 1990.

Morrison

Martin Hewitt novel and stories:

Martin Hewitt, Investigator, 1894.
Chronicles of Martin Hewitt, 1895.
Adventures of Martin Hewitt, 1896.
The Red Triangle, 1903 (novel).

Edition Cited:

Best Martin Hewitt Detective Stories. Introduction by E.F. Bleiler. New
    York: Dover, 1976.

Futrelle

Professor Van Dusen novel and stories:

The Thinking Machine, 1906.
The Chase of the Golden Plate, 1906 (novel).
The Thinking Machine on the Case, 1907.

Editions cited:

Best "Thinking Machine" Detective Stories Vol I. Intro. E.F. Bleiler. New
    York: Dover, 1973.
Great Cases of the Thinking Machine Vol II. Intro. E.F. Bleiler. New
    York: Dover, 1976.

R. Austin Freeman

Dr. Thorndyke novels and stories:

The Red Thumb Mark, 1907.
John Thorndyke's Cases, 1909 (ss).

The Eye of Osiris (The Vanishing Man), 1912.
The Singing Bone (American title: *The Adventures of Dr. Thorndyke*), 1912 (ss).
The Mystery of 31, New Inn, 1912.
A Silent Witness, 1915.
The Great Portrait Mystery, 1918 (ss).
Helen Vardon's Confession, 1922.
The Cat's Eye, 1923.
Dr. Thorndyke's Casebook (The Blue Scarab), 1923 (ss).
The Mystery of Angelina Frood, 1924.
The Puzzle Lock, 1925 (ss).
The Shadow of the Wolf, 1925.
The D'Arblay Mystery, 1926.
A Certain Dr. Thorndyke, 1927.
The Magic Casket, 1927.
As a Thief in the Night, 1928.
Famous Cases of Dr. Thorndyke (The Dr. Thorndyke Omnibus), 1929 (ss).
Mr. Pottermack's Oversight, 1930.
Dr. Thorndyke Investigates, 1930.
Pontifex, Son and Thorndyke, 1931.
When Rogues Fall Out (Dr. Thorndyke's Discovery), 1932.
Dr. Thorndyke Intervenes, 1933.
For the Defence: Dr. Thorndyke, 1934.
The Penrose Mystery, 1936.
Felo de Se? (Death at the Inn), 1937.
The Stoneware Monkey, 1938.
Mr. Polton Explains, 1940.
Dr. Thorndyke's Crime File, 1941 (includes "Meet Dr. Thorndyke" and "Art of the Detective Story").
The Jacob Street Mystery (Unconscious Witness), 1942.

Editions cited:

The Best Dr. Thorndyke Detective Stories. Intro. E.F. Bleiler. New York: Dover, 1973.
The Cat's Eye. New York: A.L. Burt, 1927.

A Certain Dr. Thorndyke. London: Hodder and Stoughton, 1927.

Death at the Inn. New York: Dodd Mead, 1937.

Dr. Thorndyke's Crime File. Ed. P.M. Stone. New York: Dodd Mead, 1941.

The Famous Cases of Dr. Thorndyke. London: Hodder and Stoughton, 1929.

The Eye of Osiris. New York: Carroll and Graf, 1986.

For the Defence: Dr. Thorndyke. London: Hodder and Stoughton, 1934.

Mr. Polton Explains. New York: Dodd Mead, 1940.

Pontifex, Son and Thorndyke. New York: Dodd Mead, 1931.

Red Thumb Mark. New York: Dover, 1986.

Silent Witness. London: Hodder and Stoughton, 1936.

The Stoneware Monkey and The Penrose Mystery. New York: Dover, 1973.

When Rogues Fall Out. London: Hodder and Stoughton, 1932.

Arthur B. Reeve

Craig Kennedy:

The Silent Bullet (English title: The Black Hand), 1912.

The Poisoned Pen, 1913.

The Dream Doctor, 1914.

The War Terror, 1915.

The Gold of the Gods, 1915.

The Exploits of Elaine, 1915.

The Romance of Elaine, 1916.

The Triumph of Elaine, 1916 (UK only).

The Social Gangster (The Diamond Queen), 1916.

The Ear in the Wall, 1916.

The Treasure Train, 1917.

The Adventuress, 1917.

The Panama Plot, 1918.

The Soul Scar, 1919.

The Film Mystery, 1921.

Craig Kennedy Listens In, 1923.

Atavar, The Dream Dancer, 1924.
The Fourteen Points, 1925.
Craig Kennedy on the Farm, 1925.
The Boy Scout's Craig Kennedy, 1925.
The Radio Detective, 1926.
Pandora, 1926.
The Kidnap Club, 1932.
The Clutching Hand, 1934.
Enter Craig Kennedy, 1935.
The Stars Scream Murder, 1936.

Other Detective Stories:

Guy Garrick, 1914.
Constance Dunlap, 1916.
The Master Mystery, 1919.
The Mystery Mind, 1921.

Editions cited:

Constance Dunlap. New York: Harper, 1913.
The Dream Doctor. New York: Van Rees P, 1914.
The Ear in the Wall. New York: Harper, 1916.
The Exploits of Elaine. New York: Harper, 1915.
The Film Mystery. New York: Grossett and Dunlap, 1921.
The Fourteen Points. New York: Harper, 1925.
The Kidnap Club. New York: Macaulay, 1932.
The Master Mystery. New York: Grosset and Dunlap, 1919.
Pandora. New York: Harper, 1926.
The Poisoned Pen. New York: Harper, 1911.
The Romance of Elaine. New York: Harper, 1916.
The Silent Bullett. New York: Harper, 1910.
The Social Gangster. New York: Harper, 1916
The Treasure Train. New York: Harper, 1917.

B. Other Detective Story Writers

Other Primary Texts Cited:

Adrian, Jack, ed. *Detective Stories from The Strand.* New York: Oxford UP, 1991.

Chesterton, G.K. *The Father Brown Stories.* London: Cassell, 1950.

Forrester, Andrew, Jr. "The Unknown Weapon." In *Three Victorian Detective Novels.* E.F. Bleiler, ed. New York: Dover, 1978.

Greene, Hugh. *The Further Rivals of Sherlock Holmes.* New York: Pantheon, 1973.

_____. *The Rivals of Sherlock Holmes.* New York: Pantheon, 1970.

Leroux, Gaston. *The Mystery of the Yellow Room.* New York: Dover, [1908] 1977.

_____. *The Perfume of the Lady in Black.* New York: Grosset & Dunlap, 1909.

Lynde, Francis. *Scientific Sprague.* New York: Scribner's, 1912.

Meade, L.T., and Clifford Halifax. *Stories from the Diary of a Doctor.* New York: Arno, 1976.

Orczy, Baroness. *The Old Man in the Corner.* New York: Dover, 1980.

Rhode, John. *The Ellerby Case.* New York: Burt, 1927.

_____. *The Murders in Praed Street.* New York: Burt, 1928.

Sayers, Dorothy, ed. *The Omnibus of Crime.* Garden City: Garden City, 1937 [1929].

Shiel, M.P. *Prince Zaleski and Cummings King Monk.* Sauk City, WI: Mycroft and Moran, 1977.

Van Dine, S.S. *The Benson Murder Case.* New York: Burt, [1926].

_____. ed. *The World's Best Detective Stories.* New York: Blue Ribbon, 1931 [1927].

II. Secondary Sources

Accardo, Pasquale. *Diagnosis and Detection.* Rutherford: Fairleigh Dickenson UP, 1987.

Adams, Henry. *The Education of Henry Adams.* Ernest Samuels, ed. Boston: Houghton Mifflin, 1974.

Altick, Richard D. *Victorian Studies in Scarlet.* New York: Norton, 1970.

Bacon, Francis. *Selected Writings*. New York: Modern Library, 1955.

Barolsky, Paul. "The Case of the Domesticated Aesthete." *Virginia Quarterly Review* 60 (1984): 438-52.

Barzun, Jacques. "Detection and the Literary Art." In *The Delights of Detection*. Ed. Jacques Barzun. New York: Criterion, 1961.

Barzun, Jacques, and Wendall Taylor. *A Catalogue of Crime*. New York: Harper & Row, 1989.

Basalla, George, William Coleman, and Robert H. Kargon, eds. *Victorian Science*. Garden City: Doubleday/Anchor, 1970.

Batory, Dana Martin. "A Look Behind Conan Doyle's *The Lost World*." *Riverside Quarterly* 6 (1977): 268-71.

Beaver, Harold. "Introduction." *The Science Fiction of Edgar Allan Poe*. Harmondsworth: Penguin, 1976: vii-xxi.

Benton, Richard P. "Gaston Leroux." *Critical Survey of Mystery and Detective Fiction*. Ed. Frank N. Magill. Pasadena, CA: Salem P, 1988.

Berg, Stanton O. "Sherlock Holmes: Father of Scientific Crime Detection." *The Journal of Criminal Law, Criminology and Police Science* 61 (1970): 446-52.

Blieler, E.F. "Introduction." *The Old Man in the Corner*. New York: Dover, 1980.

Bozeman, Theodore Dwight. *Protestants in an Age of Science: The Baconian Ideal and Antebellum American Religious Thought*. Chapel Hill: U North Carolina P, 1977.

Brome, Vincent. *Four Realist Novelists*. London: Longmans, Green/British Council, 1965.

Bruce, Robert V. *The Launching of American Science, 1846-1876*. New York: Knopf, 1987.

Calder, Robert. "Arthur Morrison: A Commentary with an Annotated Bibliography of Writings About Him." *English Literature in Transition 1880-1920*. 28:3 (1985): 276-97.

Carr, John Dickson. *The Life of Sir Arthur Conan Doyle*. New York: Vintage, 1975.

Chapple, J.A.V. *Science and Literature in the Nineteenth Century*. London: Macmillan, 1986.

Clareson, Thomas D. *Understanding Contemporary American Science Fiction: The Formative Period (1926-1970).* Columbia: U South Carolina P, 1990.

Clausen, Christopher. "Sherlock Holmes, Order, and the Late Victorian Mind." *Georgia Review* 38 (1984): 104-23.

Cosslett, Tess. *The 'Scientific Movement' and Victorian Literature.* Sussex: Harvester P, 1982.

Cox, J. Randolph. "A Reading of Reeve: Some Thoughts on the Creator of Craig Kennedy" (with "A Chronological Bibliography of the Books of Arthur B. Reeve"). *The Armchair Detective* (Jan. 1978): 28-33.

Cox, Michael. *Victorian Tales of Mystery and Detection: An Oxford Anthology.* Oxford: Oxford UP, 1992.

Dale, Peter Allan. *In Pursuit of a Scientific Culture: Science, Art, and Society in the Victorian Age.* Madison: U Wisconson P, 1989.

Dameron, J. Lasley. "Poe's Auguste Dupin." *No Fairer Land.* Eds. J. Lasley Dameron and James W. Mathews. Troy, NY: Whitston, 1986: 159-71.

Daniels, George H. *American Science in the Jacksonian Age.* New York: Columbia UP, 1968.

_____. *Nineteenth-Century American Science: A Reappraisal.* Evanston: Northwestern UP, 1972.

Dizer, John T. *Tom Swift and Company.* Jefferson, NC: McFarland, 1982.

Dove, George N. *The Police Procedural.* Bowling Green: Bowling Green State UP, 1982.

Doyle, Arthur Conan. *Memories and Adventures.* London: Hodder and Stoughton, 1924.

Eco, Umberto, and Thomas A. Seboek. *The Sign of the Three—Dupin, Holmes, Pierce.* Bloomington: Indiana UP, 1983.

Edwards, Owen Dudley. *The Quest for Sherlock Holmes.* Edinburgh: Mainstream Publishing, 1983.

Ellul, Jacques. *The Technological Society.* John Wilkinson, trans. New York: Vintage/Random, 1964.

Freedman, Benedict. "The Thinking Machine." *Mystery and Detection Annual.* Ed. D. Adams. Beverly Hills: Donald Adams, 1972: 79-85.

Fulcher, James. "Murder Reports: Formulaic Narrative and Cultural Context." *Journal of Popular Culture* 18:4 (1985): 31-45.

Gerber, Samuel M. *Chemistry and Crime: From Sherlock Holmes to Today's Courtroom.* Washington: American Chemical Society, 1983.

Gilbert, Elliot L. "Murder without Air." *New Republic* 30 July 1977: 33-34.

Goncourt, Edmund, and Jules. *Pages from the Goncourt Journal.* Trans and ed. Robert Baldrick. London: Oxford UP, 1962.

Green, Richard Lancelyn, ed. *The Sherlock Holmes Letters.* London: Secker & Warburg, 1986.

Hall, Trevor. *Sherlock Holmes and His Creator.* New York: St. Martin's, 1977.

Harrowitz, Nancy. "The Body of the Detective Model: Charles S. Peirce and Edgar Allan Poe." In Eco and Seboek, 179-97.

Harwood, John. "Arthur B. Reeve and the American Sherlock Holmes." *The Armchair Detective* (Oct. 1977): 354-57.

Haycraft, Howard. *The Art of the Mystery Story.* New York: Simon and Schuster, 1946.

_____. *Murder for Pleasure.* New York: D. Appleton, 1941.

Hayne, Barrie. "Anna Katharine Green." *10 Women of Mystery.* Ed. Earl F. Bargainnier. Bowling Green: Bowling Green State UP, 1981.

Hull, David L. *Darwin and His Critics.* Cambridge: Harvard UP, 1973.

Huxley, Leonard. *The Life and Letters of Thomas Henry Huxley.* New York: Appleton, 1916.

Huxley, T.H. *Evolution and Ethics.* Eds. James Paradis and George C. Williams. Princeton: Princeton UP, 1989.

_____. "Past and Present." *Nature* 51 (1 Nov. 1894): 1-3.

_____. *Science and Education, Collected Essays* III.45.

_____. *Selected Works of Thomas Henry Huxley.* New York: D. Appleton, 1897. Vol 2: *Darwiniana.*; Vol 4: *Science and the Hebrew Tradition.*

Irvine, William. *Apes, Angels, and Victorians.* New York: Time, 1963.

Irwin, John T. "Reading Poe's Mind: Politics, Mathematics, and the Association of Ideas in 'The Murders in the Rue Morgue'." *American Literary History* 4.2 (1992): 187-206.

252 You Know My Method

Jensen, J. Vernon. *Thomas Henry Huxley Communicating for Science.* Newark: U Delaware P, 1991.

Jones, Kelvin I. *Conan Doyle and the Spirits: The Spiritualist Career of Sir Arthur Conan Doyle.* Wellingborough, Northhants: Aquarian, 1989.

Kalikoff, Beth. *Murder and Moral Decay in Victorian Popular Literature.*

Keating, P.J. "Biographical Study." In Arthur Morrison, *A Child of the Jago.* London: MacGibbon and Kee, 1969: 11-36.

Knight, Stephen. *Form and Ideology in Crime Fiction.* Bloomington: Indiana UP, 1980.

Lardner, Ring. "The Big Town." *The Portable Lardner.* Ed. Gilbert Seldes. New York: Viking, 1946.

Laudon, Larry. "Theories of Scientific Method from Plato to Mach: A Bibliographic Review." *History of Science* 7 (1968): 1-63.

Liebow, Ely. *Dr. Joe Bell: Model for Sherlock Holmes.* Bowling Green: Bowling Green State UP, 1982.

Limon, John. *The Place of Fiction in the Time of Science: A Disciplinary History of American Writing.* Cambridge: Cambridge UP, 1990.

Loughery, John. *Alias S.S. Van Dine.* New York: Scribner's, 1992.

Maida, Patricia. *Mother of Detective Fiction: The Life and Works of Anna Katharine Green.* Bowling Green: Bowling Green State UP, 1989.

Mandel, Ernest. *Delightful Murder.* Minneapolis: U Minnesota P, 1984.

Martin, Terry J. "Detection, Imagination, and the Introduction to 'The Murders in the Rue Morgue'." *Modern Language Studies* 19:4 (1989): 31-45.

Meikle, Jeffrey L. " 'Over There': Arthur Conan Doyle and Spiritualism." *The Library Chronicle of the University of Texas at Austin.* n.s. No. 8 (Fall 1974): 23-27.

Merrill, Lynn L. *The Romance of Victorian Natural History.* New York: Oxford UP, 1989.

Messac, Régis. *Le "Detective Novel" et l'Influence de la Pensée Scientifique.* Paris: Librairie Ancienne Honoré Champion, 1929.

Morn, Frank. *The Eye That Never Sleeps.* Bloomington: Indiana UP, 1982.

Moskowitz, Sam. *Strange Horizons: The Spectrum of Science Fiction.* New York: Scribners, 1976.

Mott, Frank Luther. *A History of American Magazines 1885-1905.* Vol. 4. Cambridge: Harvard UP, 1957.

Mumford, Lewis. *Technics and Civilization.* New York: Harcourt Brace, 1963.

Murch, Alma Elilabeth. *The Development of the Detective Novel.* New York: Philosophical Library, 1958.

Murray, Raymond C., and John C.F. Tedrow. *Forensic Geology.* New Brunswick: Rutgers UP, 1975.

Ousby, Ian. *Bloodhounds of Heaven.* Cambridge: Harvard UP, 1976.

Panek, LeRoy. *Watteau's Shepherds: The Detective Novel in Britain, 1914-1940.* Bowling Green: Bowling Green State UP, 1979.

Paradis, James, and Thomas Postlewait, eds. *Victorian Science and Victorian Values: Literary Perspectives.* New York: New York Academy of Sciences, 1981.

Pasquale, Accardo. *Diagnosis and Detection.* Rutherford: Fairleigh Dickenson UP, 1987.

Peterson, Audrey. *Victorian Masters of Mystery: From Wilkie Collins to Conan Doyle.* New York: Ungar, 1984.

Poe, Edgar Allan. *The Complete Works of Edgar Allan Poe.* Vol. 17. Ed. James A. Harrison. New York: Crowell, 1902.

Pound, Reginald. *The Stand Magazine 1891-1950.* London: Heinemann, 1966.

Queen, Ellery, ed. *101 Years Entertainment.* The Great Detective Stories, 1841-1941. Boston: Little, Brown, 1941.

———. "Queen's Quorum." *Twentieth Century Detective Stories.* Cleveland: World, 1948.

Reeve, Arthur B. *The Golden Age of Crime.* New York: Mohawk P, 1931.

Reingold, Nathan. "American Indifference to Basic Research: A Reappraisal." *Nineteenth-Century American Science: A Reappraisal.* Ed. George H. Daniels. Evanston: Northwestern UP, 1972.

Rodin, Alvin E. *Medical Casebook of Doctor Arthur Conan Doyle: From Practitioner to Sherlock Holmes and Beyond.* Malabar, FL: Krieger, 1984.

Rollason, Christopher. "The Detective Myth in Edgar Allan Poe's Dupin Trilogy." *American Crime Fiction.* Ed. Brian Docherty. London: Macmillan, 1988.

Rosenberg, Samuel. *Naked Is the Best Disguise.* New York: Penguin, 1975.

Routley, Eric. *The Puritan Pleasures of the Detective Story.* London: Gollanz, 1972.

Sampson, Robert. *Yesterday's Faces.* Vol II. *Strange Days.* Bowling Green, OH: Bowling Green State UP, 1984.

Schreffler, Philip A. *The Baker Street Reader.* Westport, CT: Greenwood P, 1984.

Scarlett, E.P. "Doctor Out of Zebulon: The Doctor in Detective Fiction with an Expanded Note on Dr. John Thorndyke." *Archives of Internal Medicine* 118.2 (Aug. 1966): 180-86.

Shapin, Steven, and Arnold Thachray. "Prosopography as a Research Tool in the History of Science: The British Scientific Community, 1700-1900. *History of Science* 12 (1974): 1-28.

Shiel, M.P. *The Works of M.P. Shiel.* Ed. A. Reynolds Morse. Cleveland: privately printed, 1979: III.514.

Shelley, Mary. *Frankenstein.* Ed. Joanna Smith. New York: Bedford/St. Martin's, 1992: 53.

Simpson, Keith. *Sherlock Holmes on Medicine and Science.* Intro. Isaac Asimov; Appreciation E. Stanley Palm. New York: Magico, 1983.

Slade, Joseph W., and Judith Yaross Lee, eds. *Beyond the Two Cultures.* Ames: Iowa State UP, 1990.

Smith, Sir Sydney. *Mostly Murder.* New York: McKay, 1960.

Snow, C.P. *The Two Cultures: and a Second Look.* New York: NAL, 1963

Stewart, R.F. *...And Always a Detective.* Newton Abbot: David & Charles, 1980.

Symons, Julian. *Bloody Murder.* Harmondsworth: Penguin, 1974.

Tebbel, John, and Mary Ellen Zuckerman. *The Magazine in America.* New York: Oxford UP, 1991.

Theerman, Paul. "Natural Images of Science: British and American Views of Scientific Heroes in the Early Nineteenth Century." *Beyond the Two Cultures.* Eds. Joseph W. Slade and Judith Yaross

Lee. Ames: Iowa State UP, 1990.

Thomson, H. Douglas. *Masters of Mystery*. New York: Dover, 1978.

Tobey, Ronald C. *The American Ideology of National Science 1919-1930*. Pittsburg: U Pittsburg P, 1971.

Tracy, Jack, ed. *The Encyclopedia Sherlockiana*. Garden City: Doubleday, 1977.

Wallace, Alfred Russel. *The Wonderful Century*. New York: Dodd, Mead, 1909.

Ward, Alfred C. *Aspects of the Modern Short Story*. London: U London P, 1924.

Welsh, Susan. "The Value of Analogical Evidence: Poe's *Eureka* in the Context of a Scientific Debate." *Modern Language Studies* 21.4 (1991): 3-15.

Wood, James Playsted. *Magazines in the United States*. New York: Ronald P, 1956.

Woods, Robin. " 'His Appearance Is Against Him': The Emergence of the Detective." *The Cunning Craft: Original Essays on Detective Fiction and Contemporary Literary Theory*. Eds. Ronald G. Walker and June M. Frazer. Western Illinois UP, 1990.

Yeo, Richard R. "Science and Intellectual Authority in Mid-Nineteenth-Century Britain: Robert Chambers and Vestiges of the Natural History of Creation." *Victorian Studies* 28 (1984): 5-31.

_____. "Scientific Method and the Image of Science 1831-1891." *The Parliament of Science*. Eds. Ray MacLeod and Peter Collins. Northwood, Midx: Science Reviews, 1981.

_____. "Scientific Method and the Rhetoric of Science in Britain, 1830-1917." *The Politics and Rhetoric of Scientific Method*. Eds. John A. Schuster and Richard R. Yeo. Dordrecht: D. Reidel, 1986.

Index